Rio Bravo

Laredo, Texas

(Rio Grande)

Monterrey

Nuevo León

Ciudad Victoria

Tamaulipas

otosí

Luis Potosí

uato

Querétaro

uerétaro

Hidalgo

Pachuca

México City

Tlaxcala

Jalapa

Toluca

éxico

Tlaxcala

Morelos

Cuernavaca

Puebla

Puebla

Veracruz

Chilpancingo

Guerrero

Oaxaca

Oaxaca

Mérida

Yucatán

Quintana Roo

Campeche

Campeche

Chetumal

Tabasco

Villahermosa

Tuxtla Gutiérrez

Chiapas

# MEXICAN REBEL

# MEXICAN REBEL

Pascual Orozco
and the Mexican Revolution
1910–1915

*by*

MICHAEL C. MEYER

UNIVERSITY OF NEBRASKA PRESS

LINCOLN

Publishers on the Plains

UNP

To Goldalee

# Acknowledgments

In addition to the authors of the books and articles I consulted during the preparation of this work (see Bibliography), I gratefully acknowledge the help of many others. Professor Edwin Lieuwen, Chairman of the Department of History at the University of New Mexico, and Professor Troy Floyd of the Department of History at the University of New Mexico gave generously of their time in reading and commenting upon the manuscript during its early stages. The late Professor Miguel Jorrín, Director of the School of Inter-American Affairs at the University of New Mexico, provided encouragement and inspiration over a period of many years. Professor Leon Helguera of the Department of History at Vanderbilt University kindly consented to read the manuscript and to offer suggestions. My colleague at the University of Nebraska, Dr. David Trask, corrected several embarrassing slips. Dr. Richard E. Greenleaf, Academic Vice President of the University of the Americas, assisted me with his extensive knowledge of the organization and functioning of Mexico City archives. Lieutenant Carlos San Román and Brigadier General Juan Manuel Solís made possible many fruitful hours of investigation in Mexico City's Archivo Histórico de la Defensa Nacional. Professor Luis Muro of El Colegio de México very kindly placed an unpublished guide to the Hemeroteca Nacional at my disposal, which greatly facilitated the use of that repository. Two members of the Orozco family, Señor Emigdio Orozco, one of the general's sons, and Ingeniero Enrique Meyer Orozco, one of the grandsons, spent many hours in correspondence and interviews with me and provided access to material that was unattainable elsewhere. The staff of the Bancroft Library at the University of California at Berkeley made working in the Terrazas collection a pleasure rather than a chore.

vii

The Research Council of the University of Nebraska provided a faculty grant that financed one of several research trips to Mexico City.

Finally, my wife, Goldalee, spent many tedious days proofreading, checking the accuracy of quotations, and criticizing the text. The dedication page is but a poor expression of my appreciation.

M. C. M.

# Contents

*A section of illustrations follows page 84.*

*A map follows page 24.*

# *Abbreviations*

ABFC    Albert Bacon Fall Collection, University of New Mexico. Papers from the Senate Office Files of Senator Albert Fall Relating to Mexican Affairs.

AGN    Archivo General de la Nación. Ramo de la Secretaría de Gobernación. Various *legajos* and *expedientes*, 1910–1914.

AGO    Records of the Adjutant General's Office, Department of War. Record Group 94, 1911–1915.

AHDN    Archivo Histórico de la Defensa Nacional. File Series XI/ 481.5. Various sections and volumes, 1910–1915.

APEMO    Archivo Particular de Enrique Meyer Orozco, Monterrey, Mexico.

AREM    Archivo de Relaciones Exteriores de México. Revolución Mexicana Durante los Años de 1910 a 1920. Informaciones Diversas de la República y de las Oficinas de México en el Exterior. File Series H/513–1910–20/1, various sections and volumes, 1910–1915.

BNAM    Biblioteca Nacional, Archivo Madero. Correspondencia del Presidente Francisco I. Madero, Mayo a Junio, 1911. Four boxes.

RDS    Records of the Department of State Relating to the Internal Affairs of Mexico, 1910–1929. National Archives Microfilm Publications (Microcopy No. 274), 1910–1915.

STC    Silvestre Terrazas Collection. Correspondence and Papers, Bancroft Library, University of California, Berkeley.

# MEXICAN REBEL

# Introduction

Despite the sophistication of twentieth-century historical analysis, revolution—perhaps the most enigmatic phenomenon in a nation's historical development—is often portrayed simply as the violent reaction of downtrodden masses against an intolerable despotism. The issues are reduced to a single conceptual formula: oppression (challenge) produces revolt (response). So it is with the Mexican Revolution of 1910, the first of a series of social upheavals that subsequently swept Latin America. Although the Revolution has been the subject of countless treatises and monographs, many of the best evaluations continue to view the movement that began in November of 1910 as the spontaneous revolt of the common man against the *ancien régime*, personified in this case by Porfirio Díaz.

It is not the aim of this work to attempt a vindication of the Porfirian despotism, even if this were possible. On the other hand, although social and economic inequalities provided an environment that nurtured discontent, explanation of the revolutionary phenomenon solely on these grounds is quite untenable. Resentment of despotism and the status quo, to be sure, is a prime consideration in every revolutionary uprising, but a detailed examination of the nature of revolution will show that a series of other factors are at least of equal significance. And this was true of Mexico in 1910.

Mexico's development during its first half century of independence reflected the political turbulence and chaos that have become synonymous with the "age of caudillos" in nineteenth-century Latin American history. A series of soldier-presidents guided the nation, for better or worse, during most of this period. The struggles between liberals and conservatives, federalists and centralists, and anticlericals and proponents of clerical privilege were compounded by an attempted

3

reconquest by Spain in 1829, by invasions by France in the 1830's and 1860's, and by a disastrous war with the United States between 1845 and 1848 (after which Mexico was divested of about half of her national territory). In the period between 1824 and 1876 the presidency changed hands seventy-five times, so that continuity of policy was impossible. By 1876 many Mexicans were ready to sacrifice almost everything for peace and stability, for a semblance of national order. Although the last quarter of the nineteenth century ushered in an era of unprecedented political stability and economic growth, the country was required to make certain concessions in return. Whether the end product justified the price that was paid is a question that still divides Mexicanists.

During this period, 1876 to 1910, Mexico became the personal preserve of Don Porfirio Díaz, a mestizo from the southern state of Oaxaca. For thirty-four years Díaz governed Mexico with a type of paternalism that is completely foreign to the Anglo-Saxon political tradition. The dictator's whims were tantamount to law, and—whenever necessary—they received the official sanction of the legislative and judicial branches of the government. Criticism of the regime was not tolerated and political dissidents were thrown into jail or forced into exile.

Despite the political oppression and the preceding half century's turmoil, the country began to progress. Mexico's first experience of political stability coincided with the first major investment of foreign capital. British and United States entrepreneurs, no longer fearful that a careless utterance or an imprudent decree might occasion an insurrection, invested their pounds sterling and their dollars and brought in their technical skills. Railroads were built, telephone and telegraph lines were laid, harbor and dock facilities were enlarged, mining production was increased; and by 1894 the national budget was balanced for the first time since independence. But the political stability and economic growth of the Díaz period were accomplished at the expense of personal freedom and social justice.

During the first decade of the twentieth century, Mexican intellectuals, abandoning all hope of a major social reorientation within the framework of the existing order, began to desert the regime. Díaz, moreover, unwittingly encouraged the growth of the opposition by indicating—in an interview with James Creelman, a United States journalist—that he did not plan to run for president after his current (seventh) term expired. In 1909 the opposition began to crystallize around Francisco I. Madero, a political novice who had gained a measure of national prominence the previous year by publishing a mildly anti-Díaz tract, *La Sucesión Presidencial en 1910*. As the elections of 1910 approached, Díaz forgot his promise and again presented himself as a presidential candidate. As if to rub salt in the wound, the president chose Ramón Corral, whose name was anathema to the liberals, as his running mate. The election day found the opposition candidate and thousands of his followers in jail on political charges. To nobody's surprise the administration announced that Díaz was reelected. Shortly after the final votes were tabulated, Madero eluded his guards and, disguised as a mechanic, escaped into exile in the United States. In October, 1910, a new revolution was proclaimed, under the banner of the Plan de San Luis Potosí.

At the time of the outbreak of the new movement, less than one-fifth of Mexico's 15,000,000 inhabitants were literate. The overwhelmingly rural population lived much as it always had. Land hunger was certainly nothing new, as its origins date far back into the colonial period. The Revolution likewise cannot properly be interpreted as a reaction against the seizure of political prerogatives by Porfirio Díaz, because democratic processes had never operated in Mexico before 1910.

A leading United States Mexicanist, Frank Tannenbaum, contends that the Madero revolution was a narrowly defined movement, meager in social content, and designed primarily to engineer the overthrow of the dictator. Although this analysis is sound, it does not necessarily follow that the average Mexican peon, the element that would comprise the rank and file of the Revolutionary Army and ultimately spell its success, was in the least concerned whether one individual held the presidential office for thirty-four years or whether—according to the original terms of the constitution—the office was relinquished at the end of a four-year term. It is equally implausible that the multitudes had any common bond with Madero, the son of a wealthy *hacendado* from Coahuila and the self-acclaimed head of the imminent fight against the Porfirian dictatorship. The elegant and at times idealistic phraseology of the Plan de San Luis Potosí or the political recriminations of the various editions of *La Sucesión Presidencial en 1910* could have had but little meaning to the *serrano* of western Chihuahua, the Yaqui Indian of Sonora, or the farmer of the Bolson de Mapimí. For reasons that have not yet been adequately explained, the masses nevertheless did react. Peons and tenant farmers began to leave the countryside in the late months of 1910, swelling the ranks of the Revolutionary Army.

It is my opinion that personal grievances against state and local *jefes políticos, jefes municipales, hacendados,* and judicial officials (the natural by-product of an extremely paternalistic and oppressive social order) must have convinced the multitudes that any change would necessarily be a change for the better. It is obvious, however, that the development and growth of such a phenomenon do not occur automatically, that a spark is needed; but almost as many sparks have been suggested as there are historians to suggest them. The Creelman interview, Madero's *La Sucesión Presidencial en 1910,* the choice of Ramón Corral as Díaz' running mate in the election of 1910, the Plan de San Luis Potosí, and the fraudulent election are some of the favorite suggestions. But even with all of these factors operating in his behalf, Madero, when he crossed the Rio Grande into Mexican territory in February of 1911, might well have met the same fate as another returning Mexican savior, Agustín de Iturbide, almost a century before, had not the groundwork for his return been carefully laid by a small number of enterprising individuals in the northern state of Chihuahua.

In late 1910 one of the most active anti-reelectionist clubs in Mexico was operating in Chihuahua. Under the leadership of Don Abraham González, the Club Anti-Reeleccionista Benito Juárez was responsible for a steady stream of propaganda against the Díaz dictatorship. After the promulgation of the Plan de San Luis Potosí, the club directed its efforts toward precipitating and coordinating a series of insurrectionary movements that, according to the plan, were to begin on the evening of November 20, 1910. First, however, the anti-reelectionist club had to find a suitable local leader, a leader who could publicize the ideals of the anti-Díaz movement and make them palatable to the masses in the various districts of the state. In the District of Guerrero, in western Chihuahua, González found his candidate in Pascual Orozco, Jr. From this modest beginning in the revolutionary ranks, Orozco, in less than six months, would be a national hero whose reception in hamlets and cities throughout the entire country would often surpass Madero's. Within another year Orozco would be universally damned as a traitor to the cause of the already sacrosanct Revolution.

If Orozco had been merely the intermediary between those seeking to overthrow the established order and the only force that could effect this end—the people—his career would be of interest only to those who seek to understand how the masses were enlisted. In addition to this service to the Revolution, however, the *guerrillero* from Chihuahua was Madero's most successful general in the military campaigns against the federal forces. Although it is somewhat difficult to overlook Orozco's military contributions to the overthrow of the dictator, these services have been minimized and at times completely forgotten. The primary reason for the disparagement or the neglect is that Mexican revolutionary historiography often has been compiled by a school of historians with a pro-revolutionary bias—and Orozco subsequently turned against the Madero faction. The historian who seeks to understand or trace the source of the effective leadership during the protracted campaigns of 1910 and 1911 cannot allow himself this "commitment."

The most publicized events in the relatively short career of Pascual Orozco were his defection from the Maderist fold in March, 1912, his abortive revolt against Madero, and his subsequent recognition of the government of Victoriano Huerta. Far from being a simple matter of good or evil, of patriotism or treason, the Orozquista insurrection—at least as manifested through its pronouncements—was a succinct censure of some of the most serious shortcomings of the Madero regime and in retrospect can be viewed as a preview of subsequent anti-Maderist demonstrations, the last of which would culminate in the president's assassination. It is possible, however, that Orozco's motives did not find their way into any of the revolutionary pronouncements and that the statements that appeared over his name were no more than a subterfuge for gaining the support of all elements that were already beginning to tire of Madero's apparent inactivity.

The present study aims at something more than a biographical account of Pascual Orozco. It does not purport to be a detailed description of the Revolution in the northern Mexican states, but, by centering upon Orozco's activities in the north, it tries to shed new light upon the history of the revolutionary process in Mexico at the grass-roots level. At the same time, because I believe that General Orozco has been maligned by the pro-revolutionary school, I have assessed the various charges that have been leveled against the general. Emphasis is placed upon Orozco's rapprochement with the masses and upon the aristocratic elements that used his popularity for their own ends. In addition, the ideological content of Orozco's revolutionary plans are given special consideration because they reflect a social awareness that is strangely absent from Madero's Plan de San Luis Potosí. Orozco's contributions to the Revolution were substantial, his indiscretions notwithstanding. Even if his defection is viewed as inexcusable, his activities helped shape the course the Revolution would follow, and therefore they warrant an unprejudiced examination.

Orozco, in his role as one of the framers of the Mexican Revolution, is not the only figure worthy of additional research. Only when carefully researched studies of the activities of other important revolutionary leaders—the Flores Magón brothers, Bernardo Reyes, Emilio Vásquez Gómez, Abraham González, and Félix Díaz—can be compared will the revolutionary maze of revolts and counterrevolts, altruism and self-indulgence, political machinations and social reform be fully comprehensible.

# I

# *Chihuahua: Cradle of Discontent*

Although, on the eve of the Revolution of 1910, mutinous ferment was more advanced in the state of Chihuahua than in the remainder of Mexico, the abuses of "Diazpotismo" were not more excessive there. Abuse was present, but in the last analysis it was the operation of other factors in this north-central Mexican state that had made revolt imminent and its success at least plausible. Not a few of these factors were geopolitical in nature.

Chihuahua's comparative isolation from the rest of Mexico, its remoteness from the national capital, and its contiguity with the United States all contributed to the outbreak and growth of the revolutionary phenomenon. Moreover, in sharp contrast to the remainder of Mexico, in the first decade of the twentieth century, Chihuahua possessed a relatively large middle class of merchants, artisans, coachmen, railroad men, and clerks. There is some evidence to suggest that these middle groups maintained a limited contact with their social counterparts in the United States and, in emulation of the better-defined middle sector north of the Rio Grande, desired to better their lot.[1] As a result, the middle groups within the state were especially susceptible to the endless stream of revolutionary propaganda that saturated Chihuahua during the last few years of the Díaz dictatorship.

The proximity of the United States also meant—after revolutionary sentiment had turned to armed conflict, in November, 1910—that arms and munitions could easily be obtained across the border.[2] The physical

[1] This observation was recorded by Marion Letcher, an energetic consular agent of the United States, who was in Mexico during the period 1910 to 1915; see Records of the Department of State Relating to the Internal Affairs of Mexico, 1910–1929 (RDS), National Archives Microfilm Publication, Microcopy No. 274, Marion Letcher, Consul, Chihuahua, to Sec. of State, File No. 812.00/9484, October 17, 1913.

[2] The sale of arms to Mexican revolutionaries was legal, from the United States' point of view, until March 13, 1912, when an arms embargo was enacted. The prohibition, however, was circumvented by smuggling.

isolation of Chihuahua from the center of federal control, in turn, contributed to early revolutionary successes. The unprotected railroad lines, over which government troops had to be transported, and mile after mile of unguarded telephone and telegraph lines were easy targets even for small, unorganized revolutionary bands. Federal troops who attempted to pursue the "bandits" soon discovered that the Chihuahua desert and the mountain pockets of the Sierra Madre Occidental afforded excellent protection for *guerrilleros* engaged primarily in hit-and-run warfare. The inhospitable climate of the Chihuahua desert was still another factor which, although not a detriment to the local inhabitants, limited the effectiveness of troops from the south.[3]

The unique economic and political history of Chihuahua also provides material for building a case for the state's predisposition to revolt. In the half century prior to the 1910 uprising the fortunes of the state of Chihuahua were guided by one tremendously powerful force, the Terrazas family. First coming to prominence in the 1860's with the governorship of General Luis Terrazas, the family controlled the political machinery of the state until 1911. The founder of the dynasty, Luis Terrazas, became one of Chihuahua's leading citizens after serving as a guerrilla against the French during the war of occupation. After the expulsion of the French, when the property of collaborators was confiscated by the government and put up for sale, Luis Terrazas was able to buy the huge estate of Señor Pablo Martínez del Rio, a man who had served Maximilian in various diplomatic capacities in Europe, for practically nothing. Luis continued to acquire land throughout the remainder of the nineteenth century and he became one of the wealthiest *hacendados* in Latin America.

The political power of the Terrazas clan matched its economic status. The family cultivated excellent relations with President Díaz and used

---

[3] In April, 1911, a month before he was forced from office, Díaz delivered a message to the 25th Mexican Congress in which he explained the successes of the Revolution in Chihuahua largely in geographic terms: ". . . The protection of the mountains and the effective co-operation of men and war supplies—received from foreign parts—as well as from groups of Mexicans who have for years conspired not only against the present government but against all social order, easily explains how the revolt has kept extending through almost the whole state of Chihuahua and to several points in Sonora and Durango, in spite of the efforts to limit it made by the federal government and those of the states mentioned. . . ." The speech is quoted in *Papers Relating to the Foreign Relations of the United States, 1911* (Washington, D.C.: Government Printing Office, 1918), p. 445 (hereafter cited as *U.S. Foreign Relations*).

their influence to fullest advantage.[4] According to the United States consul in Chihuahua:

> State officers were entirely within the gift of this family, the courts were but their servile tools to such an extent, indeed, that attorneys declined cases in which a member of the Terrazas family might be an adverse party to the suit. . . . all that might be desired in the way of arbitrary and despotic power was exercised by this immensely wealthy family.[5]

The landholdings of the Terrazas family on the eve of the Revolution are estimated to have been between 1,966,184 and 2,679,954 hectares.[6] The largest single hacienda, Encinillas, comprised some 386,000 hectares and was worked by approximately 2,000 inhabitants. In addition to this immense acreage, which made the family the largest landholders in Mexico—perhaps in all of Latin America—the Terrazas monopolized the banking, industrial, and mercantile enterprises of the state. All of the Terrazas enterprises carried tax-exemption privileges.

In October, 1907, Señor Enrique Creel, a nephew and son-in-law of Don Luis Terrazas and a man who had served as interim governor of Chihuahua, was elected to a four-year constitutional governorship.[7] This term coincided at the national level with the activation of the Mexican Liberal Party and the intensification of anti-Porfirian political expression. In Chihuahua, as informal groups began to meet to discuss political abuses in Mexico City and within the state, they received encouragement and support from the famous precursors of the Mexican Revolution, the Flores Magón brothers. From their exile in St. Louis, Missouri, Jesús and Ricardo Flores Magón began to flood the state with copies of *La Regeneración*, the official organ of the liberal revolutionaries in exile; and pamphlets that denounced the old system began to circulate in Chihuahua City. Governor Creel, aware of the potential

[4] *Archivo del General Porfirio Díaz: Memorias y Documentos* (29 vols.; Mexico City: Editorial "Elede" S. A., 1947–60), XXVII, 182–183, and XXIX, *passim*.

[5] RDS, Letcher to Sec. of State, 812.00/9484, Oct. 17, 1913.

[6] This is only slightly less than the total land area of Costa Rica—or approximately the same as the total area of Connecticut, Rhode Island, Delaware, and Maryland. The huge fortune of the Terrazas family is discussed in Moisés González Navarro, *El Porfiriato Vida Social*, Vol. IV of *Historia Moderna de México*, ed. Daniel Cosío Villegas (7 vols.; Mexico City: Editorial Hermes, 1955–65), pp. 215–216.

[7] The governors of the state of Chihuahua and the dates of their terms are listed in José M. Ponce de León, *Resumen de la Historia Política de Chihuahua* (Chihuahua: Imprenta Gutenberg, 1922), and Francisco R. Almada, *Gobernantes de Chihuahua* (Chihuahua: Talleres Gráficos del Gobierno del Estado, 1929).

danger, ordered his *jefes políticos* to be on guard against revolutionary activity. Creel also distributed pictures of the Flores Magón brothers so that he could be notified immediately if they appeared in the state.[8]

These precautions were effective: there were several small insurrections between 1907 and 1909 but the political machine was able to suppress them.[9] Unfortunately, however, the dissatisfaction evidenced by the abortive revolts apparently was insufficient to make the state political machine cognizant of the fact that graft and corruption were now beginning to fall under close scrutiny. During the Creel administration the Terrazas family continued to receive government concessions on public projects. Señor Juan Terrazas was given special concessions for the construction of seven metallurgical plants in various parts of the state and for a cement plant in Ciudad Juárez; and Señor Alberto Terrazas was given special permission to construct railroads and hydroelectric and gas plants.[10]

In 1909, liberals in Chihuahua and in other Mexican states began to organize anti-reelectionist clubs. The March, 1909 nomination of the Díaz-Corral ticket to represent the "Re-electionist" Party and the subsequent refusal of Díaz to substitute Bernardo Reyes as his running mate gave great impetus to the anti-reelectionist movement. In order to promote the movement and to organize new clubs, Francisco I. Madero began to tour the country in mid-1909, and in late January, 1910, he reached Chihuahua. Upon his arrival he found that Anti-reelectionist clubs already existed in almost all of the state's major towns and cities, with the Centro Anti-reeleccionista Benito Juárez in the capital, under the presidency of Señor Abraham González, serving as a coordinating agency.[11]

[8] Silvestre Terrazas Collection (STC), Correspondence and Papers, Flores Magón Section, Jefes Políticos, Folders 5A and 5B.

[9] One of the better-known outbreaks in Chihuahua occurred in June, 1908, in the district of Galeana. The leader of this small insurrection, Práxedes G. Guerrero, was a socialist who was affiliated with the Mexican Liberal Party. Guerrero, who had no real program, armed fifty men and marched on Palomas (opposite Columbus, New Mexico) but was repulsed by a detachment of Mexican border officials; see Francisco R. Almada, *Resumen de Historia del Estado de Chihuahua* (Mexico City: Libros Mexicanos, 1955), p. 371, and Armando List Arzurbide, *Apuntes Sobre la Prehistoria de la Revolución* (Mexico City, 1958), pp. 97–99. On June 20, 1908, the government announced that another conspiracy, scheduled to begin on June 25, had been discovered and that the leaders had been arrested in Casas Grandes, Chihuahua; see Alfonso Taracena, *La Verdadera Revolución Mexicana* (6 vols.; Mexico City: Editorial Jus, S. A., 1960), I, 63.

[10] Almada, *Resumen de Historia del Estado de Chihuahua*, p. 375.

[11] The Chihuahua anti-reelectionist movement had two organs: *El Grito del*

Madero was well received in Chihuahua; the enthusiasm engendered by his visit to Hidalgo del Parral, for example, was so great that the town's merchants declared a municipal holiday.[12] Governor Creel, however, did not attach much importance to Madero's swing through Chihuahua, believing it was curiosity rather than genuine enthusiasm that attracted the large crowds to the political oddity.[13] On January 21, 1910, the Club Anti-reeleccionista Benito Juárez indicated by secret ballot that Madero and Dr. Francisco Vásquez Gómez were its choice for the nomination in the coming election.[14] This Chihuahua group was the first in Mexico officially to sponsor Madero's nomination.[15]

The national anti-reelectionist convention met in Mexico City, at the Tivolí del Elíseo, on April 15, 1910. Madero was easily nominated, but the selection of the vice-presidential candidate was more of a problem. The delegation from Chihuahua, led by Abraham González, still favored Francisco Vásquez Gómez, but other groups suggested José María Pino Suárez or General Gerónimo Treviño as possible candidates. After he accepted the presidential nomination, Madero threw his support to Vásquez Gómez, whereupon the latter was chosen as his running mate, on April 16, 1910.

Madero's presidential campaign, his arrest, his imprisonment at San Luis Potosí, and the fraudulent election of Díaz and Corral are too well known to require explication. Even before the defeated candidate issued his famous Plan de San Luis Potosí (dated October 5, 1910, but written several weeks later) it was obvious to anti-reelectionist leaders throughout the country that if the desired changes were to be effected it would be necessary to employ force. In Chihuahua, the task of coordinating revolutionary uprisings—for November 20, 1910—was assumed by the Club Anti-reeleccionista Benito Juárez. Under the direction of Abraham González, and acting through the other anti-reelectionist clubs in the state, the group in the capital contacted likely

---

*Pueblo*, which primarily attacked the Díaz-Corral ticket, and the *Correo de Chihua-hua*, which particularly denounced the Terrazas-Creel tyranny.

[12] Stanley R. Ross, *Francisco I. Madero: Apostle of Mexican Democracy* (New York: Columbia University Press, 1955), p. 90.

[13] Charles Curtis Cumberland, *Mexican Revolution: Genesis Under Madero* (Austin: University of Texas Press, 1952), p. 94.

[14] Francisco Vásquez Gómez had been the personal physician of Porfirio Díaz. Informed of his nomination by the Chihuahua club, he declined, and only after a visit from Madero did he finally allow his name to be entered as one of the vice-presidential candidates; see Francisco Vásquez Gómez, *Memorias Políticas (1909–1913)* (Mexico City: Imprenta Mundial, 1933), pp. 23–24.

[15] Ross, *Madero*, p. 91.

candidates for leadership in the various areas. In the District of Guerrero, in western Chihuahua, the club found its future leader, Pascual Orozco, Jr.[16]

Guerrero, the district in which the Revolution would subsequently flourish, was in many respects typical of northern Mexico. Mining and agriculture were the major economic activities, with agriculture employing the greatest number of persons. Most of the haciendas in the area were engaged in the raising of corn, chile, and beans. Ciudad Guerrero, the largest city in the district, had a population of 2,548 in 1900.[17] If a single characteristic distinguished Guerrero from the other eleven political districts of Chihuahua, it was the recalcitrance of its people. Guerrero was a politically active district with a definite proclivity toward revolt.

As early as August, 1879, Señor Gabriel Casavantes, from Ciudad Guerrero, had led a successful revolution against Governor Trías.[18] In 1887, when the national constitution was amended to permit re-election of the president and the state constitution was restructured to centralize still further the control of the governor, the citizens of Ciudad Guerrero rose up in armed insurrection to protest both measures.[19] In 1892 and in 1893, two more rebellions were recorded in Guerrero District.[20] In 1899, the citizens of the region had issued a strongly worded demand that Governor Luis Terrazas remove corrupt *jefes municipales* and conduct a general investigation of political administration in the district.[21] Governor Terrazas procrastinated for years before he removed a particularly hated municipal official, Luis Y. Comadurán, the *jefe municipal* of Bachíniva. Throughout the decade that preceded the outbreak of the 1910 hostilities, the governor's office had been flooded with protests from Guerrero. When Comadurán finally was removed,

[16] Some of the other military chieftains in Chihuahua were Guillermo Baca and Pedro T. Gómez, in Hidalgo del Parral; Toribio Ortega, in Cuchillo Parado; José de la Luz Blanco, in Temosáchic; and Cástulo Herrera, Ceferino Pérez, and Francisco Villa, in the Carretas–San Andrés region.

[17] José M. Ponce de León, *Chihuahua y sus Distritos: Datos Geográficos y Estadísticos* (Chihuahua: Imprenta de Simón Alarcón, 1909), p. 24.

[18] Hubert Howe Bancroft, *History of the North Mexican States*, Vol. XVI of *The Works of Hubert Howe Bancroft* (San Francisco: The History Company Publishers, 1884–89), p. 625.

[19] Francisco R. Almada, *La Revolución en el Estado de Chihuahua* (Mexico City: Talleres Gráficos de la Nación, 1964), pp. 96–98.

[20] *Ibid.*, pp. 99–103.

[21] STC, Flores Magón Section, Revolutionary Statement from Guerrero District to Señor General D. Luis Terrazas, 1899.

one of his friends was appointed to replace him, and as a result the situation in Bachíniva deteriorated further because the factor of revenge was added to the citizens' formidable list of grievances.[22] The Flores Magón brothers, realizing their revolutionary propaganda would find a receptive audience in Guerrero, by September, 1906, were corresponding with potential leaders in the district and were sending in copies of *La Regeneración*.[23]

Pascual Orozco, Jr., was born on the Hacienda de Santa Isabel near the town of San Isidro, Guerrero, Chihuahua, on January 28, 1882.[24] His father, Pascual Orozco, and his mother, Amada Orozco y Vásquez, were natives of western Chihuahua. The Orozco family had lived in Guerrero for at least three generations, and the Vásquez family were second-generation Basque immigrants.[25] Before young Pascual had reached school age, his parents moved to San Isidro, which had one of the twenty-nine public schools in the district.[26] Although rural education was woefully inadequate in Díaz' Mexico, the boy acquired a rudimentary knowledge of reading and writing during his four or five years of primary education.[27] At the age of twelve or thirteen, having virtually exhausted the educational opportunities available in San Isidro, Orozco went to work in a small store owned by his father.

In his late teens, Pascual Orozco married Refugio Frías, the daughter of Albino Frías, a politically active and respected San Isidro citizen. In 1902, at the age of twenty, Orozco left San Isidro and became a muleteer, charged with guarding ore shipments from various mines in the

[22] *Ibid.*, Guerrero District, various dates.

[23] *Ibid.*, Revoltosos, Juez del Distrito, Folder G, and Francisco Antillón to Governor Creel, Oct. 22, 1906.

[24] Joaquín Márquez Montiel, S.J., *Hombres Célebres de Chihuahua* (Mexico City: Editorial Jus, 1953), p. 221, and Daniel Moreno, *Los Hombres de la Revolución* (Mexico City: Libro Mex, Editores, 1960), p. 55. The contention that Orozco was born in Yucatán and moved with his family to Chihuahua is without validity (see, for example, "Orozco: Maker and Unmaker of Mexican Presidents," *Current Literature*, LII [June, 1912], 646).

[25] Archivo Particular de Enrique Meyer Orozco (APEMO), Arbol Genealógico.

[26] Ponce de León, *Chihuahua y sus Distritos*, p. 69.

[27] Many of Orozco's detractors have stated that he was illiterate and remained so his entire life. Although the man was not an intellectual, there is no question of his ability to read and write. I have examined correspondence from Orozco to Madero that was written in the former's hand. These documents can be examined in the Biblioteca Nacional, Archivo Madero (BNAM), Correspondencia del Presidente Francisco I. Madero, Mayo a Junio, 1911, Caja 3, folio 1570, May 14, 1911.

mountains of western Chihuahua to the foundries, many of which were near the United States border. Within a few years the enterprising youth had saved enough money to purchase a string of mules, and thus was able to offer his services to various companies for the entire transportation transaction.

Between 1902 and 1910, having worked for several large mining companies, Orozco had gained a reputation for honesty and efficiency.[28] Nils Olaf Bagge, president of the most important mining company in the region, the Companía Río de la Plata, reported that Orozco was his best packer.[29] The job was dangerous and exacting, but financially rewarding. Several years after he entered the freighting business, Orozco was able to branch out by opening a mercantile store in the small village of Estación Sánchez, which also proved to be a success. Orozco had accumulated a small fortune by 1910, most of which he would spend in revolutionary activity.[30]

Physically, Orozco was imposing; he stood six feet one inch and weighed 180 pounds—an anomaly in Mexico. His light complexion, brown hair, and preference for Texas-style clothing further emphasized the contrast with the typical rural Mexican; not even his full mustache really caused "the Mexican" to emerge. Except for a sharp nose, his facial features were soft and well suited to his personality: in personal relationships Orozco was mild-mannered and retiring, and in all formal settings shy and ill at ease. In his element—talking to a group of peons, leading guerrillas into battle, or reasoning with a company of malcontent soldiers—Orozco was at his best and demonstrated complete mastery of the situation. In an unfamiliar or undesired environment, his

[28] RDS, Letcher to Sec. of State, 812.00/9484, Oct. 17, 1913; Márquez Montiel, *Hombres Célebres de Chihuahua*, p. 221.

[29] Committee on Foreign Relations, U.S. Senate, *Investigation of Mexican Affairs* (Washington, D.C.: Government Printing Office, 1920), p. 1429 (hereafter cited as *Fall Committee*). Although the committee-hearing records contain a wealth of information that is unavailable elsewhere, they must be used only with extreme caution. For a brief analysis of some of the possible pitfalls, see Michael Meyer, "Albert Bacon Fall's Mexican Papers: A Preliminary Investigation," *New Mexico Historical Review*, XL (April, 1965), 165–174.

[30] Márquez Montiel, *Hombres Célebres de Chihuahua*, p. 211. Juan Gualberto Amaya estimated that Orozco's savings had reached $20,000 pesos by the eve of the Revolution (*Madero y los Revolucionarios* [Mexico City: 1946], p. 93. Others have estimated that the amount may have been closer to 40,000 pesos (APEMO, unidentified press clipping). Some of Orozco's savings were used to purchase a gold mine that he was working profitably immediately before the Revolution (*New York Times*, Sept. 1, 1915).

composure often left him and he would force himself to wrestle with his inadequacies.

Orozco first came to the attention of the Chihuahua political machine in October, 1906. In response to Governor Creel's many requests for information on potential troublemakers in the state, the *jefe municipal* of Temósachic, Francisco Antillón, reported that Pascual Orozco had been observed reading "anti-government literature" in San Isidro.[31] No punitive steps were taken, but Orozco's loyalties were suspect from that time. In May, 1909, a more serious charge was leveled against the muleteer: a dispatch from the *jefe político* of the district of Bravos indicated that Orozco and José Inés Salazar were purchasing arms and ammunition in the United States and bringing them into Mexico.[32] In 1909, however, Orozco's revolutionary activities in behalf of the Flores Magón brothers were sporadic and of little consequence; it was not until the following year that he abandoned his business enterprises and dedicated himself entirely to the anti-reelectionist cause.

The decision of Pascual Orozco to join the ranks of the anti-reelectionists and offer his services to Abraham González seems to have been based not upon a deep-seated feeling against the Díaz dictatorship but rather upon the personal animosity between Orozco and a rival muleteer, Captain Joaquín Chávez.[33] Chávez, an army captain by virtue of the fact that he was the commander of the Chihuahua city public security police force (which enforced the dictates of the state government), was also on the personal payroll of Señor Enrique Creel. A constant recipient of official favors, Chávez was a privileged business competitor, who at the same time made Orozco aware of political corruption at the state and local levels. It would be unjust to attribute Orozco's services to the Revolution solely to self-interested retaliation; nonetheless, his personal difficulties at the hands of the Terrazas-Creel machine made him more susceptible to the incessant bombardments of the anti-reelectionist press. By September, 1910, both of the anti-

[31] STC, Flores Magón Section, Francisco Antillón to Creel, Oct. 20, 1906.

[32] STC, Félix Bárcenos to Creel, May 18, 1909.

[33] RDS, Letcher to Sec. of State, 812.00/3414, Mar. 20, 1912; Frederick Starr, *Mexico and the United States* (Chicago: The Bible House, 1914), pp. 335–336; J. Figueroa Domenech, *Veinte Meses de Anarquía* (Mexico City, 1918), p. 118; Ramón Puente, *Pascual Orozco y la Revuelta de Chihuahua* (Mexico City: Eusebio Gómez de la Puente, 1912), pp. 24–26; Francisco Bulnes, *The Whole Truth About Mexico. President Wilson's Responsibility* (New York: M. Bulnes Book Company, 1916), pp. 154–155.

reelection organs in the state were engaged in a full-scale propaganda campaign.

Orozco committed himself to the revolutionary movement in early October, 1910. By the middle of the month he had been granted an interview with Abraham González, had received money from the head of the Chihuahua club, and had been instructed to begin recruitment in Guerrero and to be ready for action.[34] On October 31, in a second conference with González, Orozco was appointed chief of the Revolution in the District of Guerrero.[35]

Well liked in his district, Orozco encountered no difficulty in enlisting support. His reputation for bravery, uncanny skill with weapons, and superb horsemanship won him the respect of the country folk, for whom physical prowess was the true measure of masculinity. His knowledge of the terrain—acquired during eight years as a muleteer—helped instill confidence in those who had never ventured afar. From the very beginning, Orozco's attempts to enlist recruits in the revolutionary ranks met with success.

Political abuse at the local level was rampant, and one study concludes that "hate of the Terrazas family . . . was the principal factor in the revolt."[36] In addition, there was a severe crop failure in the region.[37] Finally, the strong personal appeal of Pascual Orozco, a man of the people, who had succeeded in rising above the station that apparently had been cut out for him, proved conclusive, as Orozco was able to capitalize upon the recalcitrance the district had demonstrated over many years.

[34] Alberto Calzadíaz Barrera, *Hechos Reales de la Revolución* (Chihuahua: Editorial Occidental, 1959), p. 39.

[35] Amaya, *Madero y los Revolucionarios*, pp. 103–104. The position of chief of the Revolution for the District of Guerrero did not entail full military command. The military chieftainship of the San Isidro–Guerrero area originally went to Albino Frías, Orozco's father-in-law, and Orozco was second in command. It was not until December 6, 1910, that Frías resigned his command, because of his age, and that Orozco assumed full military leadership. See Daniel Gutierrez Santos, *Historia Militar de México, 1876–1914* (Mexico City: Ediciones Ateneo, S. A., 1955), p. 66.

[36] Manuel Calero, *Un Decenio de Política Mexicana* (New York: Middleditch, 1920), p. 39.

[37] *Fall Committee*, testimony of Adolph Krauker, p. 2591.

# II

# *A Dictatorship Crumbles*

Francisco I. Madero's request for a general uprising on November 20, 1910 (Article 7 of the Plan de San Luis Potosí) was acknowledged with small insurrections in many sections of Mexico. Within a week and a half, however, Porfirio Díaz' competent *federales* had succeeded in extirpating the threat, except in a remote district in western Chihuahua.

Pascual Orozco pronounced his revolution and withdrew recognition of the federal government in San Isidro on November 19, 1910. Early the next morning, Orozco and approximately forty men,[1] most of whom had been armed by Abraham González, struck at the nearby town of Miñaca, which had been chosen because it was garrisoned only by a local police force under the command of the municipal president, Francisco Antillón. The town fell to the rebels with little resistance. Later the same day the rebel band returned to San Isidro and attacked the house of Joaquín Chávez, Orozco's old rival and the symbol of the Terrazas-Creel tyranny at the local level. Chávez had a personal body-guard of forty Tarahumara Indians, but this guard was promptly defeated by Orozco's troops.[2] Their arms and munitions were immediately confiscated, enabling Orozco to strengthen his force.

With these two minor victories behind him, Orozco decided to attack Ciudad Guerrero and to engage federal regulars for the first time. On

---

[1] The number of men believed to have been under Orozco's command during this first engagement ranges from 17 to 41; see Manuel Romero, "La Epopeya de Pascual Orozco, *Boletín de la Sociedad Chihuahuense de Estudios Históricos*, VI (June–July, 1949), 252; Taracena, *La Verdadera Revolución*, I, 110; José C. Valadés, *Imaginación y Realidad de Francisco I. Madero* (2 vols.; Mexico City: Antigua Librería Robredo, 1960), II, 290; Calzadíaz Barrera, *Hechos Reales*, p. 41; and Amaya, *Madero y los Revolucionarios*, p. 103. Amaya's figure of 41 is probably the most accurate, as he lists the names of the participants.

[2] Gutiérrez Santos, *Historia Militar de México*, p. 65.

November 21 the rebels laid siege to the capital city of the district, which was defended by a column of sixty-five men of the Third Cavalry Regiment under the command of Captain Salvador Ormachea.[3] Although the assaults of the rebels were repulsed for five days, the federal forces were unable to lift the siege. On November 25, Orozco cut all of the communication lines around Ciudad Guerrero, but not before Captain Ormachea had informed the strong federal garrison in Chihuahua City of his predicament.[4] As soon as the federal garrison in the state capital was apprised of Ormachea's untenable position, reinforcements—under General Juan Navarro—were dispatched to relieve the city.

Having been advised that reinforcements were approaching on the road from Chihuahua, the rebels divided their forces into two groups. One of the groups continued to apply pressure on Ciudad Guerrero while the second, led by Orozco, tried to divert the federal advance. On November 27, at Pedernales, a village of about 500 inhabitants, Orozco set a successful ambush and completely routed the advance guard of Navarro's column, which was under the command of Captain Manuel Sánchez Pasos.[5] Orozco's victory at Pedernales was the first important revolutionary victory over regular federal forces. The arms, munitions, and supplies that were captured at Pedernales enabled the rebel commander to return to Ciudad Guerrero and assault the plaza. The city fell to Orozco during the first week of December, 1910.

From the outset the government forces found that the revolutionary bands were not the only enemy. The people in the countryside refused them food, water, and shelter, and at times fired upon them.[6] On the other hand, rebel troops in the rural areas were afforded complete co-operation.[7] The peasantry also served the rebels as an intelligence

[3] Vito Alessio Robles, "La Primera Página Militar de la Revolución," *Todo* (March 25, 1954), p. 2; Jesús Romero Flores, *Del Porfirismo a la Revolución Constitucionalista* (Mexico City: Libro Mex Editores, 1960), p. 139.

[4] STC, Flores Magón Section, Jesús Vega Bonilla to Governor, Nov. 30, 1910.

[5] Paige W. Christiansen, "Pascual Orozco: Chihuahua Rebel," *New Mexico Historical Review*, XXXVI (April, 1961), 101; Romero Flores, *Del Porfirismo a la Revolución*, p. 140; Taracena, *La Verdadera Revolución*, I, 111; Amaya, *Madero y los Revolucionarios*, p. 108.

[6] Archivo de Relaciones Exteriores de México (AREM), Revolución Mexicana Durante de los Años de 1910 a 1920. Informaciones Diversas de la República y de las Oficinas de México en el Exterior, Expediente H/513–910–20/1, L–E [Libro Especial] 640, Sec. 16, Caja 1, from Consul, El Paso, to Sec. de Relaciones Exteriores, Mar. 13, 1911; *Mexican Herald*, Dec. 2, 1910.

[7] Alvin R. Kenner, "Mexican Revolution," *Mining and Scientific Press*, CII (May 6, 1911), 622.

service and kept them informed of the movement of government troops. It has even been suggested that this unofficial spy network was one of the main factors in Orozco's surprise victory at Pedernales.[8]

Although several other small groups in Chihuahua had revolted on or about November 20, by the end of the month the only organized group was that of Orozco. At the beginning of December he had about 800 men under his command, but the large majority were poorly armed, or carried no arms at all.[9] Calzadíaz Barrera described them as "an army of rags, without money, without any notions of military discipline, the majority badly dressed, some carried axes instead of rifles, others, far from inspiring fear, inspired pity."[10] Yet they won victories.

The Chihuahua revolution was given little publicity in the Mexico City press for the first ten days; nevertheless, rumors of the military activities in the north found their way into the capital. To quell the rumors, a leading newspaper in the capital carried the following headline on November 23, 1910: "DISORDERS IN NORTHERN MEXICO OF LITTLE CONSEQUENCE."[11] The United States government was slightly better informed, as in the last days of November Ambassador Henry Lane Wilson reported that the rebels were gaining strength in Chihuahua.[12] The state government in Chihuahua, of course, knew of the extreme danger from the outset; dispatches from the various *jefes políticos* and *jefes municipales* to the governor's office indicated profound concern.[13]

Immediately after Ciudad Guerrero fell into rebel hands (December 4, 1910), marking the fourth consecutive victory of Pascual Orozco, the *guerrillero* from San Isidro assumed full military command of the revolutionary forces in Guerrero District and issued his first revolutionary decree. The significance of this statement lies not in its content— it is a typical condemnation of the Porfirist tyranny and a general call

[8] Elías L. Torres, "Una Espía de la Revolución," *Jueves de Excélsior* (Jan. 9, 1936), pp. 24–25.

[9] Romero, "La Epopeya de Orozco," p. 253.

[10] *Hechos Reales*, p. 43. A few months later the military equipment of the rebels had improved considerably and one dispatch reported that most of the men carried Mauser rifles (RDS, Ellsworth, Consul, Cd. Porfirio Díaz, to Sec. of State, 812.00/810, Feb. 3, 1911). As late as March, however, machetes were still in use. At the beginning of March a purchase of machetes was made from the Shelton-Payne Company in El Paso (AREM, De la Barra to Sec. de Relaciones Exteriores, L–E 638, Sec. 16, Caja 1, Mar. 4, 1911).

[11] *Mexican Herald*, Nov. 23, 1910.

[12] RDS, H. L. Wilson to Sec. of State, 812.00/505, Nov. 29, 1910.

[13] STC, Flores Magón Section, Dispatches from José M. Rintoría, Jesús Vega Bonilla, and Francisco Mateus, to Governor, Nov. and Dec., 1910.

to arms—but in the fact that it was the first formal document issued by revolutionary forces actively engaged in fighting the dictatorship. The manifesto read:

> *To the Republican Maderist forces in the District of Guerrero, Chihuahua, Mexico, and to all our brothers under the banner of the Constitution of 1857 and all the laws which emanate from it.* Let it be known:
> That since the official tyranny—the Porfirist tyranny—has been responsible for so many outrages and excesses throughout the country, with utter disregard for the law, and for our moral and social customs;
> That since it is necessary to oppose this group of despots and tyrants who are solely responsible for the many evils present in Mexico with the same kind of capricious force which they use to sustain so much injustice;
> That although we love peace, we do not want the peace of slaves because without individual liberty there is no freedom in the nation;
> We have resolved to repel the brutal force which causes us so much evil and injustice with a just campaign, attempting to maintain as much order as possible and adopting as our motto the salvation of Mexico from ignominy, tyranny and abuse. We ask for the support of all good Mexicans, true democrats, and loyal republicans.

> EFFECTIVE SUFFRAGE AND NO RE-ELECTION

> *Ciudad Guerrero, December 6, 1910*
>
> PASCUAL OROZCO, JR.
> *El Jefe de las Armas* [14]

Less than a week after Ciudad Guerrero was captured by the rebels, Orozco tasted defeat for the first time. On December 11, 1910, in compliance with orders from Mexico City, federal forces under General Navarro attempted to recapture Ciudad Guerrero. They were stopped slightly short of their goal, at Cerro Prieto, where they were forced to engage the rebels. Orozco's troops at Cerro Prieto were flanked by the small revolutionary bands of Pancho Villa and José de la Luz Blanco. The cooperation of the three groups notwithstanding, their combined strength was unequal to the 1,200 well-armed soldiers of General

[14] Christiansen, "Pascual Orozco," p. 101. The document has been translated from the copy contained in Manuel González Ramírez (ed.), *Manifiestos Políticos, 1892–1912* (Mexico City: Fondo de Cultura Económica, 1957), p. 166.

Navarro.[15] After a heated battle that lasted most of the day, Orozco was forced to order a retreat. Navarro took twenty rebel prisoners and summarily issued orders for their execution at the local cemetery.[16]

During the last two weeks of December skirmishes were fought in various areas of Chihuahua. This same period also witnessed the first real attempt at organization and cooperation among the hitherto independent revolutionary groups. Bands of revolutionaries, under leaders other than Orozco, had won minor victories in late November and early December, but shortages of arms, munitions, and supplies had prohibited a consolidation of their victories.[17] As the revolt against Díaz moved into its second month, it became obvious that unless genuine cooperation among the Chihuahua rebels was effected, the *federales* would soon extinguish the last real revolutionary sparks in the country. Fully cognizant of this eventuality, rebel commanders such as José de la Luz Blanco, Cástulo Herrera, Pancho Villa, Epifanio Cos, Francisco Salido, and Pascual Orozco began to hold meetings and consult with one another. By the end of the year Orozco had emerged as the supreme military commander of the Revolution in the state of Chihuahua and was at least tacitly recognized as such by the other rebel chieftains.

The new year began well for Orozco. On January 2, 1911, in concert with several other rebel commanders, he successfully ambushed the federal detachment of Colonel Martín Luis Guzmán in the Cañón de Mal Paso. The rebel forces, after allowing Guzmán's train convoy to enter the canyon, sealed off retreat by burning several bridges over which the train had passed. As the federal convoy continued into the canyon, Orozco's men, who commanded the heights on both sides, opened fire;[18] Guzmán's force was almost totally destroyed. It was after this battle that Orozco reputedly ordered his men to gather up all

[15] Márquez Montiel, *Hombres Célebres de Chihuahua*, p. 222.

[16] Agustín Victor Casasola, *Historia Gráfica de la Revolución, 1900–1940* (6 vols.; Mexico City: Archivo Casasola, n.d.), I, 224; Tarcena, *La Verdadera Revolución*, p. 112; Calzadíaz Barrera, *Hechos Reales*, p. 47. One of the prisoners who was executed by Navarro at Cerro Prieto was Pascual Orozco's uncle, Alberto Orozco. Díaz' control of the press was exercised after the executions at Cerro Prieto. On December 15, 1910, the *Mexican Herald* reported that General Navarro, obeying his orders, had taken no prisoners; "the bayonet had completed the work of the bullet." The following day the *Herald* retracted its statements in an editorial: ". . . there can be no warrant for the statement that prisoners are butchered in cold blood or that prisoners are shot."

[17] Christiansen, "Pascual Orozco," pp. 101–102.

[18] Ross, *Madero*, p. 132.

the caps and other articles of clothing of the dead federals; the articles are said to have been sent to President Díaz with the taunt: "Here are your wrappings. Send me some more tamales."[19]

Obtaining adequate supplies was an ever present problem for the rebels. During the first month of the campaign, when the armies were small, money obtained from the anti-reelectionist clubs and delivered through Abraham González was used to purchase supplies of war. When goods had to be confiscated, the rebels would often return the following day and pay for the articles they had taken.[20] As the size of the armies and the intensity of the campaigns increased, however, voluntary contributions proved even less adequate than before. Arms and munitions captured from federal prisoners afforded some relief, but this source also proved inadequate as the revolutionary ranks continued to swell. By the first week in January the impasse had become critical and Orozco determined that only a daring move might resolve the problem. On January 7, 1911, Orozco attacked a well-defended military freight train on the Kansas City, Mexico, Orient Railroad.[21] With only fifty-six men, he stopped the train, fought a pitched battle, subdued the guards, and unloaded the supplies. He then allowed the train to continue on its way.[22]

With morale and potential bolstered by this successful seizure, Orozco devised his first scheme of real military strategy. On January 7 he ordered a quiet rebel evacuation of Ciudad Guerrero, and General Navarro, after a hard march, entered the city unopposed.[23] From his new refuge in the mountains of western Chihuahua, Orozco then allowed rumors to circulate that he was planning an all-out attack on Chihuahua City, the capital of the state.[24] The bait was accepted: military dispatches from the Chihuahua military zone commander to the Minister of War, and the minister's replies, reflected genuine fear of an impending attack on Chihuahua City.[25] By February 1 the press

[19] "*Ahí te van las hojas, mándame más tamales*"; in Amaya, *Madero y los Revolucionarios*, p. 127.

[20] RDS, unidentified Associated Press dispatch from Chihuahua, 812.00/555; Kenner, "Mexican Revolution," pp. 623–624.

[21] *Mexican Herald*, Jan. 8, 1911.

[22] Archivo Histórico de la Defensa Nacional (AHDN), Gen. Juan Navarro to Min. de Guerra y Marina, Expediente XI/481.5/61, Tomo I, folio 272, Jan. 8, 1911.

[23] *El País*, Jan. 9, 1911.

[24] Christiansen, "Pascual Orozco," p. 103.

[25] AHDN, Min. de Guerra y Marina to Chihuahua Zone Commander, Exp. XI/481.5/200, Tomo IV, folio 800, Jan. 8, 1911.

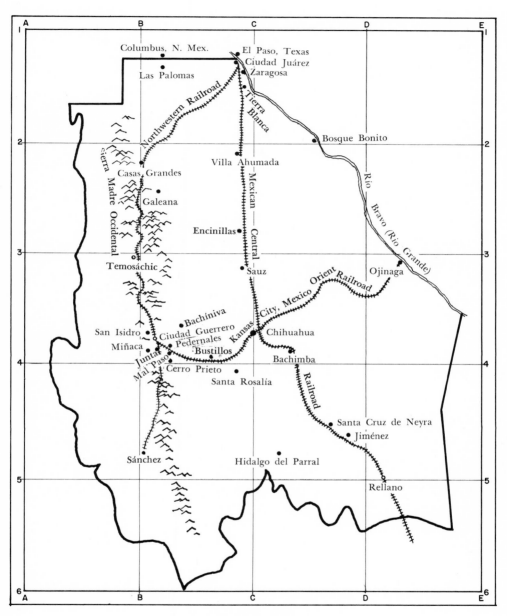

Map of Chihuahua

in Mexico City had picked up the rumors and had begun to publicize the imminence of an attack.

> ...the apparent inactivity on the part of the insurgents has been devoted to extensive preparations for the most ambitious efforts. Pascual Orozco, the younger...now has 800 men gathered within 70 miles of Chihuahua and will attack that city with a force of 1,200 men within ten days. With the younger Orozco is Pascual Orozco, the father, second in command, both appointed by Francisco Madero, and both instructed to move on Chihuahua at once.[26]

On February 1, Orozco attacked two additional trains and helped himself to their cargoes.[27] The same day the Minister of War ordered Colonel Antonio Rábago to move his large federal garrison from Casas Grandes to the capital of the state.[28] The following day Orozco began his march—not on Chihuahua as was expected, but on the border town of Ciudad Juárez. On the afternoon of February 2 he approached Ciudad Juárez with 1,500 men.[29]

As soon as Orozco's movements were detected by the federal government, President Díaz ordered the manager of the Mexican Central Railroad, Señor Ferriz, to place all his trains at the disposition of the federal troops so that they could be transported to the border city without delay.[30] Colonel Rábago, who received new orders, was directed by the commander of the second military zone to fortify the garrison of Ciudad Juárez.[31]

Although Orozco's detractors have proclaimed that he was utterly indifferent to foreign—especially United States—interests during the northern campaign, abundant documentary evidence refutes this contention. Before the attack on Ciudad Juárez, Orozco sent a special dispatch to the United States consular agent in El Paso, Thomas B. Edwards, in which he requested that the consul notify Americans, other foreigners, and noncombatants to seek a place of safety because the attack on Ciudad Juárez would begin within twenty-four hours.[32]

---

[26] *Mexican Herald*, Feb. 1, 1911.

[27] Casasola, *Historia Gráfica*, I, 229.

[28] AHDN, Min. de Guerra y Marina to Rábago, Exp. XI/481.5/62, Tomo I, folio 4, Feb. 1, 1911.

[29] *El Paso Morning Times*, Feb. 2, 1911.

[30] AHDN, Díaz to Second Military Zone Commander, Exp. XI/481.5/62, Tomo I, folio 107, Feb. 2, 1911.

[31] AHDN, Second Military Zone Commander to Rábago, Exp. XI/481.5/62, Tomo I, folio 209, Feb. 3, 1911.

[32] RDS, Edwards to Sec. of State, 812.00/723, Feb. 4, 1911.

Orozco also announced, publicly, that he would take care not to jeopardize American lives and property.[33]

The attack was scheduled for February 5, the anniversary of the adoption of the Constitution of 1857. At that time Francisco Madero, who had been in the United States since the Revolution began, was to cross into Mexican territory from El Paso to take charge of the movement, but the delay between February 2 and February 5 proved disastrous. On February 4, Colonel Rábago arrived on the outskirts of the city with a large body of reinforcements, succeeded in penetrating the rebel lines, and fortified the Juárez garrison. Advised that General Navarro also was marching on Juárez, with an additional 1,500 men, Orozco wisely gave up his plan to attack the city.[34]

By the end of January, 1911, President Díaz realized that he was losing his grip on the state. In an attempt to salvage elements that were not yet committed to the Revolution, the president called upon one of the most influential men in the state, Miguel Ahumada (governor of Chihuahua from 1892 to 1903), to assume an interim governorship. After receiving his appointment from the Díaz-controlled state legislature on February 1, 1911, the new governor made the following appeal.

> ... I lament with all sincerity the tragic events developing in the District of Guerrero whose virile sons have raised arms . . . bringing mourning and desolation to that rich and prosperous region. Guerrero today is isolated by a civil war, a war of brother against brother, a fratricidal war that must cease at all costs.[35]

The appeal had no effect. Chihuahua was beyond the point of turning

[33] *Mexican Herald*, Feb. 5, 1911. On February 10 several American newspapermen were captured and escorted to General Orozco's camp; as soon as their identity and nationality were determined they were released (RDS, Ellsworth to Sec. of State, 812.00/820, Feb. 11, 1911). Contrary to the reports perpetuated by Orozco's detractors, Americans traveling through territory under the control of the rebels were not mistreated; on the contrary, according to the reports of United States consular agents, they were treated quite well (RDS, Dye, Consul Nogales to Sec. of State, 812.00/729, Feb. 4, 1911).

[34] Orozco's intelligence was correct: Navarro had been ordered to Ciudad Juárez (AHDN, Orders to General Navarro, Exp. IX/481.5/62, Tomo I, folio 232, Feb. 3, 1911). Because the railroad between Chihuahua and Juárez had to be repaired, he did not arrive until February 15 (*Campaña de 1910 a 1911: Estudio en General de las Operaciones que han Tenido Lugar del 18 de Noviembre de 1910 al 25 de Mayo de 1911 en la Parte Correspondiente a la Segunda Zona Militar* [Mexico City: Secretaría de Guerra y Marina, 1913], p. 109; RDS, Ellsworth to Sec. of State, 812.00/735 Feb. 5, 1911).

[35] González Ramírez, *Manifiestos Políticos*, p. 171.

back, and within two weeks Francisco Madero would return to Mexican soil.

Soon after Colonel Ahumada assumed the governorship of the state, rumors began to circulate in the press of the capital that Orozco and Ahumada were old friends and that the former, since his retreat from Ciudad Juárez, had been inactive because he was contemplating turning over his troops to the new governor.[36] Orozco's "inactivity," however, had nothing to do with selling out the Revolution; he was making preparations for a new assault on the border city. When Governor Ahumada offered him a full pardon in return for abandoning the fight, Orozco promptly rejected the offer.[37]

Several days after the attempt upon Ciudad Juárez was frustrated, Madero called a rebel junta meeting in El Paso,[38] which was attended by Abraham González, Raul Madero, Roque González Garza, and other leaders. It was decided that Francisco Madero should reenter Mexico despite the failure to capture the border city. At the same meeting Madero insisted, over the protests of some of his advisers, that the prime goal of the military campaigns in the north should be Casas Grandes rather than Ciudad Juárez.[39] Accordingly, Madero crossed into Mexico on February 14, 1911, at the town of Zaragosa and began making preparations for the attack on Casas Grandes. On March 1, Madero ordered Orozco to mobilize his men, march to Galeana, and await further orders.[40] Five days later, without contacting Orozco further or requesting the cooperation of his troops, the provisional president led an attack on Casas Grandes and suffered the most severe setback of the entire northern campaign.

Madero was wounded in the battle and many of his troops were permanently disabled, taken prisoner, or killed.[41] The rebels' loss at Casas Grandes was compounded by the fact that the federal army also seized sixteen wagons of supplies and munitions and 300 horses.[42]

[36] *Mexican Herald*, Feb. 23, 1911; *El País*, Feb. 26, 1911.

[37] José Fuentes Mares, . . . *Y México se Refugió en el Desierto, Luis Terrazas: Historia y Destino* (Mexico City: Editorial Jus, S. A. 1954), p. 247.

[38] Valadés, *Francisco I. Madero*, II, 102–103.

[39] *Ibid.*, p. 103.

[40] Rosendo Salazar, *Del Militarismo al Civilismo en Nuestra Revolución* (Mexico City: Libro Mex Editores, 1958), p. 184; Amaya, *Madero y los Revolucionarios*, p. 134.

[41] *Campaña de 1910 a 1911*, p. 184; Casasola, *Historia Gráfica*, I, 231–232; Amaya, *Madero y los Revolucionarios*, p. 134.

[42] AREM, Consul, El Paso, to Sec. de Relaciones Exteriores, L–E 640, Sec. 16, Caja 1, Mar. 13, 1911.

Madero's utter failure increased his respect for such *guerrilleros* as Pascual Orozco and Pancho Villa, men who had thwarted the enemy's superiority and who on numerous occasions had emerged victorious from battles with the federals.

Immediately after the engagement at Casas Grandes, Madero moved south to consult with the two rebel leaders at Bustillos, near Ciudad Guerrero. At this temporary headquarters Orozco was awarded his first official military rank in the Revolutionary Army, as Madero appointed him colonel. In the same ceremony Pancho Villa was named major.[43] It was also at this time that Madero made arrangements for a supply line that would carry provisions from the United States border to the rebel headquarters, wherever it might be located at any given time. After several consultations with Orozco, Madero became convinced of the advisability of a new attack on Ciudad Juárez, and this project henceforth was given top priority.

The newly united Revolutionary Army began its slow march to the north at the end of March. Orozco and Villa, charged with seizing the Northwestern and the Mexican Central railroads, accomplished their objectives by early April, thereby isolating Ciudad Juárez. The progressive concentration of government troops in Chihuahua had an important effect on the fortunes of the Revolution in the other Mexican states. Almost without exception, revolutionaries throughout the republic began to increase their activities and expand the size of their armies. By early April the federal forces were once again fighting a war on many fronts.[44]

On April 19, Madero asked General Juan Navarro for the surrender of Ciudad Juárez.[45] Navarro, of course, refused. Several days later, however, Madero received two unofficial peace envoys from President Díaz, Oscar Braniff and Toribio Esquivel Obregón, and on April 22 a temporary armistice was declared and the Madero forces entered into peace negotiations.[46] The discussions for a permanent cessation of hostilities broke

[43] Valadés, *Francisco I. Madero*, II, 139.

[44] By the beginning of April, 1911, there were 5,200 armed rebels in Chihuahua, 1,000 in Coahuila, 4,000 in Sonora, 2,000 in Sinaloa, 800 in Zacatecas, 200 in Nuevo León, 1,500 in Puebla, 1,500 in Veracruz, 1,500 in Guerrero, and 1,000 in Yucatán (Taracena, *La Verdadera Revolución*, I, 127). The revolutionaries were especially active in Durango. Because Durango was in the same military zone as Chihuahua, it was left almost defenseless inasmuch as troops were concentrated farther to the north. As a result, many towns in the state of Durango fell into rebel hands during the last two weeks of April (*Campaña de 1910 a 1911*, pp. 259–262).

[45] *Mexican Herald*, Apr. 20, 1911; Casasola, *Historia Gráfica*, I, 257.

[46] *El País*, Apr. 23, 1911.

down on the key issue of President Díaz' immediate resignation; the revolutionaries insisted on this point but the representatives of the government could not acquiesce. The armistice ended without positive result on May 6, 1911.

Pascual Orozco was at Madero's side throughout the negotiations and was consulted on all of the key issues.[47] It was also during this interlude that Orozco, fully in Madero's confidence, was made a brigadier general.[48] During the ceremony in which Madero confirmed the new commission he made the following remarks in honor of the *guerrillero.*

> Everyone present today, everyone affiliated with our army, everyone who has served in one way or another has acted with heroism. But . . . we must be fair to the man who will go down in history together with the national insurrection which will have transcendental results —Pascual Orozco. He is the hero who stands out among all those who have offered their lives, who have shed their blood for the fatherland. Because of this . . . it is a genuine pleasure to reward him with the rank he deserves—that of General.[49]

The seizure of Ciudad Juárez by the Revolutionary Army and the events that accompanied the seizure constitute one of the most interesting episodes in the military revolt against the Díaz dictatorship. When the peace negotiations broke down on May 6, seasoned troops of the Revolution—under the leadership of Pascual Orozco, Pancho Villa, and the Italian filibuster José Garibaldi (grandson of Giuseppe Garibaldi, the famous nineteenth-century Italian soldier of fortune) were on the outskirts of the border city. Although plans for its seizure had been discussed for more than a month, Madero changed his mind, on May 7, and decided that instead of laying siege to the city the army should turn south. The best explanation for this sudden change of plans is that Madero feared that stray shells would fall on El Paso, Texas, and thus possibly occasion United States military intervention in Mexico.[50]

---

[47] Amaya, *Madero y los Revolucionarios*, p. 172; Casasola, *Historia Gráfica*, I, 257–258; Pascual Ortiz Rubio, *La Revolución de 1910* (Mexico City, 1919), p. 165.

[48] The ceremony during which Orozco received his new commission is described in the *El Paso Morning Times*, Apr. 28, 1911.

[49] BNAM, Informe de Francisco Madero, Caja 3, folio 1568, n.d.

[50] Valadés, *Francisco I. Madero*, II, 162; José Mancisidor, *Historia de la Revolución Mexicana* (Mexico City: Libro Mex Editores, 1959), p. 123. Although the United States had assembled troops along the New Mexico and Texas borders and intervention was a possibility, the press exaggerated the threat (see, for example, *El País*, May 6, 1911).

Madero expressed his misgivings too late, however. Violating the provisional president's countermand, Orozco ordered the attack the following day.

There are several plausible explanations for the attack. A common version is that on the morning of May 8, 1911, federal soldiers and revolutionaries began to hurl insults at one another across the trenches. The exchange of *vivas* and *mueras* soon was replaced by more vulgar utterances from both sides, utterances that culminated in the exchange of shots and a full-scale battle.[51] A less colorful but probably more accurate explanation is that Orozco simply took the initiative on his own. After the disaster at Casas Grandes, none of the northern *guerrilleros* placed much confidence in Madero as a military tactician or strategist, and Orozco—as events would demonstrate—was not above opposing the provisional president if he felt the latter was in error.[52] The indecisive, dilatory direction of Madero and the revolutionary junta in El Paso had previously denied Orozco this prize; therefore, realizing that he possessed superior manpower and fully cognizant of the strategic value of a port of entry, Orozco probably resolved that the city would not be denied him again.[53]

Orozco began the attack on Ciudad Juárez at ten o'clock in the morning of May 8, 1911. Upon learning of Orozco's insubordination, Madero informed General Navarro that the engagement was completely unauthorized and personally ordered Orozco to suspend the attack.[54] Orozco's reply was evasive: "It is impossible because our

[51] This is a common version; cf. Alfonso Taracena, *Madero, El Héroe Cívico* (Mexico City: Ediciones Xochitl, 1946), p. 129; Casasola, *Historia Gráfica*, I, 269; and Howard Cline, *The United States and Mexico* (Cambridge, Mass.: Harvard University Press, 1953), p. 124.

[52] José R. del Castillo states that Orozco decided on the evening of May 7 that he would attack on the following morning (*Historia de la Revolución Social de México* [Mexico City, 1915], p. 296). Others who accept this explanation are Amaya (*Madero y los Revolucionarios*, p. 181), Ross (*Madero*, p. 164), and Rafael F. Muñoz ("Pascual Orozco: Caudillo Olvidado," *Así* [Apr. 26, 1941], p. 19).

[53] Figures for the numerical strength of contingents in all revolutionary engagements must be used with care, but it is clear that in this case the rebels greatly outnumbered General Navarro's federal garrison. Casasola cites 900 for the federals and more than 1,500 for the rebels (*Historia Gráfica*, I, 269–270); Rosendo Salazar credits the federals with 1,116 (*Del Militarismo al Civilismo*, p. 189). The report of General Navarro appears exaggerated; he claimed he had only 675 able-bodied troops with which to defend the city against some 3,500 rebels (*Campaña de 1910 a 1911*, pp. 288–289).

[54] BNAM, Madero to Orozco, Caja 3, folio 1570, May 8, 1911.

soldiers have already captured some enemy positions. It is best to continue."[55] Orozco ordered his troops to advance to the Rio Grande, above and below the positions that had been fortified by General Navarro's federal garrison. By conducting the campaign parallel to the river rather than by a frontal assault toward the United States border, the rebel commander hoped to avoid the possibility of inadvertently shelling El Paso.[56] By noon of the first day the rebels had captured several key positions along the railroad line and had taken a few houses on the outskirts of the city. By mid-afternoon the first line of federal trenches had fallen to the rebels and by nine in the evening Orozco's troops had moved into the city itself.[57]

During the evening of the first day, Madero once again changed his mind and accepted Orozco's decision to attack. Madero demonstrated his tacit approval by demanding that Navarro surrender the city in order to avoid complications with the United States.[58]

Although sporadic fighting continued throughout the night, it was not until dawn of May 9 that the rebels renewed the attack in earnest. Orozco then changed his tactic and deployed his troops between the federal garrison and El Paso, but still along the river: if stray shells were lobbed over the border, the troops of the government would be held accountable. A good description of the military situation during the morning of the second day is recorded in a dispatch from the Mexican consul in El Paso to the Secretaría de Relaciones Exteriores in Mexico City.

10:00 A.M. Considerable losses both sides. It is said that more than fifty rebels have been killed and over twice that number have been wounded. Madero is not commanding his troops. The rebels are in control of Avenida Juárez and the federals cannot fire upon them because they are facing the American border.[59]

[55] Quoted in Vásquez Gómez, *Memorias Políticas*, p. 171. A slightly different reply, but one that conveys the same message, was recorded by José Castillo: "I will not call my men back. On the contrary, I am going to reinforce the line of fire" (*Historia de la Revolución*, p. 299).

[56] This plan of attack had been devised for Orozco's first attempt on Ciudad Juárez, and the United States officials on the border had been informed of the plan (Records of the Adjutant General's Office [AGO], National Archives, Hoyt to Adjutant General, Doc. File Box 6314, No. 1716354, A 122, Feb. 4, 1911).

[57] Amaya, *Madero y los Revolucionarios*, p. 187, and Ross, *Madero*, p. 164.

[58] *El País*, May 9, 1911.

[59] AREM, Torres, Consul El Paso to Sec. de Relaciones Exteriores, L–E 658 73–17), May 9, 1911.

By noon, the tide had turned in favor of the assaulters. All communications out of Juárez had been cut and great quantities of federal artillery and ammunition had been captured. In the early afternoon of May 10, 1911, General Navarro hoisted a white flag over the last remaining federal barracks and turned the city over to the *Ejército Libertador*.[60]

Navarro's surrender ushered in a period of complete chaos in Ciudad Juárez. As often happens after the disappearance of civil authority, looting, pillaging, and burning became commonplace. Not only did the brigands and shoplifters of the civilian populace put their talents to the test, but also unruly elements within the army relieved themselves of all pent-up inhibitions and restraint.[61] Orozco immediately issued strict orders to his men to guard stores and houses and to prevent looting,[62] and within thirty-six hours unmitigated anarchy had given way to effective military government. Then, informed that groups of bandits were passing themselves off as members of the *Ejército Libertador* and were looting and pillaging in the countryside, Orozco named Lic. Martín Castillos as a special agent of the Revolutionary Army and charged him with ferreting out the bandits and bringing them to justice.[63]

On May 11, 1911, Madero made Ciudad Juárez the provisional capital of the country and named his provisional cabinet. Two days later an episode occurred which was the first serious conflict between civilian and military authorities in the Mexican Revolution. On May 13, as Madero was presiding over a cabinet meeting at the customs house (the temporary capitol), Pascual Orozco and Pancho Villa broke into the room and made three demands of the provisional president. The first demand was that General Navarro be tried as a war criminal. The argument that ensued became quite heated and on at least one occasion revolvers were leveled at the provisional president.[64] After a few tense

---

[60] *El Paso Morning Times*, May 10, 1911. Five persons were killed and fourteen wounded in El Paso during the fighting (Albert Bacon Fall Collection [ABFC], University of New Mexico, Papers from the Senate Office Files of Senator Albert Bacon Fall Relating to Mexican Affairs, "Persons Killed or Wounded during the Juárez Battle," May 23, 1911).

[61] There is very strong evidence that riffraff from El Paso partook in the looting after the battle (BNAM, Madero to Orozco, Caja 3, folio 1547, May 14, 1911).

[62] *Mexican Herald*, May 11, 1911.

[63] BNAM, Orozco to Madero, Caja 3, folio 1574, May 14, 1911; BNAM, Hopkins to Vásquez Gómez, Caja 4, folio 2103, May 13, 1911.

[64] *Mexican Herald*, May 14, 1911; *El País*, May 14, 1911; *La Verdad*, May 18, 1912; AGO, Devore to Adjutant General, Doc. File Box 6316, No. 1716354, AG 86, May 15, 1911.

moments the discussion was resumed and Madero convinced Orozco that the bitter passions engendered by the recent campaigns would preclude an impartial trial at that time. Orozco finally acquiesced.

The charge of many historians that Orozco and Villa wanted the life of Navarro (who had ordered the execution of rebel prisoners at Cerro Prieto the previous December), although probably correct, is also misleading, for it is implied that what the two military chieftains really wanted was a lynching.[65] If Orozco had wanted the immediate execution of Navarro, he could have accomplished it during the hours between Navarro's surrender of the city and Madero's entrance on May 10, 1911.[66] Orozco had asked for a court-martial,[67] and although the result in either case might have been the same for the hated federal general, there is no reason to imply by omission that Orozco did not want to follow legitimate judicial processes. Madero himself, in a statement to the press on May 14, vindicated Orozco. Speaking of his decision to spare Navarro's life by conducting him across the border to the American side, Madero said:

> In honor of Orozco, I should say that he himself proposed to me that we should act in this manner from the beginning. And even Villa, himself, told me with all submission that whatever I did was well done. Consequently it is not true that any of the officers has demanded his life from me.[68]

Orozco's second demand was for the immediate resignation of Madero's provisional cabinet and for the naming of new ministers

[65] Christiansen, "Pascual Orozco," p. 107; Francisco Almada, "Ciudad Juárez al Través de la Revolución," *Boletín de la Sociedad Chihuahuense de Estudios Históricos*, VI (Aug.–Sept., 1954), p. 7; Cumberland, *Mexican Revolution*, p. 144; Ortiz Rubio, *La Revolución de 1910*, p. 215. Contemporary newspaper coverage is exemplified by a headline in the *San Francisco Examiner* (May 14, 1911): "CRYING DEATH TO NAVARRO OROZCO LEADS REVOLT AGAINST MADERO." The suggestion of Stanley Ross that some of Orozco's men demanded the life of the federal commander is more tenable (*Madero*, p. 167). Another version is that Villa wanted to kill Navarro and that Orozco stopped him (AGO, Steever to Adjutant General, File Box 6316, No. 1716354, May 13, 1911).

[66] Navarro, according to his official report, surrendered at 2:30 P.M. (*Campaña de 1910 a 1911*, p. 294); Madero did not enter the city until 5:00 P.M. (Amaya, *Madero y los Revolucionarios*, p. 192).

[67] *El Paso Morning Times*, May 13, 1911.

[68] *Mexican Herald*, May 14, 1911. Charles Cumberland says there is evidence that Orozco demanded Navarro's execution despite Madero's statement to the contrary, but he does not cite this evidence or indicate where it can be found (*Mexican Revolution*, p. 144, n. 134). I have found no evidence that supports Cumberland's contention.

from those who had fought in the campaigns and had given Madero his provisional capital.[69] The appointment of a civilian, Venustiano Carranza, as Minister of War probably was especially unsavory to Orozco, who had been convinced by his father and many of his friends that this position should be the reward for the services Orozco junior had rendered the Revolution. At any rate, Orozco again was forced to back down; Madero was unyielding on the point that he alone, as provisional president, had the right to name the cabinet.

Only in his last demand was the *guerrillero* successful. He complained that his men had not been paid, did not have enough to eat, and were ready to mutiny. Madero first tried to overrule this demand, stating that the banks had not yet given him the money they had promised and that therefore he could do nothing to rectify the situation. Only when Orozco threatened serious trouble did the provisional president write a check for $750 drawn on the City Bank of El Paso.[70] Madero told Orozco that the money was to be distributed among the troops and that additional funds would be available if needed.[71]

After the tension had subsided and the compromises were effected, Orozco and Madero appeared before the throng of soldiers who had gathered outside the building. To show that the forces of the Revolution were still united, the two men exchanged *abrazos* before the cheering crowd. A few days later, to ensure cooperation between the military and the civil authority, the two leaders exchanged formal letters that were distributed as flyers to the troops.[72] Madero wrote Orozco:

*Ciudad Juárez, May 15, 1911*

## SR. GENERAL PASCUAL OROZCO

MY DEAR FRIEND,

Referring to the events which occurred here on the thirteenth of this month, and which popular fantasy and our enemies have exaggerated out of all proportion in order to spread the rumor that we are divided, I am happy to clarify the matter through this letter by stating that it is true that we had a rather heated discussion because

[69] Ortiz Rubio, *La Revolución de 1910*, p. 215.

[70] BNAM, Madero to Orozco, Caja 3, folio 1573, May 13, 1911.

[71] *Ibid.*

[72] Six copies of the flyers that contain the exchange of letters have been preserved in the Biblioteca Nacional: BNAM, Dos Cartas Interesantes Cambiadas Entre el Presidente Provisional Francisco I. Madero y el General Pascual Orozco, H., Caja 3, folio 1577.

of various administrative matters, but we were far from harboring the idea of splitting and ceasing to direct all of our energy toward the triumph of the sacred cause for which we have fought with such success up until the present time.

I also want to make clear that I have never doubted your loyalty to my government nor your personal friendship toward me. This was demonstrated by the firm *abrazos* which we exchanged in public. Even if something [serious] had occurred, this would have been sufficient to blot out the slightest misunderstanding from your heart or mine. You and I are fighting for ideals and we will never be side-tracked from our purpose by any personal animosity, especially since at this time none exists. I repeat, not for a single moment do I doubt your friendship for me.

Once more I want you to know that I am your loyal friend and will always have the highest esteem for you.

FRANCISCO I. MADERO

General Orozco's reply to the provisional president appeared on the same flyer.

*Ciudad Juárez, May 15, 1911*

## SEÑOR FRANCISCO I. MADERO

## PROVISIONAL PRESIDENT OF THE REPUBLIC

MY RESPECTED FRIEND,

I take pleasure in referring to your letter of the same date.

As you wisely indicate, our political enemies and popular fantasy have given the events which took place on the thirteenth of this month proportions which they do not deserve. Popular fantasy has exaggerated them and our political enemies falsified them in order to give substance to the rumor that we are divided in the noble task of overthrowing tyranny. Nothing could be further from the truth! Our union is indestructible because in addition to the friendship and affection which one man can have for another, our sentiment demands that in this historic moment every honorable Mexican should join forces for the love of the country.

Mr. President: When the sons of Guerrero District rose up in arms with me on November 20, 1910, seconding the plan promulgated by you in San Luis Potosí, we accepted it as a harbinger of the Mexican people and swore at that time to shed our blood for the triumph of that noble enterprise. This oath we remember and today it is still more vivid in my heart and in those of my fellow companions in arms.

You can be sure of this, Mr. President, as well as of our constant loyalty and respect.

Yours respectfully,

P. OROZCO H.

If the accounts of what transpired between Orozco and Madero differ, the reasons suggested for Orozco's "insubordination" vary even more. Undoubtedly, a combination of factors acted upon the general. It is likely that he was disappointed in not having received a cabinet position, but his rise from obscurity to national prominence had been much too fast. Just as failure often results in lowering the aspirational level, success had caused it to rise. Orozco's lack of the educational qualifications for a cabinet position must have seemed less important than the respect—the adulation—of the masses. In addition, there is little doubt that Orozco was moved by the plight of his men. Finally, strong evidence suggests that persons who were interested in splitting the forces of the Revolution seized upon Orozco's discontent and encouraged him to take the stands that he did.

The former peace envoys of Porfirio Díaz, Toribio Esquivel Obregón and Oscar Braniff, were in Juárez at the time and are often singled out as the culprits.[73] In his memoirs, Esquivel Obregón says that he spoke to Orozco once on the telephone and met with him three times between the surrender of the city and the incident with Madero.[74] Madero, who believed that the two representatives of the federal government were behind the affair, told the press that "Orozco, excited by victory, . . . and by the bad advice of persons interested in causing disunion among us, committed an error which fortunately had no consequences."[75]

The conflicting evidence about the role of the unofficial representatives of the federal government in fomenting Orozco's insubordination precludes a positive determination. The federal government, of course, was immediately advised of the incident.[76] Even if the government did

[73] *El País*, May 15, 1911; *La Verdad*, May 15, 1912; Francisco Ramírez Plancarte, *La Revolución Mexicana* (Mexico City: Editorial B. Costa-Amic, 1948), p. 272; Ross, *Madero*, p. 168; Mancisidor, *Historia de la Revolución*, p. 132; Vásquez Gómez, *Memorias Políticas*, pp. 182–183.

[74] Toribio Esquivel Obregón, *Democracia y Personalismo* (Mexico City: Imprenta de A. Carranza e Hijos, 1911), pp. 60, 73–74. Obregón, however, denied having had anything to do with the incident itself (*El Tiempo*, July 10, 1911).

[75] *Mexican Herald*, May 14, 1911.

[76] AREM, Torres to Sec. de Relaciones Exteriores, L–E 685 (73–17), May 13, 1911.

not instigate the affair, it must have been immensely pleased with the first reports: if the reconciliation had not been prompt the cause of the Revolution would undoubtedly have suffered a severe setback.

The Orozco-Madero affair must be interpreted as a victory for civilian authority, which Orozco accepted unenthusiastically. The fraternity suggested by the exchange of *abrazos* and the subsequent exchange of letters was, at best, superficial, and designed only to avert a disastrous schism. Although a split was avoided, the personal enmity generated by the episode was not forgotten. Within a year the antagonism conceived in Ciudad Juárez would receive strong stimulation and would erupt in a serious revolution against the incumbent Madero regime.

# III

# *The Tenuous Armistice*

The capture of Ciudad Juárez by General Pascual Orozco was the turning point in the military campaigns against the dictator. Although skirmishes continued to be fought throughout the country, the success of the Revolution was no longer seriously in doubt. In addition to giving the forces of the Revolution an important city, a provisional capital, and an official port of entry through which arms and munitions could be legally imported, the victory had a tremendous morale factor. Their confidence bolstered by the capture of the border city, rebels in virtually every state of the country intensified their efforts. President Díaz, however, not yet convinced of the inevitable, ordered General Antonio Rábago to fortify the federal garrison in Chihuahua City.[1] Orozco left Ciudad Juárez for Casas Grandes, and began making preparations for the engagement, but the battle did not take place. Díaz succumbed to the mounting pressure and resigned on May 25, 1911. Francisco León de la Barra, Díaz' Secretary of Foreign Relations, assumed the interim presidency.

The month that followed the resignation of the dictator was a hectic period of governmental reorganization throughout Mexico. Although revolutionary governments had been established in some of the states, the elimination of most of the political relics of the old regime occurred in June, 1911. In Chihuahua, Abraham González was named interim governor, replacing the Porfirist head of the state, Miguel Ahumada. During the changeover Orozco and a large body of his troops camped at Saúz, on the Central Railroad line between Chihuahua and Ciudad

[1] AREM, De la Barra to Consul, El Paso, L–E 685 (73–17), May 15, 1911. This dispatch was sent through the consular agent in El Paso rather than through regular military channels because the rebels controlled all of the communication facilities in the state of Chihuahua.

Juárez.[2] On June 23 the force was ordered to proceed to the capital of the state.

The reception given Orozco and his 3,000 troops was extraordinary; a newspaper account described it as follows:

> General Pascual Orozco, to whom much credit is given for the early successes of the revolution, entered Chihuahua today at the head of his troops. Tomorrow, all those who have not already called for their checks . . . will receive their pay . . . and the famous aggregation which for months held sway along the border will have disappeared.
>
> The troops came into the city mounted on mules and horses of every size and age, and carrying arms of all descriptions, but in spite of their unmilitary appearance, they were given such a reception as is due a conquering army. Three military bands and more than a thousand regulars and *rurales* escorted them into town, and at the governor's palace, where Orozco was received, old officers of the regular army rubbed elbows with the newly constituted ones, apparently in the utmost accord.
>
> Generals Rábago and Villar stood with Governor González while Orozco bowed acknowledgment of the honors heaped upon him. Once or twice he tried to escape from the applauding crowd but was as often called back to face what appeared to him a more trying ordeal than any hitherto encountered during the rebellion.[3]

A few weeks later Orozco received an official appointment from the provisional government in Mexico City: he was named commander of the *rurales* in the state of Chihuahua. This modest position was rewarded with an even more modest salary: eight pesos a day.[4]

During the last week of June, however, Orozco fell victim to the great temptation of the military hero; he made a serious bid for political office—the first and only time in his life. The gubernatorial election in Chihuahua was scheduled for late August, 1911, but by the middle of June the interim governor, Abraham González, was by far the strongest candidate. At the end of June a new political organization, the Club

[2] Amaya, *Madero y los Revolucionarios*, p. 216.

[3] *Mexican Herald*, June 22, 1911. Another newspaper stated that "Orozco was dragged from his horse and carried upon the shoulders of his admirers to the reception at the governor's palace" (*El Paso Morning Times*, June 23, 1911). Still another newspaper reported that no fewer than 30,000 persons turned out to greet Orozco (*El País*, June 22, 1911). The welcome Orozco received in various towns and cities throughout Mexico—these strong appeals to human vanity—help explain some of Orozco's subsequent actions.

[4] Henry Baerlein, *Mexico, Land of Unrest* (Philadelphia: Lippincott, n.d.), p. 230.

Independiente Chihuahuense, was formed to oppose the Madero-backed candidate. This organization was colored by a wide array of political hues, but the Gonzalista supporters availed themselves of a number of popular revolutionary slogans and quickly labeled the club a party of reaction.[5] Nonetheless, it was not difficult for the newly formed group to designate a likely and extremely popular opposition candidate. On June 26 the club offered its support for the governorship of the state to Pascual Orozco, and two days later the general agreed to run.[6]

The Porfirist elements in the state certainly lent support to the Club Independiente Chihuahuense, but there is no conclusive evidence that indicates that conservative interests dominated the group: in fact, the two most important conservatives in Chihuahua, General Luis Terrazas and Enrique Creel, refused to support the club.[7] All competent political surveys of the first few months after the resignation of Porfirio Díaz indicate that opposition to Madero came from the left as well as the right, and the student with even a cursory familiarity with Latin American politics in the twentieth century knows that temporary coalitions of opposing political factions are not uncommon. It is therefore likely that the intrinsic animosity between left and right gave way to a temporary *mariage de convenance* in order to oppose the imposition of the first in a long series of "official" candidates.

The two weeks that followed his official announcement of candidacy must have been extremely difficult for the political novice. The full wrath of the interim state political machine was directed against Orozco and the charges of his pact with the old oligarchy, neatly devised and propagated by the supporters of Abraham González, were picked up and aired by the press;[8] indeed, Madero advised the *guerrillero* against presenting himself as a candidate.[9] The legalists of the official party then found that Orozco was ineligible: the state constitution stipulated that a governor must be at least thirty years of age, and Orozco was a few months short of his thirtieth birthday.[10]

On July 15, 1911, Orozco's short-lived venture into politics came to

[5] Amaya, *Madero y los Revolucionarios*, p. 262.

[6] *El Paso Morning Times*, June 29, 1911.

[7] *Mexican Herald*, July 2, 1911.

[8] *El País*, June 26, 1911; *El Paso Morning Times*, July 10, 1911; Luis Vargas Piñera, "El Gobierno Maquinó la Sublevación de Pascual Orozco Contra Madero," *Excélsior* (Sept. 4, 1938), magazine section, pp. 1–2.

[9] *El Paso Morning Times*, Apr. 24, 1912.

[10] *Mexican Herald*, July 2, 1911.

an end as he yielded to pressure from many quarters and announced his withdrawal from the gubernatorial race.[11] The following explanation was sent to the press:

> My candidacy for governor of the state of Chihuahua has caused great excitement . . . the people thinking that this has been dictated by the last official administration . . . such suspicions are not true. They should be considered only false alarms. I have decided, considering it patriotic, to make a formal resignation of my candidacy.
>
> PASCUAL OROZCO[12]

On August 21, 1911, Abraham González was elected governor of Chihuahua without opposition.[13] Although he was not in sympathy with the new administration—or perhaps because he was not—Orozco retained his position as commander of the Chihuahua *rurales*.

Orozco's short venture into Mexican political life contains a more important message. His campaign demonstrates for the first time that

[11] The statement of the generally meticulous Charles Cumberland that Orozco ran for the governorship and was "overwhelmingly defeated in a free election by the popular and able Abraham González" is incorrect. Cumberland's authority for this is the violently anti-Orozco polemic of Ramón Puente (*Pascual Orozco*, pp. 31, 41–43). Frederick Starr (*Mexico and the United States*, p. 341) makes the same error, as does Salvador Resendi (*La Revolución Actual* [Mexico City: Librería Vda de Ch. Bouret, 1912], p. 38). The contemporary press and the United States consular agent in Chihuahua reported that Orozco withdrew from the race (*El Paso Morning Times*, July 15, 1911; *El Tiempo*, July 13, 1911; and RDS, Letcher to Sec. of State, 812.00/ 3424, Mar. 20, 1912). Orozco's withdrawal is confirmed by Francisco Almada (*La Revolución en Chihuahua*, pp. 245–246). The statements of Antonio P. González and J. Figueroa Domenech that Terrazas and Creel offered the candidacy to Orozco and that the latter turned it down from the beginning is completely incorrect (*La Revolución y sus Heroes* [Mexico City: Librería de Ortega y Compañía, 1911], p. 188). Launa Smith's contention that Madero succeeded in making Orozco military and civil governor of the state is also without foundation (*American Relations with Mexico* [Oklahoma City: Harlow Publishing Co., 1924], p. 72).

[12] *El Paso Morning Times*, July 15, 1911.

[13] *Ibid.*, Aug. 21, 1911. Shortly after he won the governorship, Abraham González asked the Chihuahua legislature for a leave of absence because he had received an appointment as Secretary of Gobernación from Madero. Although the legislature complied with the request, the situation caused considerable discontent within the state. Absentee governorships and/or the substitution of a weak interim governor had been one of the most serious political abuses during the Díaz dictatorship. Now the situation was repeated under the first constitutional government that stemmed from the Revolution. The political indignation generated by this questionable political maneuver would be a factor in Chihuahua's readiness to support a number of anti-Madero movements.

the resounding phrases of political democracy, eloquently aired in Madero's Plan de San Luis Potosí, were at best a peculiar Mexican adaptation of traditionally accepted democratic principles and at worst nothing more than a charade. Political candidates in the states were free to conduct their campaigns as long as they enjoyed the endorsement of the national government in Mexico City. The birth of the concept of an "official party" does not rest, as most observers suggest, with the formation of the Partido Nacional Revolucionario (P.N.R.), the Partido Revolucionario Mexicano (P.R.M.), or the Partido Revolucionario Institucional (P.R.I.), but rather with the subtle, indirect, but nevertheless effective pressures brought to bear upon potential candidates from the moment of the initial revolutionary triumph.

As the Chihuahua political campaign was unfolding, the choice of Madero's running mate in the scheduled presidential election was fiercely debated, and the issue became so heated that the revolutionary party split into opposing factions. A group that retained the name Partido Anti-reeleccionista supported the nomination of Francisco Vásquez Gómez, while the new Partido Constitucionalista Progresista favored the selection of José María Pino Suárez of Yucatán. In late August the nominating convention, following the wishes of the presidential nominee, selected the Yucatecan as the vice-presidential candidate.

A much more serious threat came from outside the immediate revolutionary family. In June the ex-Porfirist general Bernardo Reyes returned to Mexico from a military study mission in Europe. Reyes had been ordered to return by José Ives de Limantour, Díaz' competent Minister of Finance, before the dictatorship fell. Having reached Mexico after the triumph of the Revolution, Reyes decided to ally himself with the new cause and by the end of July had presented himself as a candidate in opposition to Madero in the forthcoming election. The campaign was bitter, with serious recriminations voiced from both sides, and Reyes once was assaulted by a mob of "Maderistas." There was fear in Mexico City that Reyes, should he lose the election, might attempt to seize power by force.[14]

Almost immediately, Pascual Orozco—probably because of his earlier difficulty with Madero and his brief and unsuccessful venture into Chihuahua politics—was linked in the public mind with the Reyes

[14] Cumberland, *Mexican Revolution*, p. 166.

camp.[15] The rumor was given further credibility at the official Reyista convention in Mexico City, on September 12, 1911. The convention's closing address was delivered by Lic. Rafael Rodríguez Talavera, whose peroration was a panegyric for the "revolutionary soldier that so gallantly fought for the cause of the people—Pascual Orozco."[16] The delegates left the convention amidst cries of "¡*Viva Orozco!*" The same evening the board of directors of the Reyista Party voted to make Orozco an honorary member of the board, but Orozco declined the offer.[17] Several days after the convention, Reyes, crying fraud and coercion, withdrew from the race and went into exile in San Antonio, Texas. The primary election occurred without incident, on October 1, 1911,[18] and the Madero–Pino Suárez ticket carried the day.

Orozco, who had been completely neutral throughout the campaign, arrived in Mexico City the evening before election day. The *guerrillero*'s reception in the capital was similar to the one in Chihuahua three and a half months earlier:[19] more than 2,000 persons met the general at the railroad station and another huge crowd gathered outside his hotel. A typical example of Orozco's treatment at the hands of the pro-revolutionary school records Orozco's first visit to Mexico City. Rather than discuss Orozco's reception or his itinerary in the capital, one partisan historian preferred to project an "image":

> Orozco revealed clearly . . . the wild instincts and savage passions of the criminal. His physiognomy had the features which betray qualities inclined and sensitive to crime. His lower jaw, broad and heavy, the enormous mouth, the thin lips, the large face with broad cheekbones, the discolored skin, the scant beard, the broad straight nose, the projecting ears, and lastly the cold and repellant glances which shoot forth from faded blue eyes, show in him an aggregation of anthropological signs extremely common in the criminal man, to such an extent as to arouse in one's mind the impression of a mattoid.[20]

[15] RDS, Ross, Special Agent, Department of Justice, to Sec. of State, 812.00/2342, Sept. 2, 1911.

[16] *Mexican Herald*, Sept. 14, 1911.

[17] *El Tiempo*, Sept. 22, 1911.

[18] The primary election at the beginning of October was merely for presidential electors. The electors cast their votes two weeks later, officially confirming the election of Francisco Madero and José María Pino Suárez.

[19] Great demonstrations also occurred in Zacatecas, on September 30, when Orozco's train stopped there for the day (*Mexican Herald*, Oct. 1, 1911).

[20] Puente, *Pascual Orozco*, pp. 53–54.

Several days after Orozco's arrival in Mexico City, he had an interview with the interim president, Francisco León de la Barra. As a direct result of this interview a week later the Chihuahua general was named commander of the *rurales* in the state of Sinaloa.[21] The appointment was announced by the Secretary of Gobernación, Alberto García Granados, on October 9. Although this seemingly strange appointment has never been explained, it is not difficult to understand the president's reasoning. Bernardo Reyes was already plotting revolution from the United States[22] and because the rumors of Orozco's support of Reyes had degenerated into his alleged complicity in the imminent insurrection,[23] it seemed expedient to remove Orozco from the United States border and from the center of his vast popularity in the state of Chihuahua. Probably unaware of the political machinations behind his appointment, Orozco accepted the promotion, which was accompanied by a raise in salary to fifteen pesos a day.

The news of Orozco's new position unleashed a storm of protest in Chihuahua. Hundreds of telegrams were sent to President de la Barra requesting that Orozco not be removed from the state:[24] contrary to the president's reasoning, the Chihuahuenses believed that if a Reyista revolution broke out in the state, General Orozco was the only person who could cope with the situation. The protests notwithstanding, the new commission was not revoked, and Orozco arrived in Mazatlán early in the third week of November.[25]

Francisco Madero was inaugurated on November 6, 1911. Not only did the new administration inherit the political dissidence engendered by the De la Barra regime, but quickly—almost methodically—it seemed to cultivate its own.[26] The Reyes revolution, expected for

[21] *El Tiempo*, Oct. 3, 1911.

[22] Although Reyes' revolutionary plan was not pronounced until November 14, his activities were well known in early October. For an interesting account of Reyes' exile in the United States, see Vic Niemeyer, "Frustrated Invasion: The Revolutionary Attempt of General Bernardo Reyes from San Antonio in 1911," *Southwestern Historical Quarterly*, LXVII (July, 1963–June, 1964), 213–225.

[23] RDS, F. H. Lancaster, Special Agent, Department of Justice, to Sec. of State, 812.00/2438, Oct. 16, 1911.

[24] *El Paso Morning Times*, Oct. 10, 1911.

[25] Archivo General de la Nación (AGN), Ramo de la Secretaría de Gobernación, Leg. 21, Exp. 4, Gov. Banderas to Sec. de Gobernación, Nov. 17, 1911.

[26] During the last two months of the De la Barra interim presidency, small revolts against the federal government were reported in the states of Veracruz, Puebla, Sinaloa, Coahuila, Aguascalientes, Jalisco, Hidalgo, Michoacán, Oaxaca, and Mexico (AGN, various reports from Administradores Principales del Timbre to Sec. de Gobernación, Leg. 16, Exp. 1, Oct.–Nov., 1911).

several months, was scheduled to begin December 1, and Madero, finding little reason to accept de la Barra's evaluation of Orozco's loyalty, decided to send the Chihuahuan back to his native state. On November 20, 1911, before Orozco had completed his first week as commander of the Sinaloa *rurales*, Madero ordered him back to Mexico City,[27] and several days later the general was sent to Chihuahua.[28] Orozco was given command of the important federal garrison at Ciudad Juárez on November 27.[29] Madero's confidence in Orozco, as it turned out, was not put to a severe test immediately, for Reyes was arrested in the United States soon afterward for violation of neutrality laws.

Besides negating the chances for a successful revolution, the arrest was the first important indication that the United States, which had been very tolerant of rebel activity north of the Rio Grande during the anti-Díaz movement, was adopting a new and more stringent exile policy.[30] Immediately after Reyes' arrest, a date was set for his trial and he was released on bond. During the first week in December, reports were published in the press to the effect that "positive proof" of Orozco's complicity in the revolutionary plot would be made public during General Reyes' trial.[31] The "proof," it was said, had been obtained by a special agent of the Department of Justice, who ten days earlier had reported to the Secretary of State that he had seen five typewritten letters, over the signature of Pascual Orozco, in which the general had offered his services and the support of his men to Bernardo Reyes. The report also alleged that one of Orozco's sisters and one of his brothers were working in San Antonio for the Reyes cause.[32] Orozco's enemies were "cheated," however: Reyes jumped bond, the trial had to be canceled, and the alleged evidence was never brought to light.

Reyes reentered Mexico on December 4, 1911, still hopeful of finding mass support for his revolt against Madero. Apparently accepting Orozco's collusion a priori, the American consul in Nuevo Laredo erroneously reported that Reyes was going to join the Chihuahua

[27] AGN, Sec. de Gobernación to Banderas, Leg. 21, Exp. 4, Nov. 20, 1911.

[28] *El Tiempo*, Nov. 21, 1911.

[29] RDS, [Ross], Special Agent, to Sec. of State, 812.00/2606, Nov. 27, 1911.

[30] The United States' strict enforcement of its neutrality laws would have a profound effect on the Orozquista movement.

[31] *Mexican Herald*, Dec. 4, 1911; *El Paso Morning Times*, Dec. 4, 1911.

[32] RDS, [Ross], Special Agent, to Sec. of State, 812.00/2645, Nov. 22, 1911. The report was seemingly confirmed in a special dispatch sent to the Adjutant General (AGO, Special Report, Mexican Revolutionary Situation, Doc. File Box, 6720, No. 1849275, A 19, Nov. 22, 1911).

general, who—according to the consul—had just declared for Reyes.[33] Not only did Reyes not receive the support of Orozco, his invasion received practically no support from any quarter. In late December he surrendered to a small detachment of *rurales* at Linares, Nuevo León, and was sent first to Monterrey and then to the Prisión Militar de Santiago Tlaltelolco in Mexico City.

Orozco's "support" of the Reyes revolution appears to have been a complete fabrication. When the news of the incriminating letters was released in the press, Orozco immediately denied the charges,[34] and several days later he requested that the American consul in Ciudad Porfirio Díaz (now Piedras Negras) advise the "press of the border" that the alleged letters—if they existed—were forgeries.[35] If Orozco's denial of the accusations were his only defense, one might seriously question his integrity, but his subsequent support of Madero in another serious conspiracy indicates that as late as January, 1912, he was loyal to the government.

While Bernardo Reyes was plotting his revolution from the United States, another independent revolt was developing in a parallel fashion. Emilio Vásquez Gómez, believing he and his brother had been unjustly treated in the presidential election, began to look for support in early November. Initially unsuccessful in his bid for assistance, in December he announced his adherence to the Plan of Tacubaya. This plan, although it had been drawn up before Madero took office, was a condemnation of Madero and a "recognition" of Emilio Vásquez Gómez as president of Mexico. Once again the name of Pascual Orozco was associated with a "counterrevolution," and once again the general's allegiance was debated.

The first serious Vasquista uprising in Chihuahua occurred shortly after Madero dispatched Orozco to Ciudad Juárez to guard against the movements of Bernardo Reyes. At the end of November, Antonio Rojas, an ex-revolutionary colonel, pronounced himself in revolt and proclaimed Vásquez Gómez president of Mexico. Fortuitously for those who were addicted to attaching Orozco's name to every anti-Madero insurrection, regardless of its nature, Rojas took it upon himself to proclaim Pascual Orozco vice-president.[36] Although the

[33] RDS, Garrett, Consul, Nuevo Laredo, to Sec. of State, 812.00/2585, Dec. 4, 1911.

[34] *Mexican Herald*, Dec. 7, 1911, and *El Tiempo*, Dec. 7, 1911.

[35] RDS, Ellsworth, Consul, Cd. Porfirio Díaz, to Sec. of State, 812.00/2583, Dec. 14, 1911.

[36] R. A. Ugalde, *Vida de Pascual Orozco: Orozco, General y Caudillo* (El Paso,

general was unable to deal with Rojas personally because of his commitments in Ciudad Juárez, he dispatched a close friend and cohort, Major Juan Dozal, to put down the insurrection. Dozal accomplished his aim with little effort and brought Rojas to Chihuahua City, where he was interned in the state penitentiary.[37]

After the collapse of the Reyista movement, in late December, 1911, Orozco was able to devote his full efforts to combating the Vasquista conspiracy, and in early January, 1912, several small, poorly coordinated movements were crushed. Orozco personally led the government forces on some occasions, and dispatched competent subordinates on others. Within two weeks the Vasquista threat appeared to have been removed. In the middle of January, President Madero invited Orozco to return to Mexico City, and rumors began to circulate in Chihuahua that the general would be sent into the state of Morelos, where a third serious anti-Madero movement was being waged—by Emiliano Zapata.[38]

Orozco arrived in the capital on January 19 and was immediately received by the president, but the purpose and outcome of the meeting were not made public. When questioned by the press and by other interested parties, Madero was evasive, saying the discussion related primarily to affairs in the state of Chihuahua.[39] Although this conference is seldom discussed by those who attempt to explain Orozco's subsequent defection from the Maderist fold, it provides at least one extremely important key to the Orozquista revolt. The best evidence of what transpired between Orozco and Madero was recorded by Juan Gualberto Amaya, a historian who obtained much of his information through conversations and interviews with Orozco and Orozco's family and intimates. According to Amaya, a serious rift developed during the meeting: Madero asked Orozco to exert pressure on the Chihuahua legislature so that it would give Governor Abraham González unlimited powers,[40] which Orozco refused to do. His refusal precipitated the break between the two men.

Although there is no reason for doubting Amaya's account, there

1915[?]), pp. 13–14; J. Figueroa Domenech, *Veinte Meses*, p. 77; *El Tiempo*, Dec. 13, 1911.

[37] Amaya, *Madero y los Revolucionarios*, p. 335; Almada, *La Revolución en Chihuahua*, pp. 276–277.

[38] *El Paso Morning Times*, Jan. 21, 1912.

[39] *El País*, Jan. 20, 1912; *Mexican Herald*, Jan. 20, 1912.

[40] Amaya, *Madero y los Revolucionarios*, p. 342. A similar interpretation of the January meeting is given by R. A. Ugalde, *Vida de Orozco*, pp. 14–15.

are many reasons for assuming that additional factors were involved in the dispute. A few days after the meeting, Orozco resigned as commander of the Chihuahua *rurales*. Orozco and his advisers were fully cognizant of the importance of the position, and therefore it is unlikely that disagreement upon a single point—even sharp disagreement— would have resulted in such a momentous decision. Orozco's letter of resignation has often been reproduced [41] but it has never been analyzed for insight into the Orozco-Madero conference. The letter indicates that, among other things, Orozco was critical of Madero's political appointments. Although he did not charge Madero with nepotism (as would be done later), Orozco indicated his displeasure with Madero's cabinet and with many of his federal appointments. Earlier, Orozco had criticized Madero's wholesale acceptance of the officers of the Porfirist army, for it was obvious that these officers—even many who had joined the Revolution in its latter stages—were ideologically attached to the previous regime. An entire paragraph was devoted to appointments.

> As a private citizen I appeal to your patriotism . . . to bear in mind the immense responsibility which rests upon you. Try to surround yourself with truly impartial, learned, and patriotic men who will work with you in the great chore of saving the people in this period of transition. It is necessary that each and every one of your associates be eminently qualified through their patriotism as well as through their ability and prudence to bring a happy conclusion to the difficult and transcendental problems which exist today. The ruin or prosperity of our beloved fatherland will depend in large measure on the resolution of these problems. [42]

The political unrest in southern Mexico at the time of the meeting provides grounds for additional speculation. The intensification of Emiliano Zapata's revolution in late December and early January would appear to substantiate the claims of the Chihuahuenses that General Orozco would be sent into the state of Morelos. In late December and

[41] Ricardo García Granados, *Historia de México Desde la Restauración de la República en 1867 Hasta la Caída de Huerta* (2 vols.; Mexico City: Editorial Jus, 1956), II, 272–273; Rafael Sánchez Escobar, *Narraciones Revolucionarias Mexicanas Histórico-anecdóticas* (Tlalpan: Talleres Tipográficas de la Casa Orientación para Varones, 1934), pp. 82–83; Casasola, *Historia Gráfica*, I, 413; Amaya, *Madero y los Revolucionarios*, pp. 343–344; Muñoz, "Caudillo Olvidado," *Así* (May 3, 1941), p. 36.

[42] Quoted in Casasola, *Historia Gráfica*, I, 413. The entire letter of resignation has been translated and is included as Appendix A, pp. 136–137.

early January, Zapata seized national railroad lines, disrupted telegraph communications, took over a number of small towns, and repeatedly defeated federal regulars.[43] Orozco had successfully served Madero on two occasions against political dissidents, and it is likely that he was again urged to serve in the same capacity—and that this time he refused.[44]

Although the relationship between Orozco and Zapata has never been carefully examined, it is impossible to accept the contention that there was no connection between them;[45] a bond of sympathy between the men and their movements is obvious.[46] Although the two *guerrilleros* probably never met one another,[47] when Zapata pronounced his Plan de Ayala, on November 25, 1911, Orozco was mentioned prominently. Article 3 stated that "Pascual Orozco is recognized as Chief of the Revolución Libertadora,"[48] and only if Orozco refused to accept this position would Zapata be considered the leader of the movement. Immediately after publishing the plan, Zapata sent a personal envoy, Gonzalo Vásquez Ortiz, to Orozco with a copy of the document and a letter that urged his cooperation.[49] Although Orozco quickly dissociated himself from the Reyista and Vasquista movements, he never publicly repudiated Article 3 of the Plan de Ayala, which made him titular head of the southern revolt. As his own revolutionary plan would subsequently demonstrate, he was in close accord with the basic

[43] *El País*, Dec. 20, 1911 to Jan. 15, 1912.

[44] The author's contention is corroborated in part by Rafael Muñoz, who states that as soon as Orozco arrived in Mexico City he publicly announced that he would not fight against Emiliano Zapata ("Caudillo Olvidado," p. 36). Francisco Almada also suggests that Orozco refused to fight in Morelos (*Resumen de Historia de Chihuahua*, p. 394). Neither of these statements is confirmed by the contemporary press, however.

[45] M. Márquez Sterling, *Los Ultimos Días del Presidente Madero* (Mexico City: Editorial Porrua, S. A., 1958), p. 184.

[46] Carlos Pérez Guerrero, "Cuando Transigió Zapata," *El Universal* (Sept. 6, 1933), p. 31; *El Paso Morning Times*, Feb. 1, 1912.

[47] The contention of Octavio Paz that Orozco and Zapata attended a banquet in Mexico City is apparently without validity ("Vásquez Gómez, Pascual Orozco, y Emiliano Zapata," *El Universal* [Dec. 1, 1929], magazine section, pp. 1, 8). It has been disproved in a most convincing manner by Rafael F. Muñoz ("Pascual Orozco y Emiliano Zapata," *El Universal* [Dec. 9, 1929], p. 5).

[48] The text of the Plan de Ayala has often been reprinted; a convenient and accurate reproduction can be found in Felipe Tena Ramírez, *Leyes Fundamentales de México: 1808–1957* (Mexico City: Editorial Porrua, S. A., 1957), p. 74.

[49] Gildardo Magaña, *Emiliano Zapata y el Agrarismo en Mexico* (3 vols.; Mexico City: Editorial Ruta, 1951–52), II, 97.

principles of Zapata's measures for agrarian reform. Just as Zapata sent Orozco a copy of his revolutionary plan, the Chihuahua general sent Zapata a copy of the Plan Orozquista soon after its promulgation on March 25, 1912.[50] Zapata's reply, moreover, indicated his basic agreement with all of the major articles.[51] Under these circumstances, if Madero asked Orozco to take command of the federal troops in Morelos, it is quite certain that Orozco refused.[52]

The full details of the January 19 meeting probably will never be brought to light. One need not accept the suppositions, however, to appreciate that a serious breach did occur. This rift, although not widely publicized, was every bit as intense—and certainly more far-reaching—than the heralded incident in Ciudad Juárez the previous May. If, as some historians contend, the Ciudad Juárez affair was never completely forgotten by Orozco, the Mexico City meeting served to conjure up graphic recollections.

Orozco returned to Chihuahua City shortly after the meeting with Madero and tendered his resignation on January 26, 1912. The president refused to accept the resignation and asked the general to retain his position as head of the Zona Rural de Chihuahua at least until March because his services still were needed.[53] Indeed, on January 31 the most serious of the Vasquista uprisings occurred in Ciudad Juárez. Stores and saloons were looted, buildings were burned, and many Mexicans and Americans were forced to take refuge in El Paso.[54]

The federal government had been advised that a Vasquista revolt would occur in Ciudad Juárez, and the Mexican consul in El Paso—no doubt taken in by the endless stream of anti-Orozco propaganda—reported to his superiors that Orozco would lead the movement.[55] Nevertheless, as soon as news of the Vasquista rebellion reached Chihuahua City, Orozco asked for troops and supplies to restore order.

[50] Pérez Guerrero, "Cuando Transiguió Zapata," p. 3.

[51] Diego Arenas Guzmán, *Del Maderismo a los Tratados de Teoloyucan* (Mexico City: Talleres Gráficos de la Nación, 1955), pp. 60–62.

[52] Another indication that Orozco and Zapata were in contact was contained in a press release that was issued only a few days after the promulgation of the Plan Orozquista. The release stated that Orozco was planning to march south with his army and join Zapata on the outskirts of Mexico City for the capture of the capital (*San Antonio Light*, Mar. 30, 1912). For a number of reasons, which will be discussed later, the plan did not materialize.

[53] *Mexican Herald*, Jan. 31, 1912.

[54] *El Paso Morning Times*, Feb. 1, 1912.

[55] AREM, Llorente to Sec. de Relaciones Exteriores, L–E 817, Tomo 208, No. 203, Jan. 31, 1912.

Madero met the request and ordered Orozco to fortify the Juárez garrison. The general arrived at the border city on February 3 and made two speeches to the malcontents.[56] His influence was still so great among the army troops who had joined the revolt that he succeeded in thwarting the movement without firing a shot. The leaders of the mutiny were arrested and sent back to Chihuahua City under guard.

Orozco's detractors have had an extremely difficult task in interpreting this episode. If Orozco had been planning treachery for so many months, why did he put down a revolt against the federal government at the eleventh hour? Orozco's handling of the Juárez incident would seem to be a perfect yardstick for measuring his fidelity and his competence. Even Ramón Puente, who seeks to deprecate Orozco's achievements, could say only that Orozco "had already assumed his role of perfidy and cowardice . . . he only went to Ciudad Juárez to put himself in contact with [the leaders of the revolt]."[57] This end, of course, could have been accomplished without extinguishing the fire. Another critic states that Madero was unwise in appointing Orozco to put down the uprising because "he was no longer a Maderista"—ignoring the fact that Orozco single-handedly quelled the uprising.[58]

After Orozco split with Madero, the American consul in Chihuahua was called upon to explain the movement to the Department of State. Recognizing the incongruency of Orozco's actions—in stopping the Vasquista uprising and almost immediately afterward instigating a rebellion—the consul reported that the Vásquez Gómez revolution had taken the *científicos* by surprise and that therefore they had allowed Orozco to put it down.[59] This explanation leaves the basic problem unsolved. If the movement had taken the *científicos* by surprise—and this is doubtful—their inactivity could easily be understood. Why, then, after learning of the revolt, did they allow Orozco to take positive action in behalf of the Madero government?

The obvious answer—which perpetrators of the anti-Orozco legend will not admit—is that the general had not been an accomplice in the

---

[56] *El Paso Morning Times*, Feb. 5, 1912.

[57] *Pascual Orozco*, pp. 84–85.

[58] Romero Flores, *Del Porfirismo a la Revolución*, pp. 220–221. The same error is committed by Sánchez Escobar, who states that Madero, by sending Orozco to Ciudad Juárez, "placed the Church in the hands of Luther" (*Narraciones*, p. 85).

[59] RDS, Letcher to Sec. of State, 812.00/9494, Oct. 17, 1913. Letcher used the term "*científicos*" too loosely. His reference was merely to the Chihuahua aristocracy; some of the aristocracy were *científicos* but most were not.

anti-Madero movements between November, 1911, and January, 1912. Nor had he been a tool of conservative interests in the state of Chihuahua. Although Orozco could no longer accord Madero his full support, and wanted to leave the ranks of the Madero forces, he had publicly stated that he would temporarily retain his position as commander of the Chihuahua *rurales*, and this position required that he subdue the anti-Madero movements within the state. Orozco, in short, complied with the demands of the office with which he had been entrusted.

During the last three weeks of February, 1912, events in northern Mexico developed with startling rapidity. The governor of the state of Sonora, José María Maytorena, reported to the federal government that he had good evidence that Orozco was involved in an anti-Madero plot;[60] but the Secretary of Gobernación replied that the rumors were false.[61] At approximately the same time, the Vásquez Gómez movement, having been defeated at Ciudad Juárez, spread rapidly to other areas of Chihuahua. The towns of Galeana, Pearson, Casas Grandes, Palomas, and El Valle declared themselves in revolt against the Madero government. Lic. Aureliano González, the weak interim governor of the state, acting for Abraham González who had been named Secretary of Gobernación, was unable to contain the revolts, whereupon the legislature voted to replace him with Pascual Orozco.[62]

President Madero urged Orozco to accept the governorship,[63] but the general refused.[64] Rather than accept a position that would ally him with the federal government, Orozco again resigned his military post. This time the somewhat petulant resignation was accepted, and Agustín Estrada was named commander of the Chihuahua *rurales*. At approximately the same time, conservative spokesmen began to cultivate Orozco assiduously. By the end of the month he had agreed to turn against the Madero government and to unite various disaffected elements under his banner. Orozco pronounced his revolt on March 3, 1912.

[60] AGN, Maytorena to Sec. de Gobernación, Leg. 21, Exp. 3, Feb. 25, 1912.
[61] AGN, Sec. de Gobernación to Maytorena, Leg. 21, Exp. 3, Feb. 27, 1912.
[62] *El País*, Feb. 5, 1912, and *Mexican Herald*, Feb. 6, 1912.
[63] *Mexican Herald*, Feb. 7, 1912.
[64] RDS, Letcher to Sec. of State, 812.00/2753, Feb. 7, 1912.

# IV

## *The Birth of a Revolution*

The news of Orozco's defection was accepted without panic by an administration that after five months in power had become almost immune to political turmoil. The task of restoring order was certainly nothing new. Chihuahua, moreover, was far away from the capital, which had been threatened almost incessantly by Emiliano Zapata and his "rebellious hordes," and the competent federal army—it was thought—would be able to put down the northern rebellion in a matter of weeks. Orozquismo was nothing more than another vehicle of reaction for carrying Mexico back to a condition of nineteenth-century privilege and abuse; like all of the other attempts, it would undoubtedly end in failure.

Journalists from both the United States and Mexico used the news of the Orozquista insurrection to justify their earlier allegations about its chief and as proof that Orozco had participated in all of the anti-Madero plots of the last five months.[1] Contemporary historians, without a pretense of detachment or objectivity, used the news of the insurrection in a similar manner. Unqualified assumptions and rash generalizations became commonplace, and Orozco's total debasement was even more rapid than his rise from obscurity. Seeing not a particle of justification in the movement, theorizers soon outstripped one another in speculating on its causes. Conjectures, quickly accepted as facts, furnished a later generation of historians with so much violent anti-Orozco propaganda that the man was converted into an ogre. Only the equally derisive and unfounded anti-Madero accounts could

---

[1] An editorial comment in the *El Paso Morning Times*, Mar. 11, 1912, is typical: "Pascual Orozco, the Benedict Arnold of the Republic of Mexico, has finally temporarily delivered the state of Chihuahua over to the Red Flag gang of looters that he has been negotiating with since the close of the Madero revolution."

find anything human in the Chihuahua general; but Orozco was vindicated for the wrong reasons and the president was substituted as the monster.

The favorite hypothesis of the contemporaneous and many subsequent accounts is that Orozco revolted for money. He was an "egoist whose conscience was in his pocket."[2] "He ... converted himself into a Judas and sold himself out to the *científicos* for a checkbook."[3] The most common pecuniary explanation is that Orozco felt he had not been properly indemnified by Madero for his financial outlay to the Revolution and for the service he had rendered it, and therefore had rebelled. Many accounts do not specify the amount of money that ostensibly provoked the insurrection, and the others reveal staggering discrepancies.[4]

The Orozquista revolt has also been attributed to the malicious designs of Orozco's father. The elder Orozco, supposedly unbalanced because his son had not been appointed governor of Chihuahua, convinced the general to take up arms against the thankless first magistrate.[5] The fact that Orozco subsequently had been offered the governorship by the state legislature and had refused it did not discourage this line of reasoning.[6] For others, Orozco was intoxicated by the vision of power and desired nothing less than the ministry of war or the presi-

[2] Edward Bell, *The Political Shame of Mexico* (New York: McBride, Nast, and Company, 1914), p. 168.

[3] Conrado Gimeno, *La Canalla Roja* (El Paso, 1912), p. 10. *Rojo* or *colorado* was often used to describe the Orozquistas because of the color of their banner.

[4] The smallest figure is recorded by Dolores Butterfield, who states that Orozco received $25,000 and had asked for considerably more ("The Conspiracy Against Madero," *Forum* [July–December, 1913], p. 470). Alfonso Taracena says Orozco demanded $100,000 but received only $50,000 (*La Verdadera Revolución*, I, p. 227); and Frederick Starr accepts the same figures (*Mexico and the United States*, p. 340). Manuel Calero agrees that the demand was $100,000 but believes that Orozco received $55,000 (*Un Decenio de Política Mexicana*, p. 94). Edward Bell, often prone to exaggeration, cites the demand as $250,000, of which Orozco received only $100,000 (*Political Shame of Mexico*, p. 168).

Another version is that the money Orozco demanded was not for services rendered to the Revolution, but in payment of a debt the Madero family had owed the *guerrillero* from the days when he was a muleteer ("Orozco: Maker and Unmaker of Mexican Presidents," p. 646). The allegation that Orozco revolted for money has led at least one historian to characterize the Orozquistas as *condottiere* (see Pedro González-Blanco, *De Porfirio Díaz a Carranza* [Mexico City: Imprenta Helénica, 1916], p. 96 n.).

[5] Puente, *Pascual Orozco*, pp. 30–35.

[6] See above, p. 52.

dency itself.[7] Madero had attained the presidency via revolution, and Orozco was merely emulating Madero;[8] insatiable ambition had turned the hero into the traitor. Another report suggested that the antipathy between Orozco and Madero could be traced to the fact that "Orozco ... being a big man physically and not distinctly educated had the contempt of his class for the dwarfish and scholarly Madero."[9]

These oversimplifications are only a few examples of the distortion that characterized much of the historiography of the Revolution. Unfortunately, even many recent scholars have been deceived by the volume of the propaganda that was disseminated in the early years of the conflict and have unwittingly contributed to the perpetuation of the inaccuracies.[10]

The causes of Orozquismo were multiple and varied. Attempts to discover a solidarity of interests within these causes are misled. Orozquismo contained humanitarianism and misanthropy, benevolence and rancor, avid commitment and indifference. The fact that the leaders did not pursue a common end was a source of considerable strength—it widened the base of support—and also a weakness—it was impossible to reconcile the discordant personal and ideological aims.

One of the most important aspects of the Orozquista revolt, and a factor that is prerequisite for a sound understanding of the origin and early growth of Orozquismo, is its relationship to Chihuahua conservatism. Almost without exception, Mexicanists have equated the conservative movement in Chihuahua after Diaz' overthrow with *cientificismo*, the Mexican adaptation of the positivism of Auguste Comte, Herbert Spencer, and John Stuart Mill (which was prevalent during the last two decades of the dictatorship). This confusion undoubtedly stems from the fact that the *cientificos* and the Chihuahua aristocracy, for the most part, were oblivious to the needs of the Indians and mestizos. In 1912, most of the land barons and the moneyed elite

[7] Adrian Aguirre Benavides, *Madero el Inmaculado* (Mexico City: Editorial Diana, S. A., 1962), p. 456; Starr, *Mexico and the United States*, p. 343; Otilio Orestes, "Una Farsa la Campaña de V. Huerta," *Novedades* (July 8, 1962), p. 12.

[8] Valadés, *Francisco I. Madero*, II, 236–237.

[9] RDS, Letcher to Sec. of State, 812.00/3414, Mar. 20, 1912. It is only fair to state, however, that most of Letcher's suggestions are not this fanciful.

[10] Aside from many of the early anti-Madero accounts that conceded justifications for the Orozquista movement, several recent studies have acknowledged that its justification is at least a possibility; see Jesús Silva Herzog, *Breve Historia de la Revolución Mexicana* (Mexico City: Fondo de Cultura Económica, 1962), p. 223, and William L. Sherman and Richard E. Greenleaf, *Victoriano Huerta: A Reappraisal* (Mexico City: Mexico City College Press, 1960), p. 51, n. 16.

of Chihuahua were not *científicos* but merely conservatives who had given full support to the Díaz dictatorship and who were interested in slowing the pace of social and economic reforms.

That the former supporters of the dictator and of the Terrazas clique lent assistance to Orozco's revolt is undeniable; if it had not been for the financial support of the aristocratic elite, the movement would have been no more dangerous for Madero than the Reyista and Vasquista uprisings. The fact that some of the resources of the aristocracy were originally placed at the disposition of the rebels, however, made the movement a much more serious menace to the already established concept of revolutionary orthodoxy. This support also helps explain why the government was unable to extirpate the movement after a year of concerted effort.

The conservatives' interest in Pascual Orozco began in Ciudad Juárez in May, 1911, when the *caudillo* first displayed his antagonism toward Francisco I. Madero. From that time forward the eventuality of a split between the two men was viewed with more than casual interest by the forces of reaction. If, during the next eight months, the conservatives were uncertain about the man they hoped to cultivate, Orozco's vast popularity—which was demonstrated time and again during his many trips throughout most of the country—must have been reassuring. Moreover, Orozco's prestige with the army was demonstrated by the ease with which he aborted the Vasquista uprising in Ciudad Juárez on February 3, 1912.

It is impossible to state categorically when spokesmen for the right began to cultivate Orozco. It is possible that the initial efforts were made in late 1911;[11] it was not, however, until late January or early February, 1912, that undivided attention was directed toward this task. There are several possible explanations for the intensified campaign to gain the *guerrillero*'s support in early 1912. First, it is likely that news of the disagreement between Orozco and Madero at the January 19 meeting had reached Chihuahua and encouraged those hoping to sow further seeds of discontent. In addition, Governor González had announced a plan of progressive taxation on large landholdings and a plan to collect back taxes.[12] Because both of these measures were directed against the Chihuahua aristocracy, time was of the essence. Agreement with Orozco probably was reached in late February. Although it has been stated that Luis Terrazas turned over a large

[11] This is the contention of José Mancisidor (*Historia de la Revolución*, p. 178).
[12] RDS, Letcher to Sec. of State, 812.00/3414, Mar. 20, 1912.

amount of money to Orozco (in the Club Extranjero of Chihuahua),[13] it is likely that most of the negotiations were conducted by Gonzalo Enrile, who served as intermediary between the financial and military leadership of the proposed movement.[14]

Orozco's decision to embark on a new revolution was not made for the same reasons that motivated the Terrazas-Creel clique. The *guerrillero*, to whom the inner workings of politics would always remain a mystery, never realized that his backers would not allow a reform program to become operative if his revolt were successful. In late February, Orozco saw that pockets of rebellion, once again labeled Vasquista, had sprung up all over the state of Chihuahua. His fellow irregular officers in revolt against Díaz, men such as Emilio Campa, José Inés Salazar, and Demetrio Ponce, had already taken up arms. Although the Mexican press refused to attach any importance to these movements, they were, nonetheless, a clear reflection of the growing discontent with the Madero government.

The charges the Vasquista revolutionary junta in El Paso hurled at Madero and that Orozco's conservative "friends" confided to him in private made good sense. Perhaps, as a scholar has recently suggested, Orozco read more into the Plan de San Luis Potosí than Madero had intended,[15] but the charges of nepotism, indecision, corruption in state and municipal elections, and failure to understand the essence of Mexico's dilemma could not be denied. Other questions were raised. Had not Díaz, the defender of the status quo, merely been replaced by a regime of liberal inefficiency? Was not the presidency of Madero the enthronement of a new privileged class?

Indeed, Madero's family had been awarded a parasitic monopoly on the functions of government. His close relatives had been given cabinet positions and his distant relatives had been given offices in the various state political machines. Madero's explanation that he had appointed his relatives to high positions because he knew they were honest was insufficient, even for the simple *guerrillero*. The worst abuses of the dictatorship had been curbed but the inadequacies remained. What had the peons been awarded for their participation? They had suffered

---

[13] Taracena, *La Verdadera Revolución*, I, 239.

[14] Ramón Prida, *De la Dictadura a la Anarquía* (Mexico City: Ediciones Botas, 1958), p. 368, n. 1; Ross, *Madero*, p. 259; *El Paso Morning Times*, Apr. 17, 1912. Gonzalo Enrile was one of the few conservatives in the Orozquista revolt who was a *científico*.

[15] Robert E. Quirk, *The Mexican Revolution, 1914–1915* (Bloomington: University of Indiana Press, 1960), pp. 4–5.

most and benefited least from the Revolution. They were destitute and without hope; the *tiendas de raya* still kept them in a condition of debt peonage. The ideals of the Plan de San Luis Potosí, for which the revolutionaries had offered their lives, and the promises of the revolution already were proved ephemeral. The Mexican Revolution had already found its Bonaparte.

Although the charges against Madero were exaggerated, each contained at least a grain of truth that made it believable. Orozco didn't realize that a basic social reorientation could not be effected in a matter of months, even if all factors were propitious. Orozco, however, might not have yielded to the pressure had not the aristocracy held out a special piece of bait. Convinced that Orozco would prove a supple instrument for their designs, the vested interests persuaded the *guerrillero* that he alone, of all the revolutionary chieftains, could bring order out of chaos and guarantee compliance with the letter and spirit of the Plan de San Luis Potosí. It was Orozco who had placed Francisco I. Madero in the presidential chair—a fact that the people had recognized in their demonstrative receptions throughout the length of the country.

The subterfuge was facilitated by other factors, which contributed to the gradual development of a hero complex. Soon after Orozco's recognition as the most effective military leader in the struggle against the Díaz dictatorship, a mountain in the vicinity of Ciudad Juárez had been dubbed Mount Orozco in honor of the rebel chief.[16] After Díaz had resigned and Orozco had become even more renowned, an El Paso jewelry company manufactured and sold "Orozco souvenir spoons."[17] Adulation was expressed in wide and various forms:[18] women offered themselves freely to the general;[19] wine manufacturers in the Rhineland used his picture on the labels of their product;[20] civic clubs throughout Mexico were named in his honor;[21] and popular *corridos* acclaimed his exploits.[22] Even the sophisticated literary community of Mexico City could not resist the temptation to glorify the *guerrillero*'s

[16] *El Paso Morning Times*, Apr. 27, 1911.

[17] *Ibid.*, July 2, 1911.

[18] See Amaya, *Madero y los Revolucionarios*, p. 377.

[19] *Ibid.*

[20] *Ibid.*

[21] AGN, Santiago D. Rodríguez *et al.* to De la Barra, Leg. 21, Exp. 4, Aug. 12, 1911.

[22] Vicente T. Mendoza, *El Corrido de la Revolucíon* (Mexico City: Talleres Gráficos de la Nación, 1956), pp. 31, 34–35.

deeds.[23] Many foreign reporters described Orozco as a Robin Hood who possessed the physical attributes of a Hercules. The banality of some of their articles defies description:

> He shoots straight—missing nothing. He hurls his lariat at the plunging steer and brings it down. The wiry horse of the country obeys him by instinct, for he can master it in its most furious mood. . . . On the back of a galloping horse, says one authority, he can hit a swinging bottle tied to a tree. He can lasso a horse forty feet away and pull it to its knees without assistance. This, to be sure, is an exhibition of skill rather than of strength; but the physical strength of Orozco is, likewise, unusual. He has been known to relieve five toiling peasants of a bag of ore to which their combined energies proved unequal, and tossed it easily into a pack. Fortunately, like most giants, Orozco has been created gentle. He would not injure a fly. In all the years of obscurity during which he took pack trains through the mountains he was never reported to his employers, we are told, for maiming a horse or striking a peón.[24]

The sum total of these attributes, whether insignificant or humorous, was of telling effect when magnified by the agents of the aristocracy. As the vanity of the ex-muleteer was meticulously inflated, he too began to believe that the future of the country lay in his providence. His vision simply had been clouded by caprice and intrigue.

Perhaps the most important factor in the events that led to Orozco's break with Madero was the formal request on February 18, 1912, from the revolutionary leaders who already were in open rebellion; and again the appeal to the ego is obvious. The request first cited some of the significant events in the overthrow of Porfirio Díaz; then continued:

> The name of Pascual Orozco, the first *guerrero*, the most audacious, the one who was bold enough to confront all dangers, sacrificing himself in honor of the country, has become a symbol of the insurgent, the prototype of the epic Mexican who knows how to fight for liberty.
>
> The Revolution has been betrayed but your deeds, your sacrifices, will not be in vain. [The Revolution] has become rooted in the hearts of the people, it has been fertilized in new sacrifices, in the new mortal fight in which we are engaged. The sons of Chihuahua again have begun to fight for that which their brothers died.

[23] "*El penacho de Cyrano de Bergerac brillaba sobre la humilde frente de Pascual Orozco*" (Chucho Urueta, quoted in Calero, *Un Decenio de Política Mexicana*, p. 94).

[24] "Orozco: Maker and Unmaker of Mexican Presidents," pp. 645–646.

You, Señor General, have declared publicly that the present administration has not complied with its promises, has not surrounded itself with honest men, and has not done anything for the cause of the country.

Your declarations show the road which must be followed and justify the road which we have chosen. . . . The name of Pascual Orozco, we are sure, will continue to mean the first insurgent. Therefore, . . . we give you supreme command of all of our forces and acclaim you Caudillo and General-in-Chief of the Ejército Libertador.[25]

The document was signed by five of the leading officers of the revolt: General Emilio P. Campa, General José Inés Salazar, Colonel Lino Ponce, Colonel Demetrio Ponce, and Major Enrique Portillo.

By the end of February a storm of indignation had been excited, and Orozco decided to join the movement as its commander-in-chief. On March 1, 1912, Orozco issued a long statement in which he explained again his reasons for resigning his position in the federal government.[26] Stylistically, the statement was vague, extremely banal, and flamboyant, but it was designed so as not to alienate potential allies. The names of Benito Juárez and Cuauhtémoc were invoked, with the ringing cries of liberty and patriotism, in an attempt to gain the support of the masses. Two days later, on March 3, 1912, Orozco formally attached himself to the rebel cause[27] and withdrew his allegiance from the state and national governments.[28] He then ordered the confiscation of all imports through Ciudad Juárez that were bound for the federal government,[29] and, in excellent revolutionary fashion, released all political prisoners in the state penitentiary and disarmed all local police forces.

The ineffectual Vasquista movement was renamed Orozquista. Orozco and Vásquez Gómez cooperated for a short time, but after several months a split occurred and Orozco assumed full control of the revolution. The reason for the schism appears to have been that Vásquez Gómez had presidential ambitions that Orozco was unwilling

[25] The document is reproduced in its entirety in Amaya, *Madero y los Revolucionarios*, pp. 370–371.

[26] Orozco's statement is reproduced in González Ramírez, *Manifiestos Políticos*, pp. 540–541.

[27] *El País*, Mar. 4, 1912; *El Tiempo*, Mar. 14, 1912; *El Paso Morning Times*, Mar. 14, 1912.

[28] RDS, Letcher to Sec. of State, 812.00/3191, Mar. 4, 1912.

[29] AHDN, Ramírez to Sec. de Guerra y Marina, Exp. XI/481.5/68.

to support.[30] General Orozco's decision to join the movement was extremely significant. The new military leadership, the new financial backing, and the mass support attracted by the magnetism of the general's name converted hitherto loosely joined revolutionary bands into an effective military organization.

Orozco's decision to lead a revolutionary movement against the government of Francisco Madero did not have a mercenary base. In addition to his profitable transport company, a mercantile store, and a producing gold mine, the general had received a handsome offer from an American mining company with interests in Chihuahua.[31] Because his old rival, Joaquín Chávez, was dead, several Mexican companies also had made him lucrative offers. Orozco was not a financial magnate but his financial future was assured. As Ricardo García Granados observed: "It would be . . . as absurd to attribute the revolutionary movement which he [Orozco] began to the personal ambitions of the caudillo as it would be to attribute the Revolution of 1910 to the personal ambitions of Madero or the Revolution of Tuxtepec to the ambitions of Porfirio Díaz."[32] It is quite certain that Pascual Orozco had been duped, but naiveté should not be misconstrued as treason.

A provocative but indeterminable socioeconomic appraisal has been advanced by Andrés Molina Enríquez: "At the bottom of it all, the differences [between Orozco and Madero] . . . were nothing more than a blind collision between the interests of the *Criollos Señores* that Madero represented in reality and the interests of the *mestizos*, or at least the Indian-mestizos, that Orozco represented without knowing it."[33] Whatever the validity of this explanation, if Orozco had not been convinced that the Revolution had begun to veer from the path delineated in the Plan de San Luis Potosí, the machinations of the vested interests, subtle as they might have been, probably would not have been successful. Orozco revolted against Madero for the same reason he had

[30] ABFC, R. Gómez Robelo, Special Representative of the Revolutionary Army, to A. B. Fall, Group R.

[31] *Mexican Herald*, Jan. 31, 1912. Senator Albert Bacon Fall of New Mexico, an acquaintance of Orozco, used his influence with the Concheno Mining Company to see that Orozco was given an exclusive contract for transporting supplies and the ore that was extracted at the company's mine (ABFC, statement of Senator Albert Fall, Aug. 23, 1912, item 2250).

[32] *Historia de México*, II, 273.

[33] *Revolución Agraria de México*, Vol. V: *El Principio de la Verdadera Revolución* (Mexico City: Talleres Gráficos de la Nación, 1936), p. 65.

revolted against Díaz: in his unsophisticated way he desired the implementation of a revolutionary program that would satisfy the awakened aspirations of the Mexican people.[34] He had not lost contact with the masses, despite his tenuous alliance with the Chihuahua aristocracy.

Orozco, after he had committed himself to the new rebellion, allowed his name to be affixed to a series of revolutionary statements that condemned the Madero regime. The first official documents of the revolutionary headquarters, provoked by a presidential decree that had suspended constitutional guarantees only a few days after Orozco joined the movement, were three manifestos that were issued on March 13, 1912, over the name of Pascual Orozco, general-in-chief.[35] The first statement was that Madero and all members of his immediate family would be court-martialed for the crimes of nepotism and the misapplication of national funds. The second decree stated that all public officials who failed to adhere to the principles of the revolution would be summarily executed. The third statement declared null and void all loans and concessions of the Madero government after the date of the decree, and it disavowed all contracts and concessions between the national government and members of the Madero family.

The three decrees were followed, on March 25, by the Plan Orozquista, a highly significant but little-studied revolutionary document.[36] Because the plan contained vehement personal condemnations of Madero (many of which were unjustified) and employed a number of clumsy images and vague references to obscure biblical sites and mythological personages, its importance is sometimes slighted.[37] Poorly written,[38] repetitive, violently anti-United States, ultranationalistic—almost to the point of absurdity[39]—the plan, nevertheless, deserves

[34] Luis Lara Pardo, "Pascual Orozco," *Excélsior* (Aug. 18, 1953), p. 6.

[35] RDS, Letcher to Sec. of State, 812.00/3309, Mar. 15, 1912.

[36] The Plan Orozquista is sometimes called the Pacto de la Empacadora because of the building in Chihuahua City in which it was signed. The plan, which can be found in Silva Herzog, *Breve Historia*, I, 246–259, has been translated by me and is included as Appendix B, pp. 138–147.

[37] Christiansen, "Pascual Orozco," p. 111; Cumberland, *Mexican Revolution*, pp. 193–194.

[38] Although the authorship of the plan has not been firmly established, it is probably the work of Gonzalo Enrile, one of Orozco's confidants, and José Córdova, the general's personal secretary.

[39] The inclusion of the anti-United States expressions proved highly embarrassing to the leadership of the movement. A week after the plan was issued, Orozco was

careful study. Indeed, the significance of the strictures of the Madero regime does not rest with the specific denunciations or the irrelevant polemics, but rather with the positive program of reform the plan envisioned. One recent study that recognizes the significance of the Plan Orozquista concludes that—in addition to being more socially advanced than the Plan de San Luis Potosí, the Plan de Tacubaya, and the Plan de Ayala—it also established a number of important precedents for the Constitution of 1917, the document most observers believe represents the philosophical culmination of seven years of civil strife.[40]

In the political sphere, after withdrawing recognition of Francisco Madero and Pino Suárez, the Plan Orozquista anticipated the Constitution of 1917 by calling for the abolition of the office of vice-president: the president of the senate was to assume the presidency in case of the chief executive's death or disability (Article 16). The plan also recognized that a four-year presidential term was insufficient and extended the term to six years (Article 25).[41] Other political reforms included a provision for the effective autonomy of the municipalities (Article 28) and another provision for the suppression of the *jefes políticos* (Article 29). The plan also demanded that freedom of expression, in all of its forms, be made effective (Article 37).

An interesting article, one that anticipated the scourge of militarism that would afflict Mexico for the next several decades, reproached

---

called upon by leading Chihuahua conservatives to repudiate these sections and to assure the "press of the border" that he was not catering to a movement that fostered anti-American sentiment. In early April in a statement to the press, Orozco "clarified" his position (see *El Paso Herald*, Apr. 3, 1912; RDS, Letcher to Sec. of State, 812.00/3526, Apr. 4, 1912; ABFC, Memorandum to the Senate Committee on Foreign Relations, Group F). Orozco also sent an apology to President William Howard Taft (RDS, Orozco to Taft, 812.00/3538, Apr. 5, 1912).

There was good reason for the Orozquistas to repudiate the anti-American portions of the document and to offer an official apology. At the time that the original statements were released, Orozco was trying to win the support of Washington so that arms and munitions could be legally imported to the rebels through Ciudad Juárez. The exigencies of the situation made it imperative that the government of the United States be assured that United States citizens residing in Mexico would not be the subjects of wanton persecution. Despite this assurance, all requests for assistance were rejected.

[40] Silva Herzog, *Breve Historia*, I, 219–220. Frank Brandenburg also notes that the Plan Orozquista embodied a well-rounded program of social reform (*The Making of Modern Mexico* [Englewood Cliffs, N.J.: Prentice-Hall, 1964], p. 49).

[41] The framers of the Constitution of 1917 retained the provision for the four-year presidential term; it was not until 1928 that the decision was made to expand the term to six years (Tena Ramírez, *Leyes Fundamentales*, p. 911).

Madero for having enacted a bill for compulsory military training.[42] The plan stated that compulsory military service would be justified only in the event of a foreign war (Article 21), but the states were charged with organizing and maintaining small national-guard units— large enough to guarantee law and order (Article 22).

The most important proposals, however, were a series of suggested socioeconomic reforms. The Plan Orozquista called for the immediate repression of the *tiendas de raya* (Article 34–I) and for the payment of all workers in legal tender (Article 34–II). The plan also envisioned a ten-hour working day (Article 34–III),[43] placed severe restrictions on child labor (Article 34–IV), and held out the promise of higher wages (Article 34–V) and improved working conditions (Article 34–VI).[44] As if anticipating the surge of economic nationalism that would soon sweep over Mexico, the plan also called for the immediate nationalization of the railroads and the utilization of Mexican nationals in their operation (Articles 32–33).

Mexico's endemic land problem did not escape notice. Because more than 90 per cent of Mexico's rural population was landless in 1912, and because exaggerated *latifundia* was thought to be the key to many other socioeconomic problems, agrarian reform figured prominently. Provisions for the redistribution of land were cautious but comprehensive. Persons who had resided on their land for twenty years were to be given title to it (Article 35–I); other titles were to be revalidated (Article 35–II); lands illegally seized from the peasantry (a common practice during the Díaz regime) would be returned (Article 35–III); and all uncultivated and nationalized lands would be repartitioned (Article 35–IV). The most important provision called for the expropriation of the land of *hacendados* who did not regularly keep all of their land under cultivation (Article 35–V). (Payment for the expropriated lands would be raised through agricultural bonds, bearing 4 percent interest [Article 35–VI].)

Comparison of the Plan de San Luis Potosí, the Plan de Tacubaya, and the Plan de Ayala with the Plan Orozquista reveals that the former lacked balanced, well-formulated programs of reform. Madero's Plan de San Luis Potosí was primarily political in nature; it showed

---

[42] This bill had gone into effect during the first week of December, 1911 (*El Tiempo*, Dec. 2, 1911).

[43] Article 123 of the Constitution of 1917 provided for an eight-hour day.

[44] Although the Madero government had organized a Department of Labor (under the Secretaría de Fomento) by March, 1912, virtually nothing had been done to alleviate the plight of urban laborers.

that its author was an advocate of administrative reform, but of little else: its references to agrarian reform were few, and vague. The Plan de Tacubaya, like the first part of the Plan Orozquista, was a condemnation of Madero for his failure to live up to the principles of the Plan de San Luis Potosí, but its most "constructive" offering was the presidency of Emilio Vásquez Gómez. The widely heralded Plan de Ayala of Emiliano Zapata contained several valuable proposals for agrarian reform but it overlooked other important areas in which reform was badly needed.

The ideas contained in the Plan Orozquista were not original; many of its principles can be traced to the manifesto of the Mexican Liberal Party published in St. Louis, Missouri, July 1, 1906, by Ricardo and Enrique Flores Magón.[45] The Plan Orozquista, however, was the first comprehensive and well-developed plan of reform to emanate from the Revolution and to be promulgated on Mexican soil.[46] Because of the heavy emphasis that has been placed upon the social and economic aspects of the revolutionary phenomenon in recent years, it is strange that the plan has not been recognized as such.

The Orozquista insurrection was prompted and financed, at least in part, by reactionary elements in Chihuahua but its statement of revolution was inspired by the manifesto of the Mexican Liberal party. It is likely that the aristocracy could have accepted most of the political reforms proposed by the plan and not seriously compromised their privileged position, but the economic and social reforms were inimical to the license they had enjoyed throughout the period of the Díaz dictatorship. Soon after the Orozquista rebellion broke out, the American consul in Chihuahua City, Marion T. Letcher, provided a key to this problem when he reported that the fulfillment or nonfulfillment of the promises made by Madero had nothing to do with the movement.[47] In a like manner, from the point of view of the far right, the program for social and economic reform outlined in the Plan Orozquista had nothing to do with the new rebellion. The Chihuahua

[45] See Silva Herzog, *Breve Historia*, I, 76–107. A short but excellent account of the political thought and revolutionary activities of the Flores Magón brothers can be found in Lyle C. Brown, "The Mexican Liberals and Their Struggle Against the Díaz Dictatorship," *Antología MCC* (1956), pp. 318–362 and *passim*.

[46] It is significant that the original slogan of the Orozquista revolt, "*Tierra y Libertad*," soon was changed to "*Reforma, Justicia, y Libertad*" (Almada, *Resumen de Historia de Chihuahua*, p. 345).

[47] RDS, Letcher to Sec. of State, 812.00/3414, Mar. 20, 1912. I assume that the consul was referring to the position of the vested interests within the state.

aristocracy encouraged the formulation of a liberal document in an attempt to entice mass support and—more importantly—to attract the leadership that would give the movement the name they desired. The intrigue succeeded in both of its aims.

It is ironic that a plan born in prevarication and nurtured in deceit should have had a strong and positive influence on the program of social and economic reform that would be realized in Mexico within the next three decades. This unexpected effect of the Plan Orozquista was only one aspect of the total phenomenon of Orozquismo: the military campaigns that followed from Orozco's decision to join and lead the new revolution helped provide the setting from which General Victoriano Huerta would emerge as a military hero and a trusted aid of the president.

# V

## *Orozquismo*

At approximately the same time that the Orozquistas were setting up their headquarters, issuing their first decrees, and formulating their revolutionary plan, the first military engagements of the new campaign were beginning to unfold. The initial rebel victories over the federal forces converted the nonchalant attitude that had attended the news of Orozco's defection into profound concern, and the government soon faced a critical situation.

The most important victory of the Vasquistas, before the two movements were merged, was the seizure of Ciudad Juárez on February 27, 1912. The border city had been taken by General Emilio P. Campa, almost without a fight, after government troops had withdrawn—presumably to avoid an international incident with the United States.[1] Several small towns in Chihuahua also were in rebel hands at the time Orozco withdrew his recognition of the federal government. Orozco's first military contribution to the new cause was made on March 3, 1912—the same day that he formally committed himself to the revolution. The general's adversary in this engagement was Pancho Villa, who had been his fellow officer and subordinate in the struggle against the Díaz dictatorship.

Although Villa's apologists laud the fact that their protagonist remained loyal to the "Apostle of the Revolution" when almost everybody else in northern Mexico was turning against him,[2] there is evidence

[1] Taracena, *La Verdadera Revolución*, I, 236; Casasola, *Historia Gráfica*, I, 424.

[2] Haldeen Braddy, *Cock of the Walk* (Albuquerque: University of New Mexico Press, 1955), pp. 99–100; Ernest Otto Schuster, *Pancho Villa's Shadow* (New York: The Exposition Press, 1947), pp. 115–116; Martín Luis Guzmán, *Memorias de Pancho Villa* (Mexico City: Compañía de Ediciones, S. A., 1960), pp. 104–111; Juan Barragán Rodríguez, *Historia del Ejército y de la Revolución Constitucionalista* (2 vols.; Mexico City: Talleres de la Editora Stylo, 1946), I, 231; Calzadíaz Barrera, *Hechos Reales*, pp. 85–89; *El País*, Mar. 5, 1912.

that Villa desired to join the Orozquista revolt and that his offer of assistance was not accepted by Orozco.[3] At any rate, Governor González ordered Villa, who was encamped at Bustillos, seventy-five miles west of Chihuahua, to bring his 600 troops to the capital of the state.[4] Orozco engaged Villa on the outskirts of Chihuahua City early in the morning of March 3 and routed him.[5] Two days later the Secretary of War in Mexico City, General José González Salas, a capable career soldier, resigned his cabinet position to take the field against Orozco.[6] Meanwhile, Madero, who had issued a call for volunteers, in a bellicose address to the cadets of the national military academy lashed Orozco for his defection, labeled him a traitor to the Revolution, and vowed that when the "ex-revolutionary" was apprehended he would receive the most severe punishment the president could inflict.[7] During the first ten days of March, Orozco made extensive preparations for a series of military campaigns.

Rebel recruitment efforts met with considerable success in Chihuahua. A visitor to the city in early March reported that the general was receiving volunteers every day.[8] A partial explanation was recorded by the American consul in Chihuahua who stated that "the pay of Orozco's soldiers is two pesos a day. Few could earn two pesos a day at any peaceful occupation."[9] The salary factor, however, does not explain recruitment success entirely. In April, Orozco sent an agent, Epifanio Ruíz, to recruit men in the city and the state of Aguascalientes,[10] but the attempt was not notably successful. Orozco had be-

[3] The antipathy and mutual distrust between Orozco and Villa, apparent even during the struggle against Porfirio Díaz, could have led Orozco to refuse Villa's services. Several sources assert that Villa's request to join the Orozquista revolt was answered by the statement: "*No se admiten bandidos en las filas de este movimiento*" (Márquez Montiel, *Hombres Célebres de Chihuahua*, p. 224; Amaya, *Madero y los Revolucionarios*, p. 373; and Ugalde, *Vida de Orozco*, p. 31).

[4] RDS, Letcher to Sec. of State, 812.00/3192, Mar. 4, 1912.

[5] *El País*, Mar. 5, 1912. It is likely that many persons in the city who would otherwise have remained neutral during the battle gave active support to Orozco in order to avoid the horrors of a sack by the Villista troops (Resendi, *La Revolución Actual*, p. 46).

[6] AGN, Protestación de González Salas, Leg. 18, Exp. 10, Mar. 8, 1912.

[7] *Mexican Herald*, Mar. 6, 1912, and *El Tiempo*, Mar. 6, 1912. A conflicting report, to the effect that Madero sought to appease Orozco immediately after the battle of Chihuahua and dispatched Roque González Garza to make peace with the rebel, is without validity ("A Procession of Presidents," *Outlook*, CIX [Feb. 10, 1915], 304).

[8] RDS, Ellsworth to Sec. of State, 812.00/3297, Mar. 14, 1912.

[9] RDS, Letcher to Sec. of State, 812.00/3414, Mar. 20, 1912.

[10] AREM, Llorente to Sec. de Relaciones Exteriores, L–E 746 (92–52), May 2, 1912.

come a symbol in Chihuahua which undoubtedly explains his great following within his native state. For the men who had fought under him in the previous armed insurrection, it was Orozco alone who had been responsible for the overthrow of the dictatorship.[11] Orozco's call to arms was therefore answered once again.

Ramón Puente's explanation of Orozco's recruitment success—"the ex-revolutionary soldiers still had the desire for adventure"[12]—is a gross oversimplification. Fighting, of course, had become a way of life for many, but if other factors, such as those suggested above, were not involved, why did the "ex-revolutionary" soldiers decide not to cast their lot with the federal regular or irregular forces? Actually, in addition to more volunteers than could profitably be used,[13] a large number of federal troops also joined the rebel cause. They were always more than welcome for two reasons: they did not have to be trained, and they almost always brought their own arms with them.

Orozco announced, on March 6, that he was planning to march on Mexico City with a force of 8,000 men.[14] The boldness and confidence of this announcement caused Madero great consternation. The presidential response was vacillation. Several days after Orozco's pronouncement was released to the press, Madero commissioned Señor Juan Sarabia to negotiate with the rebels. The envoy was instructed to consent to all of Orozco's demands for reform if he could convince the general to lay down his arms.[15] Orozco, interpreting the offer as a sign of fear and weakness, refused to negotiate and continued to take possession of small towns and villages in Chihuahua. One of the most important early engagements occurred at Santa Rosalía, where the Orozquista general José Inés Salazar dislodged a large and well-entrenched federal garrison.[16] Other rebel victories, at Jiménez and Santa Cruz de Neyra, placed the forces of the rebellion in control of the entire state, with the exception of Hidalgo del Parral, by the middle of the month. The victory of Orozco's lieutenant, Benjamín Argumedo,

[11] Luis Lara Pardo, "Orozco Contra Madero," *Excélsior* (Aug. 22, 1953), p. 6.

[12] *Pascual Orozco*, p. 82.

[13] Several hundred men were not accepted because arms were scarce, and troops without weapons were a liability rather than an asset (Resendi, *La Revolución Actual*, p. 66).

[14] *El País*, Mar. 7, 1912.

[15] *El País*, Mar. 8, 1912. Sarabia had served the federal government as an unsuccessful negotiator during the previous year also.

[16] José Fernández Rojas, *De Porfirio Díaz a Victoriano Huerta, 1910–1913* (Guadalajara: Tip de la Escuela de Artes y Oficios del Estado, 1913), p. 144; Almada, *Resumen de la Historia de Chihuahua*, p. 396.

at Mapimí, Durango, in the middle of March, made the federal government more aware than ever of the significance of the steady southern thrust.

The Orozquista revolt received a severe setback on March 14, 1912—not from the federal army but in a joint resolution of the United States Congress. The resolution, originally introduced in the Senate by Elihu Root, stipulated the following:

> . . . Whenever the President shall find that in any American country conditions of domestic violence exist which are promoted by the use of arms and munitions of war from the United States, and shall make lawful proclamation thereof, it shall be unlawful to export, except under such limitations and exceptions that the President shall prescribe, the arms or munitions of war from any place in the United States to such country, until otherwise ordered by the President or by Congress.[17]

The same day the resolution was approved, President William Howard Taft found that "such conditions of domestic violence" existed in Mexico and he prohibited all future shipments of arms.[18] The arms embargo, a severe blow to the Orozquistas, had the effect of converting Ciudad Juárez, hitherto an official port of entry, into a strategic liability. The United States government allowed non-military supplies to pass through El Paso for several months after the arms embargo went into effect, but in May the border town was completely sealed off.[19]

Orozco's immediate response to the arms embargo was an all-out effort to lure federal army officers and men to the rebel cause in order to bring his campaigns to a successful conclusion before the full effect of the embargo could be felt. Major Adolfo Ramírez, a federal commander taken prisoner at the battle of Santa Cruz de Neyra, sent the following dispatch to the Mexican Department of War:

> The afternoon of the nineteenth [March] my men and I were led to the headquarters of Pascual Orozco, Chief of the Revolution. The meeting had as its purpose the object of inviting us to join his forces. In a very correct manner, but at the same time in very strong terms,

[17] *U.S. Foreign Relations, 1912*, p. 745.

[18] *Ibid.*, pp. 745–746.

[19] Charles Cumberland, "Mexican Revolutionary Movements from Texas," *Southwestern Historical Quarterly*, LII (July, 1948–April, 1949), 322–323. It has been suggested that President Taft offered Madero United States railroad facilities for transporting Mexican troops across Texas to combat the Orozquistas (Cline, *United States and Mexico*, p. 129).

we unanimously informed him that we could not adhere to his wishes because our convictions, our military honor, and our respect for the army prohibited us from doing that. In addition we told him that if he set us free we were obliged to join the first federal force that we met.[20]

One week after the arms embargo was made operative by President Taft, General Orozco named a chief of operations for the neighboring state of Sonora. After considerable thought and several consultations with his field officers, his choice fell upon Marcelino Villareal, to whom he gave the title "Commander-in-Chief of the Revolution in the State of Sonora." Orozco's fear of the repercussions of the embargo was reflected in Villareal's letter of appointment. In addition to being given authority to recruit soliders, Villareal was ordered "to import ammunition and other supplies of war in any way possible."[21] The implication was that he should smuggle arms across the Arizona border.

Knowing the full effect of the embargo would soon preclude such an operation, Orozco decided to begin the difficult drive to Mexico City. On March 20, as part of their southern thrust, the rebels captured the last federal stronghold in Chihuahua, Hidalgo del Parral.[22] The federal government's counteroffensive had begun on March 8, as General González Salas left Mexico City at the head of a column of 2,000 men.[23] Madero went to the railroad station to wish the troops success and to quell the rumors that he would ask congress for a leave of absence in order to take the field against Orozco.[24]

Advance columns of the opposing forces exchanged fire in a number of skirmishes during the third week of March, but the major encounter was delayed until March 23 at Rellano. The first battle of Rellano—one of the two most important engagements in the Orozquista revolt—was fought by armies of roughly equal size,[25] and the prize, according to most observers, was Mexico City. The forces of the government were

[20] AHDN, Ramírez to Sec. de Guerra y Marina, Exp. XI/481.5/68, T. I, folio 18, Mar. 19, 1912.

[21] AGN, Orozco to Marcelino Villareal, Leg. 12, Exp. 1, Mar. 22, 1912.

[22] *El País*, Mar. 21, 1912.

[23] *Ibid.*, Mar. 9, 1912. At Torreón, General González Salas would be joined by other contingents that were already in the field, bringing his total to approximately 6,000 men.

[24] *El Tiempo*, Mar. 9, 1912.

[25] It is possible that the rebel forces held a slight numerical advantage, but the figures for the opposing armies are at such variance that a definitive statement is impossible.

divided into three main columns: one under the command of General Trucy Aubert, the second under General Joaquín Téllez, and the third under Generals González Salas and Aureliano Blanquet. The rebels, likewise, congregated their best leadership for the encounter: Orozco, the supreme commander, and Generals Emilio Campa and David de la Fuente.

In the first engagement the federal artillery drove a large Orozquista force into the mountains north of Rellano.[26] Hoping to follow up his advantage, General González Salas ordered his supply train and a large number of troops to advance along a railroad line and prepare for a second attack. While the arms, munitions, and men were being loaded aboard the train, the Orozquista general, Emilio Campa, ordered that a locomotive in the rebels' possession be loaded with dynamite and sent down the track. As the federal train began moving north, it collided with the rebels' unmanned locomotive and caused a great explosion. Twenty-two federal soldiers were killed, seventy were wounded, and many supplies were destroyed.[27]

The rebels immediately took advantage of the panic that followed. Orozco ordered his artillery commander, David de la Fuente, to fire upon the confused federal troops. Under the bombardment, many government troops tried to flee, and General Blanquet was forced to order his loyal troops to fire upon the deserters.[28] To complicate matters still more González Salas lost contact with his support wing, under the command of General Trucy Aubert, and late in the afternoon ordered a retreat to Torreón, rather than waiting for reinforcements.[29] González Salas, rather than face the charges his superiors in Mexico City undoubtedly would hurl at him, committed suicide.[30] In a special hearing

[26] Fernández Rojas, *De Díaz a Huerta*, p. 148.

[27] García Granados, *Historia de México*, II, 279; Fernández Rojas, *De Díaz a Huerta*, p. 148. An interesting account of this episode is recorded by Rubén García in "La Máquina Loca," *El Nacional* (Oct. 7, 1934), magazine section, p. 1.

[28] Casasola, *Historia Gráfica*, I, 428; Fernández Rojas, *De Díaz a Huerta*, p. 149.

[29] The official report of the battle of Rellano was written by General Téllez and is found in AHDN, Exp. XI/481.5/68, T. I, folio 28, May 1, 1912, and folio 493, Apr. 12, 1912.

[30] Strong evidence suggests that González Salas had been informed by a rebel prisoner that the *máquina loca* was going to be used against his troops and that he didn't take sufficient precautions to avoid the disaster (Sánchez Escobar, *Narraciones*, p. 108; García, "La Máquina Loca," p. 1; Aguirre Benavides, *Madero el Inmaculado*, p. 457; Alfonso Corona del Rosal, "Las Fuerzas Armadas de la Revolución," in *México, Cincuenta Años de Revolución*, Vol. III: *La Política* [Mexico City: Fondo de Cultura Económica, 1961], p. 326).

several weeks after the battle, General Aureliano Blanquet testified: "What could be expected? We attacked in the German fashion and they fought us like Mexicans."[31]

The news of the federal defeat at Rellano was withheld from the press for several days, and when the story was released it was shamefully distorted.[32] The press contributed to the capital's steadily growing panic by reporting that General Orozco was continuing south at the head of a column of 14,000 men.[33] The reports were completely erroneous. The American ambassador, Henry Lane Wilson, apparently basing his information on the Mexico City press—and perhaps on his personal desires—expressed the opinion that the Madero government probably would fall.[34] President Madero immediately convoked a special cabinet meeting that named Victoriano Huerta to replace González Salas as field commander against Orozco. Huerta accepted the commission, asking only that he be allowed to make all arrangements for the next campaign.[35] The request was granted.

Despite the fearful reports, Orozco was not marching on Mexico City; he had turned his army northward. The mythmakers have cited Orozco's decision not to march on the capital after his victory at Rellano as proof of his incompetence in military affairs: the capital of the country lay practically at his feet and he was not intelligent enough to realize it. Rather than follow up "the victory of irresponsibility and appetite,"[36] "the Orozquista troops decided to celebrate their mass assassination in the bars and casinos."[37] "The orgy lasted too long and they couldn't march on the capital."[38] Another account is that Orozco lacked the courage to continue the drive on Mexico City: not

[31] Quoted in García Granados, *Historia de México*, II, p. 280.

[32] *El País*, Mar. 27, 1912, and *El Tiempo*, Mar. 26, 1912.

[33] *El Tiempo*, Mar. 30, 1912. Orozco's maximum strength was never more than 8,000 men.

[34] RDS, Wilson to Sec. of State, 812.00/3430, Mar. 29, 1912.

[35] [Victoriano Huerta?], *Memorias del General Victoriano Huerta* (Mexico City: Librería de Quiroga, 1915), p. 10.

[36] Valadés, *Francisco I. Madero*, II, 239.

[37] Romero Flores, *Del Porfirismo a la Revolución*, p. 223. Orozco's decision not to march on Mexico City has been likened to a similar decision a century earlier, as the Chihuahua general has been called "*un nuevo Hidalgo en las puertas de México*" (Luis Vargas Piñeres, "Pascual Orozco Forzado a Sublevarse," *Excélsior* [Sept. 11, 1938], magazine section, p. 1).

[38] Lara Pardo, "Orozco Contra Madero," p. 16. The American consul in Chihuahua City later stated: "Had the rebel commander been other than a stupid incompetent he would have marched straight to Mexico City without much difficulty" (RDS, Letcher to Sec. of State, 812.00/9484, Oct. 17, 1913).

knowing that González Salas had committed suicide, he feared the federal commander was organizing his troops for a vicious counterattack.[39]

Orozco's decision not to march on Mexico City was not the result of military incompetence, cowardice, or a desire to visit the Chihuahua brothels; indeed, the entire campaign, culminating in the victory at Rellano, had been managed with extraordinary skill. Orozco's decision was based upon the exigencies of the moment and the judgment that the arms embargo was beginning to obstruct the effectiveness of the rebel war machine. Even the enemy has vindicated Orozco's decision. Governor Venustiano Carranza of Coahuila, who watched Orozco's movements carefully because of a possible invasion of his own state, reported shortly after the battle of Rellano that Orozquismo was an inappreciable threat because Orozco lacked arms.[40] There is little question that Orozco would have taken Mexico City if his troops had had sufficient supplies and ammunition.[41]

The United States arms embargo was a partial cause of another equally serious rebel problem—insolvency. When Ciudad Juárez was open to arms shipments, war equipment was purchased in large quantities,[42] but the reserves were quickly expended after the embargo went into effect. As in the revolution against Díaz, Mexico's long border with the United States provided ample opportunity for smuggling, but illegal arms shipments, besides being unreliable, were extremely costly because of the risks involved.[43] Although Orozco tapped many sources for financing his rebellion, all were soon exhausted.

In addition to his own mine, La Soledad, which yielded some 30,000 pesos,[44] after Chihuahua was firmly under his control, Orozco decreed that the railroads in the state were nationalized and that receipts from all railroad transactions were to be paid to his treasury.[45] Mining

[39] Ramón Puente, *La Dictadura, la Revolución y sus Hombres* (Mexico City: Ediciones Bocetas, 1938), p. 232; Prida, *De la Dictadura a la Anarquía*, p. 370.

[40] *El Tiempo*, Apr. 12, 1912.

[41] Many other contemporary sources, not Orozquista in sympathy, justify the decision to turn north; see ABFC, J. W. Pender to Albert Bacon Fall, Oct. 2, 1912, and *San Antonio Light*, Dec. 22, 1912.

[42] AGO, Steever to Adjutant General, Doc. File Box 6807, No. 1875135, A 144, March 9, 1912.

[43] The arms embargo resolution provided a fine of not more than $10,000 or imprisonment of not more than two years, or both, for violation of the law (*U.S. Foreign Relations, 1912*, p. 745).

[44] Resendi, *La Revolución Actual*, p. 86.

[45] *El Paso Morning Times*, Mar. 10, 1912.

and export taxes also were earmarked for support of the revolution.[46] The contributions of the Chihuahua conservatives, approximately 1,200,000 pesos,[47] were obtained in an indirect manner, for Orozco forced the banks of the state to turn over that amount to him. As a pretense of legality for the forced loans, the state legislature, long under Orozco's thumb, voted a bond issue of 1,200,000 pesos as security.[48] The aristocracy made only mild and very proper protests. Of the 1,200,000 pesos, only 45,000 pesos is attributable directly to the Terrazas-Creel clique. This amount was obtained from the Banco Minero de Chihuahua, which at that time was under the directorship of Juan Creel, the younger brother of Enrique Creel.[49] Orozco, in his negotiations with the Banco Minero, stipulated that expenditure of the 45,000 pesos could not be authorized by anyone but himself.[50]

Some of the *caudillo*'s subordinates attempted to cope with the financial dilemma in their own way. In March, General Antonio Rojas robbed the Banco Nacional in Ciudad Juárez, but he was arrested on Orozco's orders and sent to the penitentiary in Chihuahua City.[51] All of the fund-raising devices, whether legal or illegal, were insufficient for keeping an army of approximately 8,000 men in food and clothing, meeting payrolls, and paying the exorbitant prices demanded for the illegal supply of arms and ammunition.

After the victory of the rebel forces at Rellano, Orozco deemed it imperative that the vulnerabilities of his movement be concealed from the government, and at the end of March he brashly demanded Madero's resignation. Also, as a display of strength, which was meant to disguise his weakness, Orozco mailed leaflets to leading businessmen in Mexico City. Informing them he would be in the capital within two weeks, he also assured them that he would respect their property rights.[52]

[46] *U.S. Foreign Relations, 1912*, pp. 908–910.

[47] Starr, *Mexico and the U.S.*, p. 343.

[48] *El Paso Morning Times*, Mar. 29, 1912.

[49] STC, Manuel Prieto to Enrique Creel, Oct. 9, 1912.

[50] STC, Pascual Orozco to Sr. Gerente del Banco Minero, Apr. 11, 1912.

[51] RDS, Ellsworth to Sec. of State, 812.00/3279, Mar. 14, 1912. The violently anti-Orozco *El Paso Morning Times* observed on March 25: "In spite of the fact that he is universally regarded as a traitor to his government, General Pascual Orozco has given to the world an exhibition of the fact that he still has a faint idea of the eternal fitness of things when he had General Antonio Rojas restored to his former quarters in the Chihuahua state penitentiary."

[52] *El Tiempo*, Mar. 28, 1912.

The rebel leadership perceived that the sole solution to their problem —repeal of the arms embargo—lay with the United States. In early April, in a long letter to President Taft, Orozco outlined the history of the revolt against Díaz and gave a number of reasons for the new rebellion. After informing the president of the charges against Madero, the general then made his appeal:

Now will you please tell us what the attitude of Americans would be if such a man were elected President to rule your nation? Would you keep him and let him do as he pleased? We know that such a thing would be impossible in the United States because the Congress is really independent and the representatives are genuinely interested in the public welfare . . . therefore they would impeach the President immediately.

In Mexico such a solution is impossible because the present representatives are the same ones who acted under the previous administration. . . . The executive gives all the orders and he is supported right or wrong . . . .

All we ask for is the immediate reestablishment of peace and the immediate resignation of Madero. . . . We want to sustain our present form of government. We do not want anarchy as the Maderists say. We realize that certain of the promises made by Madero are not possible and it is not for those that we disapprove of his conduct. Although some say that he has not had time to carry out his program, we do not think he needed any time to be honest with the public wealth, with public elections, or to let the press be really free.

We do not want but continuingly increasing friendship with the United States. The present conduct of the United States is creating resentment because it is helping Madero to rule. We beg you, Mr. President, to consider our reasons, weigh them carefully, and act impartially. Be neutral . . . do not help either side.

Yours very respectfully,

PASCUAL OROZCO, JR.[53]

The appeal was ignored, and one week later Orozco decided to change his tactics; he foolishly attempted to force the United States into complying with his demands. He informed the United States consular agents in Chihuahua that American consuls stationed in the territory he controlled would not be recognized until the United States

[53] RDS, Orozco to Taft, 812.00/3582, Apr. 4, 1912.

government recognized the belligerency of the revolutionary movement.[54] This dispatch too was ignored.

In mid-April, Orozco received a message from the United States, but it was not what he was awaiting. After the battle for Hidalgo del Parral —between Pancho Villa, commanding a force of federal irregulars, and the Orozquista general José Inés Salazar—a United States citizen, Thomas Fountain, was executed.[55] The death of Fountain did not occur during the battle itself but was ordered by Salazar after Villa had been driven from the city.[56] Fountain, one of Villa's irregulars, was arrested, quickly courtmartialed, and shot—despite the protests of the American consul.[57] The State Department instructed the consul in Chihuahua City to inform Orozco—"unofficially"—that the government of the United States demanded that American citizens taken prisoner during the campaigns of the Revolution be dealt with in accordance with all accepted principles of international law.[58]

Orozco's reply was caustic. Forgetting that he hoped to persuade the United States to reopen Ciudad Juárez to arms shipments, the general sent a dispatch, directly to President Taft, in which he stated that "Fountain's execution was ordered because he was fighting us, handling a rapid-firing machine gun in the ranks of Villa's army, without consideration of what nationality he was."[59] Several days later, after

[54] RDS, Edwards to Sec. of State, 812.00/3575, Apr. 12, 1912, and Letcher to Sec. of State, 812.00/3576, Apr. 12, 1912.

[55] Fountain had a long record of revolutionary activity in Mexico. As early as 1906 he had participated in the rioting that accompanied the famous strike in Cananea, Sonora (STC, Flores Magón Section, Hermanos Baca to Gov. Creel, Nov. 8, 1906).

[56] The *El Paso Morning Times* of April 12, 1912, incorrectly attributed Fountain's execution to orders from Orozco—even though the general was not in the immediate vicinity at the time. This charge was picked up and aired by Figueroa Domenech (*Veinte Meses de Anarquía*, p. 110). The United States Department of State later investigated the matter fully, and nowhere in the massive amount of information is there any evidence that Orozco ordered the execution. The only valid charge that can be leveled against the general is that he bore a moral responsibility for the conduct of his subordinate officers.

[57] ABFC, Memorandum of Outrages upon United States Citizens, Group F; RDS, Huntington Wilson, Acting Sec. of State to Senator Albert B. Fall, 812.00/3610, Apr. 15, 1912. The report of the Fountain killing was sent to Senator Fall not merely because of his special interest in Mexican affairs but because Thomas Fountain had been born in Mesilla, Doña Ana County, New Mexico. The other senator from New Mexico, Thomas Benton Catron, also received a copy of the report (RDS, H. Wilson to Catron, 812.00/3610, Apr. 15, 1912).

[58] RDS, State Dept. to Letcher, 812.00/3595A, Apr. 14, 1912.

[59] RDS, Orozco to Taft, 812.00/3613, Apr. 15, 1912.

Orozco had conferred with Marion T. Letcher, the American consul in Chihuahua,[60] the general notified Washington that he had instructed his subordinates to respect the lives, property, and interests of foreigners.[61] Then, in a letter to the Acting Secretary of State, Orozco apologized—and made another appeal.

> The American consuls on the territory occupied by the revolution, and the citizens of your country and other nations . . . enjoy every protection they merit and I shall pay the best attention to all complaints and petitions that they may see fit to lay before me. . . . It has been my special care to recommend to my associates and subordinates to make it their rule to hold the lives and interests of foreigners in the most profound respect. . . . I beg leave to say to you that the armed movement I am leading meets all the conditions required by International Law [for de facto recognition]. . . . I think I am in a position to obtain recognition of belligerency, which act, on the part of your government, would be the first step toward the initiation of frank relations with the present *de facto* government, represented by the revolution which will beyond doubt triumph because it is supported by public opinion and justice. . . . I take pleasure in saying that I am ready to listen and attend to all suggestions, requests, or claims that your government may be pleased to bring before me through any channel that your Department may deem appropriate. . . .
>
> *Reform, Liberty and Justice*
>
> PASCUAL OROZCO, JR.[62]

The execution of Thomas Fountain, in addition to embarrassing the Orozquista leadership, disconcerted the Madero regime—although the affair could have been used to the advantage of the federal government. As it turned out, an amazingly inopportune statement by Pancho Villa excluded the possibility of a solid Washington–Mexico City front against the northern revolutionaries. When informed of Fountain's death, Villa—in a statement that was quickly picked up by the State Department and the American press, said that he would kill American prisoners taken from the rebels if Orozco killed American prisoners

---

60 *U.S. Foreign Relations, 1912*, p. 792.

61 RDS, Orozco to H. Wilson, 812.00/3670, Apr. 19, 1912. Statements from American citizens in Mexico reveal that Orozco was more mindful of foreign interests after the conference with Letcher (ABFC, statement of Louis Hess, n.d.).

62 AGO, Orozco to H. Wilson, Doc. File Box 6808, No. 1875135, A 282, Apr. 18, 1912.

taken from the federals.[63] The response of Washington was to send a reminder of international obligations, as it had to Orozco, to the Madero government.[64]

The last attempt of Pascual Orozco to gain a modus vivendi with the United States as a preliminary to reopening Ciudad Juárez to the shipment of arms occurred in late April. In the middle of March, Orozco had sent Manuel Luján and Juan Prieto Quemper to Washington as envoys extraordinary.[65] Luján, on April 20, sent a letter to the Secretary of State in which he conveyed the respects of General Orozco and informed the Secretary that he would be honored to present his credentials whenever the government of the United States was disposed to receive them.[66] Although an appeal to extend Orozco de facto recognition and to lift the arms embargo was made on the floor of the United States Senate by Albert Bacon Fall at approximately the same time, the government ignored Luján's letter.[67]

Orozco also appealed for recognition to the senators, deputies, and local officials of the Mexican government. From the beginning of the movement the general had had the support of small citizen armies in a number of Mexican states,[68] but he had found government support

[63] RDS, State Dept. to Letcher, 812.00/3595A, Apr. 14, 1912.

[64] The Orozquista campaigns produced another incident that involved a United States citizen. On September 29, 1912, Herbert L. Russell was robbed and killed by two Orozquista officers at the Hacienda San Juan de Michis in the state of Durango, and Russell's widow subsequently brought suit against the Mexican government for $100,000. The claim was disallowed, as the Mexican consul argued that (1) the Orozquistas were merely rebels, not true revolutionaries; (2) they had no revolutionary plan; (3) they had never constituted a genuine threat to the Mexican government; and (4) the movement did not contribute to the establishment of a government, de jure or de facto, in the Mexican republic. Although each item was obviously incorrect, the claim was denied (*Opinions of the Commissioners Under the Convention Concluded September 10, 1923, Between the United States and Mexico as Extended by the Convention Concluded August 17, 1929* [Washington, D.C.: Government Printing Office, 1931], pp. 44–45, 59, 133–134).

[65] RDS, Letcher to Sec. of State, 812.00/3313, Mar. 15, 1912; *Mexican Herald*, Mar. 21, 1912.

[66] RDS, Luján to Sec. of State, 812.00/3313, Mar. 15, 1912.

[67] Albert Bacon Fall, *Claims Against Mexico* (Washington, D.C.: Government Printing Office, 1912), pp. 12, 44.

[68] In the Laguna district of Durango more than 6,000 rebels declared for Orozco in early March (RDS, Hamm, Consul Durango, to Sec. of State, 812.00/3222, Mar. 13, 1912). The victory over González Salas won additional support for Orozco (RDS, Hamm to Sec. of State, 812.00/3499, Mar. 29, 1912). Dispatches from United States consular agents and the American ambassador in Mexico City reveal that Orozco had considerable support in the states of Colima, Zacatecas, Mexico,

only in Chihuahua. In order to win greater official support, which would give his movement at least a pretense of legality, a special appeal was made on April 6, 1912.[69] Officials were advised that only if they intervened in behalf of the Revolution would the terrible calamities that beset the nation be brought to an end. The legislature of Chihuahua decided to blaze the trail and on April 12, 1912, convened in extraordinary session and withdrew recognition of the national government in Mexico City.[70] The response of the other states was worse than the lack of response from Washington. At the end of April the Mexican Congress passed a new military appropriations bill earmarked for the trouble in the north. Orozco, with something less than complete objectivity, censured the allocations and stated that Mexicans would have to continue killing other Mexicans.[71]

Throughout April a series of minor engagements was waged in which neither side gained a clear advantage, but the rebels and the government seemed to be preparing for a showdown. Madero's call to arms after the defeat at Rellano and the suicide of General González Salas was answered by the formation of volunteer contingents in many states. In Sonora, in response to Madero's appeal, the most famous military figure of the Revolution, Álvaro Obregón, resigned as municipal president of Huatabampo and began his military career.[72] The volunteer battalions of the north, especially those in Sonora and Coahuila, would be extremely valuable in the final defeat of the

---

Puebla, Chiapas, and Veracruz (RDS; Kirk, Consul Mazanillo, to Sec. of State, 812.00/3316, Mar. 14, 1912; H. L. Wilson to Sec. of State, 812.00/3323, Mar. 20, 1912, and 812.00/3330, Mar. 21, 1912; Canada, Consul Veracruz, to Sec. of State, 812.00/5191, Sept. 30, 1912). For an interesting account of the Orozquista movement in the state of Michoacán, see Félix C. Ramírez, *La Verdad Sobre La Revolución Mexicana: Segunda Etapa* (Mexico City: Casa Ramírez Editores, 1958), pp. 23–42. A pro-Madero interpretation of the rebellion in Durango can be found in Arnulfo Ochoa Reyna, *Historia del Estado de Durango* (Mexico City: Editorial del Magisterio, 1958), pp. 321–324.

[69] AREM, Srs. Diputados y Senadores de la Cámaras Federales y Locales, L–E 746 (92–39), Apr. 6, 1912. On March 28, 1912, one of Orozco's aides, Gonzalo Enrile, asked for the support of the national legislature, but Orozco's name did not appear on the request (González Ramírez, *Planes Políticos*, pp. 107–108).

[70] RDS, Letcher to Sec. of State, 812.00/3773, Apr. 12, 1912. The document that withdrew recognition of the federal government is reprinted in González Ramírez, *Planes Políticos*, pp. 109–110.

[71] *El Tiempo*, Apr. 30, 1912.

[72] Álvaro Obregón, *Ocho Mil Kilómetros en Campaña* (Mexico City: Fondo de Cultura Económica, 1960), pp. 7–8; José María Maytorena, *Algunas Verdades Sobre el General Álvaro Obregón* (Los Angeles, 1919), pp. 13–14.

Orozquista army and would later form the basis of a new revolutionary contingent, the Ejército Constitucionalista.[73]

On April 10 the government began a major offensive. General Victoriano Huerta and a large body of well-trained and well-equipped federal regulars left Mexico City and moved north to Torreón, where a temporary headquarters was established.[74] Shortly after their arrival in Torreón, Huerta's forces were joined by a large body of irregulars under the command of Pancho Villa. On April 28, General Huerta announced an amnesty for all Orozquistas who would lay down their arms within two weeks. The offer was not a sign of weakness, but a well-calculated scheme: Huerta was fully aware that the arms shortage and lack of finances weakened the rebels daily.

General Huerta assisted by Generals Trucy Aubert and Joaquín Téllez (both of whom had fought the Orozquistas at the first battle of Rellano), planned his campaign slowly and deliberately. A talented artillery specialist, Colonel Guillermo Rubio Navarte, was added to the staff,[75] and United States military attachés accompanied Huerta to Torreón in an advisory capacity.[76] Although 400 men declared they would not fight against Pascual Orozco and had to be disarmed and sent back to Mexico City under guard,[77] the loss did not greatly alter Huerta's plans; the addition of several volunteer brigades brought his total fighting force to slightly more than 8,000 men. Orozco and his subordinates, Cheché Campos and José Inés Salazar, mustered a force of approximately the same size. Preliminary engagements during the first week of May were indecisive, but in the first major engagement— on May 12, at Conejos—the Orozquistas were defeated and driven back. Orozco's lack of arms already had proved telling.

The most important battle occurred two weeks later—on the same field where Orozco had defeated González Salas only two months before. The second battle of Rellano (May 22–23), which marked the beginning of the decline of Orozquismo, began on the morning of May 22. It soon became apparent that the rebels would be unable to withstand the superior federal artillery fire. Handicapped by a lack of ammunition, the rebel lines were repeatedly cut down by Colonel Rubio

---

[73] Barragán Rodríguez, *Historia del Ejército*, I, 169.

[74] *El Tiempo*, Apr. 11, 1912, and *Mexican Herald*, Apr. 11, 1912.

[75] Ross, *Madero*, p. 264; Casasola, *Historia Gráfica*, I, 446.

[76] The assistance of the United States military attachés was not disclosed at the time but was brought out subsequently in a Senate investigation of Mexican affairs (*Fall Committee*, testimony of Nelson O'Shaughnessy, II, 2707).

[77] RDS, Garrett to Sec. of State, 812.00/3900, May 6, 1912.

Navarte's well-placed artillery. In addition, Huerta had been informed of the exact size of Orozco's force and the number of his artillery pieces and other heavy weapons.[78]

The battle lasted into the night of May 22, but the government army was unable to dislodge the rebels from their trenches. On the morning of May 23, in a dispatch to the Department of War, Huerta stated: "The battle has now lasted twenty hours and we are continuing to fight. I believe that with the movements we are carrying out we will be able to seize their positions before the day is out."[79] General Huerta's assessment of the situation proved sound. At 2:37 P.M. he reported: "Our troops have just succeeded in taking the last and most important enemy position. Rellano is in our hands."[80] Huerta was among the first to realize that from his own personal point of view the victory was as important politically as it was militarily.[81] He had suddenly become a military hero with a national reputation.

Orozco's defeat at the second battle of Rellano did not signify the end of the Orozquista revolution but its chances for success were greatly lessened. Throughout May and June, as the rebel forces were pushed steadily northward by Victoriano Huerta, the rebels destroyed railroad lines, bridges, and other communication facilities to impede the federal pursuit. In early June the Orozquistas enjoyed a temporary comeback as Huerta was forced to retreat because of a supply problem.[82] Several towns were recaptured, only to be lost again within a few days.[83]

At the end of June, General Orozco decided to make a stand at Bachimba. As the opposing forces began preparing for the encounter, the Orozquistas were preoccupied with the problem that had spelled their defeat at the second battle of Rellano: the lack of arms and ammunition. In addition, the series of demoralizing defeats suffered after the second battle of Rellano had prompted desertions,[84] and it was a depleted, underarmed rebel force that met the federals on July 3, 1912. Surprisingly, Orozco was able to wage battle the entire

[78] Jesús J. Tiscareño, "Porque Venció Huerta a Pascual Orozco," *El Legionario*, III (Oct., 1953), 13.

[79] AHDN, Huerta to Sec. de Guerra y Marina, Exp. XI/481.5/68, T. I, folio 68, May 23, 1912.

[80] *Ibid.*, Exp. XI/281.5/68, T. I, folio 71, May 23, 1912.

[81] [Huerta], *Memorias*, p. 12.

[82] *El País*, June 5, 1912.

[83] *Ibid.*, June 9, 10, 1912.

[84] RDS, Letcher to Sec. of State, 812.00/4357, June 28, 1912.

day before he was forced to order still another retreat.[85] Chihuahua City was the next halt of the Orozquistas, but in a matter of days Huerta set them running again. The last stand of Orozco's army was Ciudad Juárez, and by the third week in July it was the only important town under the rebels' control.[86] The final defeat came on August 16, 1912, when federal troops captured the border city.[87]

The reportage of the Orozquista revolt, from beginning to end, was one-sided. Understandably, the federal government wished to avail itself of every means for ending the fratricidal strife and reestablishing national solidarity, but its Machiavellian techniques were unjustifiable.

[85] The news of Orozco's defeat at Bachimba was so well received in Mexico City that President Madero decided to hold a gala reception and banquet in Chapultepec Castle to mark the occasion. The affair was described in a colorful manner by Edith O'Shaughnessy, the wife of the United States *chargé d'affaires* in Mexico City, who was a guest at the banquet (*Intimate Pages of Mexican History* [New York: George H. Doran Company, 1920], p. 279).

[86] *El Correo*, July 22, 1912.

[87] *El Correo*, Aug. 17, 1912. The entire military campaign of the Orozquista insurrection was the subject of a very popular *corrido* in 1913:

> *Cuando el gobierno supo la rebelión de Orozco*
> *dispuso enviar las tropas que fueran necesarias,*
> *y el mando de las fuerzas le dió a González Salas,*
> *Ministro de Guerra con tres columnas varias. . . .*
> *Llegó hasta Torreón con ánimo esforzado*
> *y comenzó su avance sin grande precaución,*
> *dándole tiempo a Orozco de esperarlo en Rellano*
> *donde quedó deshecho y en triste situación.*
> *Causó a González Salas mortal abatimiento*
> *el ver así deshecho su ejército brillante*
> *que sacando del cinto un arma disparóse*
> *cayendo muerto al punto, junto de su ayudante. . . .*
> *Huerta reunió en Jiménez los restos de las tropas*
> *forzó la disciplina y al recibir refuerzos*
> *rumbo a Conejos fuése con grande contingente,*
> *haciendo huir a Orozco con sus bisoños tercios.*
> *Sagaz le siguió Huerta con paso cauteloso,*
> *buscando punto bueno donde irlo a atacar*
> *y en Bachimba se encuentran por fin los dos rivales*
> *y se da una batalla con grande mortandad. . . .*
> *Tomaron a Chihuahua, Ahumada, y Ciudad Juárez*
> *y todo aquel estado volvió al orden legal.*
> *Y Orozco con su escolta se internó en Arizona*
> *quedando en paz entonces a poco de llegar. . . .*

The *corrido* is found in Mendoza, *El Corrido de la Revolución Mexicana*, p. 58.

The tightly controlled capital press constantly belittled Orozco's victories or exaggerated his defeats. Frequently, he was reported killed or captured, and retractions were never printed. The forces of the government were portrayed as pious and idealistic, representative of the best manhood of Mexico, while the opposition was characterized as *provocateurs*, gangsters, murderers, and renegades. Atrocities were attributed to the rebels but never to the government forces. Orozco— among other charges—was accused of placing unarmed federal prisoners in the first line of his attack to draw out the enemy's fire—at the same time to save his troops the trouble of executing them.[88] Another charge was that Orozco sadistically ordered prisoners executed at the rate of ten a day, ostensibly to save the cost of their sustenance.[89] (Why didn't he order them all killed at once?) Official Mexican War Department reports, many of them written by escaped prisoners, do not substantiate these charges; indeed, because he hoped to win them over, Orozco treated his prisoners humanely.[90]

On January 14, 1913, the *Mexican Herald*, in an attempt to demonstrate Orozco's "depravity," published a page-one story on the fate of the federal general José de la Luz Blanco, whom the Orozquistas had "hanged to a tree . . . [and] riddled with bullets."[91] Ten days later the *Herald* printed a small, inconspicuous statement to the effect that General Blanco had indeed been captured by the Orozquistas but had been released unharmed.[92] However, because most of the "atrocity" stories concerned lesser figures, retractions were seldom necessary.

There were, of course, frequent allegations of brigandage, pillage, and plunder. One source, in a parody on the famous revolutionary slogan "*Sufragio Efectivo, No Reelección*," suggested that the Orozquista slogan should be "*Saqueo Efectivo, No Devolución*."[93] The United States ambassador in Mexico City, Henry Lane Wilson, the United States consuls in Ciudad Juárez and Chihuahua City, and

[88] *La Verdad*, June 5, 1912.

[89] Calero, *Decenio de Política Mexicana*, p. 96.

[90] AHDN, Ramírez to Sec. de Guerra y Marina, Exp. XI/481.5/68, T. I, folio 18. Salvador Resendi went out of his way to report that Orozco treated prisoners exceptionally well, at times even quartering them in the Hotel St. Francis in Chihuahua City (*La Revolución Actual*, p. 83). Mrs. Edith O'Shaughnessy, who must be considered a pro-Huerta source, also states that Orozco "treated prisoners so well that they could be counted on to promptly swell the ranks of his followers" (*Intimate Pages of Mexican History*, p. 163).

[91] *Mexican Herald*, Jan. 14, 1913.

[92] *Mexican Herald*, Jan. 24, 1913.

[93] Gimeno, *La Canalla Roja*, p. 12.

Pascual Orozco, November, 1910.

Porfirio Díaz (President of Mexico, 1876–1910), 1910.

Madero's staff prior to the capture of Ciudad Juárez. Front row, left to right: Venustiano Carranza, Francisco Vásquez Gómez, Francisco Madero, Abraham González, José María Maytorena, A. Fuentes, and Pascual Orozco. Back row, left to right: Francisco Villa, Gustavo A. Madero, Francisco Madero, Sr., Giuseppe Garibaldi, Frederico González Garza, José de la Luz Blanco, Juan Sánchez Azcona, Alfonso Madero, and two unidentified persons.

Pancho Villa, 1910.

Emiliano Zapata, about 1910.

Rebel snipers at the battle for Ciudad Juárez, captured against Madero's orders.

Americans watching the battle from El Paso, May 10, 1911.

Francisco I. Madero entering
Ciudad Juárez in 1911.

Oscar Braniff, Pascual Orozco, Francisco Villa, and Giuseppe Garibaldi after the surrender of Ciudad Juárez, May, 1911.

Madero and Orozco in 1911, at the temporary headquarters in Bustillos.

Pascual Orozco, Sr., Eduardo Hay, Pascual Orozco, Jr., Madero, Abraham González, and José de la Luz Blanco during Orozco's first visit to Mexico City, November, 1911.

Victoriano Huerta, President of Mexico, February 1913–July 1914.

Huerta and Orozco exchanging *abrazos* after Orozco's announcement of support, March, 1913. This picture was subsequently widely circulated with the caption "Un Judas abrazando el otro."

Pascual Orozco, with his chiefs of staff, preparing to leave for Chihuahua to fight the Constitutionalists.

Pancho Villa leading his *dorados* during the Constitutionalist Revolution.

Pascual Orozco shortly before his death.

other observers, apparently influenced by the hostile press, sent unfavorable reports to Washington on Orozco's attitude toward the United States. The Secretary of War, Henry L. Stimson, reported that Orozco was so bitter against the United States for enforcing the arms embargo that he was planning to invade New Mexico.[94] Henry Lane Wilson reported that Orozco had so mistreated American citizens that the Department of State should consider sending troops into the state of Chihuahua.[95]

Had the reports to Washington been based upon the reports of the "victims" rather than upon a partisan press, it would have been clear that most of the charges were not well founded. In July, 1912, Senator Albert Fall of New Mexico was charged by the Senate to study the claims of American nationals for the damages they had sustained during the Revolution. Fall's investigation revealed that the federal troops, not the Orozquistas, were responsible for most of the rapine, brigandage, and other excesses.[96]

Another special report, prepared for the United States Senate in October, 1912, found that

> The extent of robberies committed are . . . greatly exaggerated by the newspapers. Horses and other property have been taken by parties without authority and in many cases by parties not connected with either of the armies. Many have been later returned or paid for. The Revolutionaries [Orozquistas] in a majority of cases issue receipts or promise to pay for the property taken. These receipts are accepted in payment of customs duties or taxes and the transaction often turns out to be quite satisfactory to both parties.[97]

A third investigation, conducted several years later, interrogated a number of Americans who had resided in Chihuahua throughout the Orozquista revolution. In this testimony—the most valid single source of information on the Orozquistas' treatment of foreigners—Henry Hobart Knox, a consulting mining engineer, denied that Orozco had

94 RDS, Stimpson to Sec. of State, 812.00/4455, July 20, 1912. The rumor appears to have been circulated by a hysterical citizen of Las Cruces, New Mexico (ABFC, Telegram from George W. Frenger to Sen. Albert B. Fall, Aug. 2, 1912). Although Fall notified General Leonard Wood of the rumor, neither Fall nor Wood attached much importance to it (ABFC, Wood to Fall, Aug. 6, 1912, item 3180).

95 RDS, H. L. Wilson to Sec. of State, 812.00/3590, Apr. 13, 1912.

96 Fall, *Claims Against Mexico*, p. 12. The statement of Senator Fall should not, in itself, be accepted as definitive; it is possible that he was biased on the other side.

97 RDS, Special Report prepared by J. R. Clark, Jr., "The Mexican Situation," 812.00/5301/2, Oct. 1, 1912.

perpetrated outrages and robberies.[98] Similarly, Nils Olaf Bagge, the president of one of the most important mining companies in Chihuahua, testified that Orozco had respected Americans and their property.[99] George C. Carothers, who had been an American consular agent in Mexico between 1910 and 1913 and a special representative of the State Department for several years, not only testified that Orozco had been friendly to Americans, but, in addition, volunteered that he had striven to protect private property.[100] Although Orozco's concern for American lives and property was based upon expediency and not upon affection for the nation that had halted his supply of arms and ammunition, there is no basis for the charges that the rebel chieftain was disdainful of United States' interests.

The propaganda campaign against the man who opposed the "Apostle of the Revolution" also represented Orozco as a thief, a sexual pervert, a traitor, a hedonist, and a murderer. Accusations were printed in the press and were repeated in leaflets that were distributed in centers of his popularity—as in a flyer distributed among the Spanish-speaking community of El Paso.

> It is well known by the majority of us that General Pascual Orozco, Jr., is a traitor. . . . We have been deceived. The rebels have been defeated time and time again and thousands of our friends have lost their lives on the fields of Cuatro Ciénegas, Conejos, Rellano, and recently Bachimba. Their families have been left without support while our General is enjoying orgies and drunkenness aboard his special train which is always ten kilometers from the line of fire. . . . Orozco has deposited $500,000 in the banks of El Paso . . . money paid for with the lives of our friends. . . . Are we going to continue offering our lives for this traitor?[101]

Despite the unwarranted harangues and vilifications, which began with Orozco's declaration of revolt and did not cease until Madero had succumbed to another coup (in February, 1913), Orozco maintained a large following. Emiliano Zapata, also in arms against the Madero government, declared his support of the northern revolution

[98] *Fall Committee*, II, 1417–1418. Henry Knox had every reason to dislike General Orozco. When the rebel commander was forced to retreat before Huerta's onslaught, he destroyed more than 200 miles of railroad track between Ciudad Juárez and Chihuahua. The destruction of the railroad lines was very costly to the mining interests.

[99] *Ibid.*, II, 1419.

[100] *Ibid.*, II, 1763–1764.

[101] AGO, Steever to Adjutant General, Doc. File Box 6808, No. 1875135, A 392, July 9, 1912.

in late May, 1912,[102] and continued to support it. Official reports, from both the Mexican and the United States governments, indicate that Orozco also had a large following among Mexicans in the United States.[103] In October, 1912, when Orozco's father, Colonel Pascual Orozco, was arrested in El Paso for violation of the United States' neutrality laws, sympathy demonstrations were conducted in his behalf.[104] That the diatribes were not wholly successful is also attested to by the loyalty of Orozco's troops. When the Orozquista army suffered its last major defeat (at Ciudad Juárez, in August, 1912), it divided into a number of small guerrilla bands and continued to fight in northern Chihuahua.

In late August and early September, 1912, Orozco led guerrilla attacks against a number of federal garrisons in northern Chihuahua. Orozco's largest band, consisting of approximately 1,000 men, defeated the federals at Ojinaga on the evening of September 11,[105] and the town served the rebels as a capital until January, 1913. Orozco, however, was wounded in the engagement,[106] and a few days later crossed into the United States.[107] Informed of the *guerrillero*'s move, United States border officials were ordered to apprehend Orozco for questioning in connection with the execution of Thomas Fountain at Parral the previous April.[108] Orozco eluded the border officials, and in early November he traveled to St. Louis, Missouri, in an attempt to enlist support.[109] At the end of November he moved to the Los Angeles area, presumably on the same mission.[110] In early December he was back in

[102] RDS, Zapata to Montgomery Schuyler, Representative of the Government of the United States of the North, 812.00/4331, June 25, 1912.

[103] AREM, Carrillo, Consul Los Angeles, to Sec. de Relaciones Exteriores, L–E 746 (92–39), June 25, 1912; RDS, Special Agent, Los Angeles, to Sec. of State, 812.00/5679, Nov. 28, 1912.

[104] *San Antonio Light*, Sept. 26, 1912.

[105] AHDN, Gen. José de las Cruz Sánchez to Huerta, Exp. XI/481.5/68, T. I, folio 168, Sept. 1912; AGO, Steever to Adjutant General, Doc. File Box 6808, No. 1875135, A 581, Sept. 14, 1912.

[106] *El País*, Feb. 5, 1913.

[107] AHDN, unidentified dispatch, Exp. XI/481.5/68, T. I, folio 162, n.d.

[108] AGO, Steever to Adjutant General, Doc. File Box 6808, No. 1875138, A 582, Sept. 15, 1912.

[109] AREM, Fernández, Consul St. Louis, to Sec. de Relaciones Exteriores, L–E 746 (92–39), Nov. 10, 1912.

[110] RDS, [James Ganor], Special Agent, Dept. of Justice to Sec. of State, 812.00/5679, Nov. 28, 1912; *El Paso Morning Times*, Nov. 25, 1912. From the beginning of the movement, Los Angeles had been a center of Orozquista support in the United

Chihuahua, coordinating the guerrilla efforts of his subordinates—such men as José Inés Salazar, Marcelo Caraveo, Antonio Rojas, and Juan Porrás.

Orozco, who returned to Mexico in poor health, suffered periodic attacks of rheumatism that kept him from active participation in the military maneuvers that were being waged under his banner. He was still recognized as Commander-in-Chief of the Revolutionary Forces, however.[111] Although most accounts state that Orozquismo lost its vital force with the rebels' loss of Ciudad Juárez, Juan Barragán—one of the few military historians who is thoroughly familiar with the documentary collection in Mexico City's National Defense Archives—believes that although Orozquismo lacked organization in January, 1913, it was still a significant force.[112] It might be added, however, that its lack of organization preserved it as a threat: if the Orozquista army had been centralized at that time, it could have been annihilated in a single engagement.

Throughout January, 1913, Antonio Rábago, the commander of the Second Military Zone, reported that the rebels were intensifying their guerrilla activity.[113] By the middle of the month the seemingly revitalized rebel force was threatening Ciudad Juárez and Chihuahua City.[114] The federal forces, it seems, were either unable or unwilling to pursue the many semi-independent Orozquista bands. It also seems that Victoriano Huerta, already toying with the idea of rebelling against Madero, did not want to extinguish the anti-Maderist revolt in northern Mexico, and therefore did not employ the full potential of the federal war machine in the northern campaigns.[115] The American

States (AREM, Carrillo to Sec. de Relaciones Exteriores, L–E 746 (92–39), July 29, 1912; RDS, [James Ganor], Special Agent, Dept. of Justice to Sec. of State, 812.00/4628, Aug., 1912).

[111] *Mexican Herald*, Jan. 17, 1913.

[112] *Historia del Ejército*, I, 20.

[113] AHDN, Rábago to Sec. de Guerra y Marina, Exp. XI/481.5/69, T. I, folios 29–60, Jan. 11, 1913, and folios 108–118, Feb. 3, 1913.

[114] *Mexican Herald*, Jan. 17, 1913.

[115] Reports from a number of independent sources—as early as September, 1912—suggest that Huerta was not pursuing the northern campaign with great vigor. The same reports also suggest an Orozco–Huerta alliance (RDS: Letcher to Sec. of State, 812.00/5056, Sept. 5, 1912; Garrett to Sec. of State, 812.00/4933, Sept. 15, 1912; Bielasky, Dept. of Justice, to Sec. of State, 812.00/5028, Sept. 14, 1912; Steever to Sec. of State, 812.00/5031, Sept. 18, 1912; and statement of H. L. Swain, "Conditions in Mexico," 812.00/7757, n.d.). The possibility of a Huerta–Orozco alliance in late 1912 has also been explored in Manuel Bonillas, *El Régimen Maderista* (Mexico City: Talleres Linotipográficas de El Universal, 1922), pp. 18–19.

consul in Chihuahua reported: "General Huerta and the federal army generally were in hearty sympathy with the enemies of the Madero government throughout this trying period and . . . were in treasonable communication and correspondence with these enemies."[116]

President Madero, on January 24, declared a five-day armistice and opened negotiations with the Orozquistas.[117] Orozco's reply was issued on January 26, through Ricardo Gómez Robelo, the secretary of the Orozquista movement.[118]

As representative of General Pascual Orozco, Jr., and the military and civil bodies of the Revolution, I manifest to the people of Mexico that the basis for the restoration of peace must be the resignation of Francisco I. Madero and his cabinet. The formation of the [new] executive power will be as follows: President, Jerónimo Treviño; Foreign Relations, Francisco León de la Barra; Gobernación, Alberto García Granados; Fomento, Jorge Vera Estañol; War, Samuel Cuellar; Hacienda, Toribio Esquivel Obregón; Communications, Félix Díaz; Public Instruction, Francisco Vásquez Gómez; and Justice, Namesio García Naranjo. Pascual Orozco declines any benefit and so will every one of us for the country's sake.[119]

This recommendation of a provisional president and cabinet indicates that conservative influence in the Orozquista movement persisted until the very end. With the exception of Namesio García Naranjo, a respected but not widely known journalist and a deputy in Congress, the cabinet was decidedly conservative. Treviño had been a governor of Nuevo León and Minister of War under Porfirio Díaz. Francisco León de la Barra had served the dictator as Secretary of Foreign Relations and had been the interim president in 1911. Alberto García Granados was Secretary of Gobernación under De la Barra, and Esquivel Obregón had served the Porfirist regime as a peace negotiator in April and May of 1911. Jorge Vera Estañol was Díaz' Secretary of Education and later his Secretary of Gobernación. General Samuel García Cuellar had been Chief of Staff late in the Díaz regime. The only member of the proposed cabinet who had actively opposed Madero was Félix Díaz, the nephew of the ex-dictator, who at that

[116] RDS, Letcher to Sec. of State, 812.00/9484, Oct. 17, 1913.
[117] *Mexican Herald*, Jan. 25, 1913.
[118] Gómez Robelo, who had been arrested for violation of neutrality laws, issued the statement after having been released on bail (*New York Times*, Jan. 12, 1913).
[119] *El País*, Jan. 29, 1913, and *Mexican Herald*, Jan. 28, 1913.

time was serving a term in the penitentiary of Tlaltelolco for having led an abortive anti-Maderist revolt in the state of Veracruz.

Although the Orozquista offensive in late January, 1913, caused apprehension in Mexico City, Madero could not accede to the rebels' demands. He had put down the revolts of Bernardo Reyes, Vásquez Gómez, Emiliano Zapata, Félix Díaz, and Orozco's earlier thrust, and there was no reason to assume that he would be unable to weather another insurrection. The armistice ended on January 28, and northern Chihuahua again became a battlefield.[120] Within two weeks, however, Madero fell victim to a new plot on his own doorstep. Not only was the office of president seized from him, but his life was taken in the bargain. Even while the army insurrection was developing in Mexico City the Orozquistas continued to apply pressure in the northern part of Chihuahua.[121]

Orozquismo, as was noted earlier, was compounded of multiple causes, under leaders who pursued various ends; its successes and failures, therefore, must be gauged on several different scales. From the conservatives' point of view, Orozquismo served its purpose: the substantial, if somewhat sporadic, financial assistance given the Orozquistas by the Chihuahua aristocracy proved an excellent investment for those who wanted to dampen reform or bring it to a standstill.[122] As the movement progressed, it of course lost its ideological overtones, and the force behind it became more and more apparent. The federal government, forced for eleven months to combat the Orozquista insurrection, exhausted the national treasury; and Orozquismo in the north and Zapatismo in the south diverted much talent and energy from the conspicuous demands of social and economic reform. The question of Madero's social consciousness becomes mere pedantry in the face of the obstacles Orozquismo placed in his path. Even if the president had been keenly receptive to the needs of early twentieth-century Mexican society, there was little he could have done.

[120] *Mexican Herald*, Jan. 29, 1913.

[121] AHDN, General Jefe de la Segunda Zona Militar to Sec. de Guerra y Marina, Exp. XI/481.5/69, T. I, folios 108–118 and folios 125, Feb. 3, and Feb. 13, 1913.

[122] Enrique Creel and Luis Terrazas denied that they had made contributions to the Orozquista effort (STC, Martín Falomer to Enrique Creel, Sept. 30, 1912, and Carta Abierta de Luis Terrazas, Jan. 28, 1913). Nevertheless, the family had offered no resistance when the forced loan was made on the Banco Minero de Chihuahua nor had it offered to cooperate with the Madero government in an effort to prevent Orozco from securing the funds.

To equate Orozquismo solely with the desire to restore the *"pax Porfiriana,"* however, would be a mistake. Even if it were granted that the movement was engineered entirely by clandestine forces hostile to the notion of twentieth-century liberalism, more than 8,000 men—most of whom had fought in the 1910–1911 campaigns against Porfirio Díaz— did not suddenly decide they had been in error. The charge that Orozco's army was comprised of self-serving opportunists is un- tenable, unless one believes that all of the revolutionary contingents between 1910 and 1920 were similarly motivated.[123] The men who comprised the Orozquista force—and those of other revolutionary bodies both before and after it—were of various economic and social backgrounds.[124] Far from consisting solely of a group of implacable reactionaries, Orozco's army combined the antagonisms of an impres- sive array of Madero's adversaries. Although most of the rank and file had no appreciation of the revolution's political subtleties, most of them had been convinced by General Orozco—who had been con- vinced by the aristocracy—that the cause for which they had earlier fought had been betrayed by President Madero.

An interesting method for assessing the relationship of Orozquismo to the counterrevolution is by analyzing the reaction of the old regime to the movement of 1912. I have found no statement of Porfirio Díaz that bears directly on the Orozquista revolt, but Ramón Corral, a Porfirist governor of Sonora and the dictator's last vice-president, commented upon the 1912 movement. In a letter to Rosendo Pineda, one of the founders of Mexican *cientificismo*, Corral indicated that Orozquismo was not a counterrevolution; Mexico, according to Corral, would have been worse off than ever if Orozco or Vásquez Gómez had been successful. At the same time, Corral recognized the military capabilities and the personal attractiveness of the Chihuahua rebel and acknowledged that he could have been of great value in a true counter- revolution. He added, however, that it would have been indispensable that Orozco "change color."[125]

Orozco never fathomed the political overtones of the movement to which he gave his name and leadership. His close contact with the president, with cabinet officials, and with a number of state governors did not contribute to the cultivation of any political genius. In January,

[123] This charge against the Orozquista army was made by Sánchez Escobar, *Narraciones*, p. 113.

[124] RDS, Ellsworth to Sec. of State, 812.00/3297, Mar. 14, 1912.

[125] The entire letter is quoted in González Ramírez, *Planes Políticos*, lxiv–lxv, n. 13.

1913, the general from western Chihuahua had no better understanding of the complicated game of Mexican politics than he did when he left his mules and took up arms in November, 1910. As the Orozquista campaigns began to take their toll of lives and the press castigated the leader of the movement, Orozco's fight became a personal vendetta. Statements from the Orozquista headquarters, which were issued over the general's name, denounced Madero viciously for the type of war he was waging: government troops were charged with cutting the ears off the Chamula Indians in Chiapas, of pouring artillery fire on towns abandoned by the rebels, of outraging and murdering defenseless women, and of executing persons on the mere suspicion that they were rebel sympathizers.[126] These indictments are at best a series of half-truths, and are no more justifiable than the anti-Orozco diatribes,[127] but they indicate that ideologies were pushed aside in favor of specific charges that could easily be understood by the rank and file—and by the general. Without the introduction of such unequivocal charges it is doubtful that the military revolt could have endured for seven months after the series of defeats that was sustained in May and June of 1912.

Although Francisco Madero fell before an apparently unrelated military coup in February, 1913, Orozquismo contributed to his downfall. The civil war had generated an instability that undermined confidence in the Madero regime, and the apparent inability of the national government to put down the revolt increased the discontent. Although it might be argued that Zapatismo produced the same effect, it was the concentration of federal troops in northern Mexico that permitted the movement in nearby Morelos to grow. Although there were no carefully formulated attempts at cooperation, the two movements complemented one another in forcing the government to wage war on two fronts. For those, therefore, whose only motivation was the over-

---

126 ABFC, "Orozco," n.d.

127 I have intentionally stressed the anti-Orozco propaganda more than the falsifications of the anti-Madero forces. The full machinery of the incumbent regime and a censored press were used to disseminate the government's vituperations; the charges of the Orozquistas, on the other hand, were relatively unheard. Although the distortions of both sides are equally objectionable on moral grounds, those of the Maderists, because of their wide circulation at the time and their present availability, have been seized upon by a number of historians who have fabricated the anti-Orozco myth. A similar evaluation of revolutionary reportage has been suggested by Lowell Blaisdell, *The Desert Revolution, Baja California, 1911* (Madison: University of Wisconsin Press, 1962), pp. 58–60.

throw of a regime, Orozquismo must be judged at least a partial success.

Only in one important aspect was the Chihuahua insurrection a failure. The Plan Orozquista, of March, 1912, attracted several genuine liberals early in the movement—persons who were interested in implementing the declaration's reform program. Because the plan was only a ruse for widening the base of support, it would have not been implemented even if the Orozquistas had been able to step into the political vacuum caused by Madero's overthrow. As the revolt progressed, and as it became evident that the movement was directed by reactionaries, the liberals abandoned the cause. Their defection was indeed vindicated in February, 1913, when the Orozquista headquarters, almost to a man, gave its support to Victoriano Huerta.

Although Orozquismo and social reform were incompatible, the artifice of the arch-conservatives, including the *científicos*, was turned against them, for the Plan Orozquista was of major interest to the constituent assembly of 1917. Orozquismo helped delineate the path the revolution would follow.

# VI

## *Orozco and Huerta*

On Sunday, February 9, 1913, Mexico City was rocked by artillery fire. Citizens of the capital, for the first time since the outbreak of the Revolution, were made acutely aware of the destructive force of the intermittent civil strife that for almost two and a half years had plagued the remainder of the country. But neither the Orozquistas nor the Zapatistas had descended upon the city; the shelling that awoke the inhabitants of the capital at dawn was the culmination of a carefully planned *coup d'état* that had originated within Madero's federal army. More than 2,000 troops of the federal garrison in the capital defected with General Manuel Mondragón and turned against the president. Although Madero had been warned that many of his leading officers were planning this act of treachery, he had refused to heed the warning.

The first task of the new, ready-made rebel army was to secure the release of two anti-Madero political prisoners: Bernardo Reyes and Félix Díaz. After this was accomplished, the army was readied for an assault on the national palace, which was defended by a group of some 200 loyal troops under General Lauro Villar. General Bernardo Reyes, who led the charge on the national palace, fell before one of the first machine-gun blasts, and the assault was repulsed. The anti-government forces were forced to retreat westward across the city and to take refuge in the old armory of the Ciudadela, where a temporary headquarters had been established by Félix Díaz and Manuel Mondragón. The episode that followed is universally labeled the blackest page of the Mexican Revolution.

President Madero, when he arrived at the national palace later in the morning of February 9, found that his loyal commander Lauro Villar had been wounded during the first encounter and was unable to continue in his command position. The president then made a momentous decision: he named General Victoriano Huerta commander-in-chief against the "Felixistas." Huerta's principal distinctions up until this time were that he had conducted a fairly successful campaign against Emiliano Zapata in the state of Morelos and that he had defeated Pascual Orozco at the second battle of Rellano. On this occasion, however, Madero's distress became Huerta's opportunity.

For ten days (*la decena trágica*) Mexico City's business district was a battleground. Artillery fire exchanged between the loyal troops in the national palace and the Felixistas in the Ciudadela leveled buildings and killed and wounded hundreds of innocent civilians. All traffic in the center of the city came to a halt; telephone service was interrupted; shopkeepers closed their doors. On February 17, when Madero summoned Huerta and asked when the fighting would cease, Huerta assured the president that peace would be restored on the following day. February 18 began, as had each of the preceding nine days, with artillery and machine-gun fire, but the fighting stopped shortly before three o'clock in the afternoon: Huerta had withdrawn recognition of the federal government and, together with his troops, joined forces with the Felixistas.[1] Madero and his vice-president, José María Pino Suárez, were arrested the same day, and their resignations were secured several days later. On the night of February 22, 1913, the ex-president and his vice-president were assassinated while being transferred from the national palace to the penitentiary. Circumstantial evidence indicates that Victoriano Huerta was at least indirectly responsible for the two murders.

The agreement by which Victoriano Huerta joined the revolutionaries is known as the Pact of the Embassy (sometimes the Pact of the Ciudadela) because the negotiations apparently were conducted under the aegis of the American ambassador in Mexico City, Henry Lane Wilson. Huerta was to assume the provisional presidency and Félix Díaz was to succeed him as soon as an election could be held. The support of the Reyistas was to be rewarded with a number of important cabinet positions. The first constitutional government to emanate from the Revolution had been overthrown by a well-planned and -executed military coup.

Immediately after Victoriano Huerta assumed the provisional presidency, sides were chosen for a new series of military campaigns. Most of the state governors and the former interim president Francisco de la

[1] Casasola, *Historia Gráfica*, II, 502.

Barra accepted the usurpation and extended their support to the new federal regime. Resistance was encountered almost immediately, however, in the northern Mexican states of Coahuila, Chihuahua, and Sonora. The center of the anti-Huerta movement, which soon would be dubbed the Constitutionalist Revolution (because the coup was considered unconstitutional), was in Coahuila, where Governor Venustiano Carranza withdrew recognition of the federal government on February 19, 1913. Carranza's decision was especially significant because a large body of armed troops from the recent Orozquista campaigns was still under his command.

The following day, in Hermosillo, Sonora, another veteran in the fight against Orozquismo, Álvaro Obregón, offered his services and those of his men to Governor José María Maytorena. The governor of Sonora vacillated, however, in the belief that an anti-Huerta movement in his state would be inopportune. This fence-straddling was not acceptable to Obregón;[2] during the week that followed, Obregón and many of his followers exerted constant pressure on Maytorena and finally forced him to ask the state legislature for a temporary leave of absence. The new interim governor, General Ignacio Pesqueira, succumbed to the demands of Sonora's anti-Huerta forces and on March 5, 1913, signed a bill that withdrew recognition of the federal government.[3]

The third pocket of resistance developed in the state of Chihuahua. Officially, the state remained within the federal fold for a time, as the anti-Huerta governor, Abraham González, was replaced by General Antonio Rábago, who assumed the title of military governor.[4] Before the end of March, however, a formidable anti-Huerta campaign was being waged by Pancho Villa, who had returned from a self-imposed exile in the United States for the express purpose of leading the movement. The formal denunciation of Huerta came on March 28, 1913.[5]

The defection of these three large and important northern states made it imperative that the new federal government of Victoriano Huerta enlist the unqualified support of all other military contingents within the country. The two largest and most important uncommitted

[2] Obregón, *Ocho Mil Kilómetros*, pp. 28–29.

[3] *Ibid.*, p. 32.

[4] Antonio Rábago was succeeded as military governor of Chihuahua by General Salvador Mercado, a federal career officer.

[5] STC, Chihuahua Denuncia los Espureos de Huerta y Rábago, Mar. 28, 1913. The act of defection was not signed by Villa, but by Toribio Ortega, Melchor T. Vela, and Juan Anaya.

fighting forces in Mexico immediately after the *decena trágica* were those of Emiliano Zapata in Morelos and Pascual Orozco in Chihuahua. Although Orozco had sent a telegram of congratulations to Huerta and Félix Díaz the day after the successful coup,[6] his active support of the new government remained in question for some time. As soon as Huerta assumed the provisional presidency, an all-out effort was made to secure the allegiance of the Orozquista forces, which Huerta hoped would also persuade the recalcitrant Zapata to lay down his arms, pledge support of the national government, and send his men back into the fields.

Huerta's first attempt to gain Orozco's support was the tentative appointment of David de la Fuente, Orozco's leading artillery commander during the Orozquista insurrection, as Minister of Communications and Public Works. De la Fuente, an engineer by profession, also commanded the respect of the Chihuahua general, but the president was mistaken if he thought Orozco would be taken in by this obvious enticement. De la Fuente did not accept the cabinet position[7] and Orozco did not announce his support of the new government. It would be necessary to attract Orozco in another manner.

A week after the resignations of Francisco Madero and José María Pino Suárez, Orozco's submission became even more important. The large body of troops directly under Orozco's command, an obvious threat in itself, might participate with the groups that already were in revolt in northern Mexico; moreover, a large body of revolutionaries in the state of Durango had declared it was awaiting direction from Orozco: only upon Orozco's explicit instructions would it announce its support of the Huertista government.[8] Huerta thereupon dispatched three commissioners, Ricardo García Granados, Esteban Maqueos Castellanos, and Antonio Herrejón López, to negotiate with Orozco and to determine his conditions for his recognition of the new regime.[9] The conference between the representatives of the government and the Chihuahua general was held at Villa Ahumada and Orozco stipulated five conditions: Orozquista soldiers, because they had contributed to the overthrow of Madero, were to be paid up to date from the federal treasury; pensions were to be established for the widows and orphans of those who had been killed in the anti-Madero campaigns; agrarian

[6] *El Imparcial*, Feb. 2, 1913.
[7] *El Imparcial*, Feb. 21, 1913, and *El País*, Feb. 23, 1913.
[8] RDS, Mann to Sec. of State, 812.00/6733, Feb. 24, 1913.
[9] *El Imparcial*, Feb. 24, 1913.

reform laws were to be quickly enacted to grant land to the "great masses of the poor"; the government was to pay the debts contracted by the Orozquistas for supplies; and Orozco's soldiers were to be employed as *rurales*.[10] Huerta was amenable to all of the demands, and Orozco, as soon as he was informed that his requests would be met, announced his unqualified support of the federal government, on February 27, 1913.[11]

Orozco's decision to ally himself with the government of Victoriano Huerta subjected him to new abuse.[12] The Orozquista rebellion against Madero was suddenly rendered still more odious by an equally serious act of treason. Orozco's submission to the government of the usurper is again explained by his lack of political awareness. Having no understanding of political ideologies, the Chihuahuan again was prey to interests who sought to use his popularity for selfish ends. While conducting a military campaign, Orozco was a man of methodical calculations and minute reckoning; when forced to make a political decision, however, his sagacity and discrimination gave way to a confused naiveté. After Madero had been removed by Huerta's coup Orozco's course, so he thought, was a matter of simple alternatives: he would join the new government or he would turn to the enemies who had been pursuing him in northern Mexico for the last six months. Neither Carranza in Coahuila nor Obregón in Sonora made a bid for Orozco's support—and it is unlikely that Orozco would have been amenable to an alliance with either. Having been given reasonable assurances that Huerta would meet his demands, Orozco decided to cast his lot with the government forces.

Orozco's rationale was recorded publicly on only one occasion: in urging Emiliano Zapata's cooperation with the new government, Orozco stated that, although he was not completely in accord with the Huerta government, he had accepted the regime as the best basis for

[10] *Fall Committee*, testimony of Dr. Allen Tupper, I, 520; *El Imparcial*, Mar. 7, 1913; [Jan Leander DeBekker], *De Como Vino Huerta y Como se Fué: Apuntes para la Historia de un Régimen Militar* (Mexico City: Librería General, 1914), p. 237.

[11] RDS, H. L. Wilson to Sec. of State, 812.00/6433, Feb. 28, 1913.

[12] The violently anti-Orozco *El Paso Morning Times* did not change its editorial policy during the Huerta period; the fact that Orozco accepted the usurper added fuel to the fire. His first act of treason (his revolt against Madero) was compounded by the second (his, acceptance of Huerta). The negotiations between the representatives of the government and Orozco were shamefully misrepresented: Orozco was charged with demanding 2,500,000 pesos cash as the price for submission (*El Paso Morning Times*, Mar. 5, 1913). Orozco's only defense was his denial (*New York Times*, Mar. 7, 1913), which the border-city newspaper did not even print.

the reestablishment of peace.[13] Orozco knew that years of civil strife could sap the vitality of the nation and believed that peace could be quickly restored if he supported the government. Implicit in Orozco's thinking was the conviction that any anti-Maderist group was necessarily dedicated to the ideals of the Revolution.

Orozco, after having made his decision to join Huerta, sent his personal secretary, Colonel José Córdova, to the capital to confer with the president. Córdova held several conferences with the Minister of Gobernación, Alberto García Grandos, and with Huerta, after which he again pledged the cooperation of Orozco and all of Orozco's subordinates in the pacification of northern Mexico.[14] Huerta immediately put Orozco's submission to use: on March 3 he sent a harshly worded telegram to Governor Maytorena of Sonora and demanded that the governor clarify his position at once—or General Orozco would be sent into the state with 3,000 well-trained, seasoned troops.[15] Several days later, Maytorena, also being urged by the Obregón faction to take a positive stand against the federal government, requested a leave of absence from the state legislature.

On March 8, a large body of Orozco's men was sent into the state of San Luis Potosí, where still another small rebellion had broken out against the Huerta government.[16] At approximately the same time, Orozco offered the services of between 3,000 and 4,000 men to General Antonio Rábago, the military governor of Chihuahua. If his men were supplied with arms and ammunition, Orozco said, they could be sent immediately into Sonora or Coahuila.[17]

Early in the second week of March, Orozco and several of his lieutenants (Marcelo Caraveo, Cheche Campos, Benjamín Argumedo, Pascual Orozco, Sr., and others) left Chihuahua City for the capital. The entourage was greeted with reverential awe all along the way, and a large celebration greeted its arrival in Mexico City, on March 12.[18] An official welcome was extended by Alberto García Granados and Enrique Zepeda, the governor of the federal district.[19] A representative of General Félix Díaz, Fidencio Hernández y Bravo Betancourt, who

[13] Magaña, *Emiliano Zapata*, III, 130–131.

[14] *El Imparcial*, Mar. 3, 1913, and *New York Times*, Mar. 4, 1913.

[15] *New York Times*, Mar. 5, 1913.

[16] *El Imparcial*, Mar. 9, 1913.

[17] AHDN, Maqueos C. [Castellanos?] to Sec. de Guerra y Marina, Exp. XI/481.5/69, T. II, folios 253–254, Mar. 8, 1913.

[18] *El País*, Mar. 13, 1913, and *El Imparcial*, Mar. 13, 1913.

[19] *El Imparcial*, Mar. 13, 1913.

delivered a welcoming address, said the success of the anti-Madero revolution was due to the relentless series of Orozquista campaigns in the north rather than to the battle waged in Mexico City during the *decena trágica*.[20] In the week that followed, Orozco attended several conferences with President Huerta and his cabinet. The results of the meetings were threefold. Orozco received a brigadier generalship in the federal army; he was charged with suppressing the rebellion in the state of Sonora; and, in addition, he was to use his influence to secure, if possible, the peaceful submission of Emiliano Zapata.

The choice of Pascual Orozco to attempt a reconciliation with Zapata must have been based on the esteem the recalcitrant *suriano* had for the Chihuahua *guerrillero* (Article 3 of the Plan de Ayala recognized Orozco as the commander-in-chief of the forces that had vowed not to lay down their arms until compliance with revolutionary promises was guaranteed). The capitulation of Orozco had prompted similar submissions in other Mexican states, and Zapata's was especially important. However, because Orozco had already been charged with the personal command of the government's military operations in northern Mexico, Huerta and his advisers decided to send the father, Colonel Pascual Orozco, to Morelos as a peace commissioner. The elder Orozco left the capital on March 21 and arrived at Cuernavaca the same day.[21] Zapata's response, upon being informed of the mission, was unexpected; he demanded, as a prerequisite for negotiation, that all federal troops be immediately withdrawn from the state and that Orozco junior be sent as the representative of the federal government.[22] Huerta refused to acknowledge the conditions, and the younger Orozco sent a letter to Zapata that did not even mention them.

> I suppose that by this date [March 25, 1913] my father, Colonel Pascual Orozco, has had the satisfaction of greeting you and of stating the object of his commission from the federal government and from myself.
>
> This letter will be placed in your hands by Ignacio Ocampo, Blas Sobrino, and Fabián Padilla. [These men] have been given extensive instructions to negotiate with you so that you can patriotically, and in a dignified manner, set aside your hostile attitude and contribute with your prestige, and with the forces under your command, to the reconstruction of nationalism.
>
> PASCUAL OROZCO, JR.[23]

[20] *El País*, Mar. 13, 1913.
[21] *El Imparcial*, Mar. 22, 1913.
[22] *Ibid.*, Mar. 23, 1913.
[23] Quoted in Magaña, *Emiliano Zapata*, III, 117–118.

In the meantime, the elder Orozco, not in the least discouraged by Zapata's attitude, decided to proceed with his mission. On March 24 he reached Zapata's headquarters, at the Hacienda de Temilpa, and was received by the leader of the southern rebels. Orozco presented his credentials from the Huerta government, a long letter from his son that urged cooperation, and a statement that outlined the basis on which the Orozquista forces had aligned themselves with the new regime; he urged Zapata to accept similar conditions.[24] Zapata's formal reply, sent not to the president but to Pascual Orozco, Jr., was both eloquent and caustic:

> ... You tell me that the government of Huerta has emanated from the Revolution as if the defection or disloyalty of the army, which originated this regime, deserves the designation which you place upon it. ... Has the Revolution triumphed or the enemies of the Revolution? Our answer is obvious. The Revolution has not triumphed. ... If Madero betrayed the Revolution, you have done the same. You don't offer liberty to the people—you offer chains. Huerta represents the defection of the army. You represent the defection of the Revolution. ...
>
> EMILIANO ZAPATA [25]

The reply left no room for negotiation, and it was obvious to Huerta and Orozco that Carranza, Obregón, and Villa—in northern Mexico—had secured an important (though undeclared) alliance with the rebels from Morelos. Zapata remained obdurate. Although there was never any formal cooperation between the Zapatistas and the Constitutionalists,[26] the fact that the federal war machine had to work in two directions limited its effectiveness. The Madero government had been militarily exposed on two sides; the Huerta government would soon find itself in exactly the same situation.

At the end of March the Mexican press published a startling and strangely premature report that the federal peace commissioners to Morelos, including Orozco senior, had been murdered on the direct order of Emiliano Zapata.[27] It was not, however, until several days later—during the first week of April—that Colonel Orozco and his fellow commissioners were arrested by order of Zapata and accused

---

[24] *Ibid.*, pp. 124–128.

[25] *Ibid.*, pp. 150–153.

[26] Quirk, *Mexican Revolution*, p. 56.

[27] *El Imparcial*, Mar. 31, 1913; *El País*, Mar. 31, 1913; *El Paso Morning Times*, Apr. 1, 1913.

of treason to the Revolution; the specific charge was that the peace mission was simply a tactic for putting the Zapatistas off guard so that federal troops could defeat them and capture their leader. The trial, which was conducted during a series of campaigns between the federal forces and the Zapatistas, was a travesty of justice. There was no conclusive evidence, but the peace commissioners were found guilty of the trumped-up charge and were imprisoned. Several months later, apparently incensed by federal excesses during the capture of the town of Cuautla, Morelos, Zapata ordered the elder Orozco shot.[28]

The complete dissolution of Zapata's esteem for Orozco junior was announced in an official statement issued from the Zapatista headquarters on May 30, 1913. Article 3 of the Plan de Ayala was amended to read:

> Pascual Orozco is declared unworthy of the honor conferred upon him by the revolutionary groups of south and central [Mexico]. . . . BECAUSE OF HIS COLLUSION AND COMPROMISE WITH THE ILLICIT, OMINOUS PSEUDO GOVERNMENT OF HUERTA, he has fallen from the esteem of his fellow citizens, to the point of being of no account. . . . He is a traitor to the principles to which he swore allegiance.
>
> As a consequence, according to the principles contained within this plan, the caudillo of the Ejército Libertador of south-central [Mexico], Emiliano Zapata, is recognized as head of the Revolution.[29]

The efforts of the federal peace commission in Morelos were viewed from the beginning with more than casual interest by Orozco junior. When the first negative reports began to filter into Mexico City, and later—when the news of Colonel Orozco's arrest was announced—rumors began to circulate to the effect that the general from Chihuahua was going to take personal command of the federal forces in Morelos.[30] Huerta did not attempt to squelch the rumors; he merely stated that he

[28] Baltasar Dromundo, *Emiliano Zapata* (Mexico City: Imprenta Mundial, 1934), p. 88; Taracena, *La Verdadera Revolución*, II, 75; Magaña, *Emiliano Zapata*, III, 287. Several years later, in a conference with Francisco Villa, Zapata boasted of having shot the elder Orozco and said he was sorry he had not been able to shoot the son as well (González Ramírez, *Planes Políticos*, p. 118).

[29] Porfirio Palacios, *Emiliano Zapata* (Mexico City: Libro Mex Editores, 1960), pp. 125–126. The revision of Article 3 can also be found in González Ramírez, *Planes Políticos*, p. 84.

[30] RDS, Burnside, Military Attaché Mexico City, to Sec. of State, 812.00/7349, Apr. 7, 1913; *El Noticioso* (Guaymas), Apr. 10, 1913; *El Paso Morning Times*, Apr. 1, 1913.

was going to send approximately 6,000 troops into Morelos "under an active and competent leader." [31] The president, however, had different plans for Orozco. Although the Zapatista movement was serious, the three-pronged movement in northern Mexico was a more immediate threat. Rather than submit to Orozco's understandable desire for personal vengeance, the pragmatic Huerta commissioned the Chihuahuan to lead a large and well-trained expedition directly north into his native state.

The story of Pascual Orozco's role as a Huertista general has never been related, but it is only through an analysis of Orozco's military career in 1913 and early 1914 that the most salient military aspects of the Constitutionalist revolution can be fully understood. To dismiss this important period with the statement that "Orozco became the workhorse among Huerta's generals" [32] is to miss the point. Without Orozco's deft determent of Pancho Villa's *dorados* in Chihuahua, the Constitutionalist movement would not have been a three-pronged race. Had not Orozco's irregular forces impeded Villa's well-equipped war machine long enough for Obregón and Carranza to effect a series of victories, the bandit chieftain would undoubtedly have arrived in the capital many months before his cohorts to the east and the west, and the Revolution would have assumed a very different complexion.

Orozco remained in Mexico City throughout April, readying his irregular troops for the northern campaign. The expedition got under way on May 9, 1913. [33] Five days later the important city of Zacatecas was captured without a fight; the rebel troops abandoned the city as Orozco's forces approached. [34] On May 19 Orozco's irregulars suffered a temporary setback as they were ambushed and defeated by the Constitutionalists at Fresnillo. [35] Orozco ordered a retreat to Zacatecas, where he reorganized his force for the northern thrust. [36] A second major goal in the northern advance was realized during the last few days of May when Orozco, after winning a series of small skirmishes, took the city of Torreón.

Torreón served Orozco's troops as a temporary headquarters during June, although, in the middle of the month, the general was ordered by

[31] RDS, H. L. Wilson to Sec. of State, 812.00/7101, Apr. 1, 1913.
[32] Christiansen, "Pascual Orozco," p. 116.
[33] *El Paso Morning Times*, May 10, 1913, and *El Imparcial*, May 10, 1913.
[34] *El Imparcial*, May 14, 1913.
[35] *Ibid.*, May 20, 1913.
[36] RDS, Gaston Schmutz, Consul Aguascalientes, to Sec. of State, 812.00/7658 and 812.00/7729, May 19 and 22, 1913.

the Secretary of War to continue northward in order to join the federal garrison of General Salvador Mercado in Chihuahua as quickly as possible.[37] The northern advance was delayed for several weeks, however, as Orozco was forced to dispatch teams of men to repair bridges and communication facilities north of Torreón—ironically, the same bridges which he had destroyed exactly one year earlier, during his retreat from General Huerta after the second battle of Rellano.[38]

General Orozco's 1,192 officers and men left Torreón and began the march to Chihuahua on July 1, 1913.[39] The steady northward advance was the most spectacular series of federal victories since the outbreak of the Constitutionalist movement five and one-half months earlier. During the first two weeks of July, Orozco won successive victories at the villages of Jaral Grande, Estación Dolores, Estación Díaz, Ortíz, Jiménez, and Bachimba.[40] Follow-up victories occurred at Ciudad Camargo, where Orozco defeated the large garrison of Colonel Rosalío Hernández,[41] and at Mapula, where 170 Constitutionalists were left dead.[42] On July 11 the capture of a Constitutionalist supply train yielded the irregulars an abundant supply of arms and munitions[43] and enabled them to win an important victory over rebel commanders Manuel Chao and Trinidad Rodríguez at Santa Rosalía.[44] Continuing northward, the victorious federal army entered Chihuahua City on July 22.[45] The Secretary of War was so pleased with the success of the mission that Orozco's force, almost to a man, received decorations and

[37] Salvador Mercado had replaced General Antonio Rábago in May. His position was practically untenable from the beginning as the rebels of Francisco Villa had captured every important city in the state, with the exception of the capital and Ciudad Juárez, early in the month (RDS, Letcher to Sec. of State, 812.00/7427 and 812.00/7438, May 3 and 9, 1913). The Constitutionalists had not been nearly as successful in the state of Coahuila. Carranza, constantly fighting a defensive battle, by August was forced to move his provisional government from Coahuila to Sonora. The battles between government troops and Constitutionalists in Sonora were not spectacular, but Obregón had been able to gain a good foothold in the state.

[38] *El Imparcial*, June 14, 1913.

[39] AHDN, Orozco to General Jefe de la División del Norte, Exp. XI/481.5/69, T. II, folio 399, Aug. 26, 1913.

[40] *Ibid.*, folios 399–400, Aug. 26, 1913; *El Paso Morning Times*, July 23, 1913.

[41] Barragán Rodríguez, *Historia del Ejército*, I, 245.

[42] *New York Times*, July 13, 1913.

[43] AHDN, Orozco to General Jefe de la División del Norte, Exp. XI/481.5/69, T. II, folios 399–400, Aug. 26, 1913.

[44] *Ibid.*, folios 400–401, Aug. 25, 1913; *El Paso Morning Times*, July 19, 1913.

[45] RDS, Letcher to Sec. of State, 812.00/8127, July 23, 1913; AHDN, Orozco to General Jefe de la División del Norte, Exp. XI/481.5/69, T. II, folio 401, Aug. 25, 1913.

commendations for their efforts on behalf of the government.[46] Shortly after his arrival in Chihuahua City, Orozco was made a general of brigade.[47]

Orozco's reinforcement of General Mercado's federal garrison, coupled with his series of victories along the way, removed the immediate danger of the capture of Chihuahua City by the Constitutionalist army of Pancho Villa. Not content with this momentary security, however, Orozco began a campaign of military recruitment. The general's popularity apparently had not waned in his native state, and his recruitment efforts were highly successful.[48]

Soon after Orozco arrived in the Chihuahua capital a serious rift developed in the federal garrison. Throughout the first two years of the Revolution the relationship between federal regulars and federal irregulars had been characterized by professional jealousy, which sometimes undermined the effectiveness of the federal war machine, but during August and September this rivalry was intensified at the Chihuahua garrison by the personal animosity between Orozco and Mercado. General Salvador Mercado, by virtue of his titles as commander of the Second Military Zone and military governor of the state of Chihuahua, was clearly in the command position. Orozco, unaccustomed to occupying a subordinate military role, opposed Mercado on many command decisions, and almost all of his suggestions for the defense of Chihuahua were rejected by his superior.[49] The situation was extremely delicate because Orozco's well-trained and loyal irregulars constituted 75 per cent of the federal fighting force, while Mercado's largely untested regulars, in addition to having demonstrated alarming inefficiency, comprised only the remaining 25 per cent.[50]

The generals' antagonism was not a secret; even the American consul in Chihuahua mentioned it in his reports to the Department of State,[51] and it is certain that the enemy also knew of the situation. Press releases from the Constitutionalists stated (incorrectly) that the

[46] AHDN, Blanquet to General Jefe de la División del Norte, Exp. XI/481.5/69, T. II, folio 432, Nov. 26, 1913.

[47] *New York Times*, Aug. 24, 1913.

[48] *El Paso Morning Times*, Aug. 19, 1913.

[49] Juan Gualberto Amaya, *Venustiano Carranza, Caudillo Constitucional* (Mexico City, 1947), p. 58.

[50] Gutiérrez Santos, *Historia Militar de México*, p. 297. Many years later, Mercado attempted to explain the rivalry by stating that Orozco's irregulars had no discipline and had resented his attempts to weld them into an efficient fighting force (STC, Mercado to Silvestre Terrazas, Feb. 2, 1919).

[51] RDS, Letcher to Sec. of State, 812.00/8220 and 812.00/8640, July 29 and Sept. 1, 1913.

"*Científico* Party" wanted to place Orozco in the governor's chair, but that the federal regulars refused to accept the proposal.[52] Although the statement was entirely false, it indicates that the Constitutionalists knew Orozco did not have the support of the regulars in the federal garrison. If Orozco had hoped to nudge Mercado out of the state of Chihuahua, he received a sobering setback on September 15, 1913, when the state legislature was suspended because Mercado had not called for new elections the previous June.[53] Mercado's executive function as military governor now included legislative matters as well. Chihuahua was to be ruled by decree, under a military dictatorship, in the person of General Salvador Mercado. Orozco made no attempt to appease Mercado, and an uneasy truce prevailed for several months.

In late September, Orozco successfully conducted a series of small operations in his native area of San Isidro.[54] The following month he defeated a large rebel garrison at Las Palmas, then reinforced the federal army at Ciudad Juárez.[55] Orozco also won a major victory over the Villistas, near Santa Rosalía, and dynamited five enemy troop trains.[56] A few days later he inflicted still another defeat on the rebels, at Chuviscar.[57] The federal victories, however, had been deceptive, for Villa had been making final preparations for the expulsion of all government troops from the state. Early in November the Constitutionalist commander began concentrating his troops for a major assault on the two important federal strongholds: Chihuahua City and Ciudad Juárez. The attack on Chihuahua began on November 5, but Villa, after two days of fighting, was unable to penetrate the federal lines;[58] Orozco and Mercado had cooperated to expel the intruder. After the unsuccessful assault on Chihuahua, Villa moved directly north and attacked Ciudad Juárez early on the morning of November 15. By noon, General Francisco Castro's federal garrison had surrendered.[59] Villa's capture of the border city completely changed the complexion

[52] *El Paso Morning Times*, Aug. 19, 1913.

[53] AGN, Varios, 1913–1914, Sec. 1, No. 91, Sept. 18, 1913.

[54] *El Imparcial*, Sept. 19, 1913.

[55] *Ibid.*, Oct. 20, 1913.

[56] *Ibid.*, Nov. 8, 1913.

[57] AHDN, Mercado to Sec. de Guerra y Marina, Exp. XI/481.5/69, T. II, folios 528–553, Nov. 12, 1913.

[58] Clarence C. Clendenen, *The United States and Pancho Villa: A Study in Unconventional Diplomacy* (Ithaca, N.Y.: Cornell University Press, 1961), p. 42.

[59] RDS, Edwards to Sec. of State, 812.00/9749, Nov. 15, 1913; *El Paso Morning Times*, Nov. 15, 1913.

of the Constitutionalist movement; Chihuahua City was the only remaining federal stronghold in the state.

The pressure that now was placed upon the federal garrison in Chihuahua City stimulated the Orozco-Mercado rivalry. Orozco, as soon as he learned of the Constitutionalist victory at the border, wanted to move north and engage the Villistas. Mercado vacillated, giving the Constitutionalists time to recuperate.[60] When permission finally was granted, it was too late; Villa's troops were ready. The detachment sent to recapture Ciudad Juárez was repulsed at Tierra Blanca on November 24.[61]

The final split between Orozco and Mercado occurred on November 26, 1913, when the military governor, although he had ample arms and ammunition,[62] announced his decision to withdraw his garrison from Chihuahua without engaging the enemy. The decision caused panic in the city, for the Chihuahuans were aware of the excesses General Francisco Villa often permitted himself and his troops after the capture of a coveted prize.[63] As soon as Mercado's decision was announced, the merchants of the capital asked him not to abandon the city.[64] When the commander refused to acknowledge the request, they offered him three million pesos to be used for strengthening the city's defense.[65] Pascual Orozco also opposed the decision to evacuate.[66] Enticement,

[60] It has been suggested that Mercado, fearing a spectacular Orozquista victory might compromise his position, did not want Orozco's troops to win major successes against the Villistas (Amaya, *Venustiano Carranza*, p. 59). The extent of the bitterness between Orozco and Mercado was revealed when Mercado was arrested and interviewed by the press. A series of charges, most of which were not valid, was leveled at Orozco during this interview. The details of the interview and the nature of the charges will be discussed below.

[61] *El Paso Morning Times*, Nov. 24, 1913. The tightly controlled press of Mexico City reported—incorrectly—that General Orozco had been victorious at Tierra Blanca and had captured Ciudad Juárez and driven the Villistas from the city (*El Imparcial*, Nov. 26, 1913). An excellent description of the battle of Tierra Blanca is recorded in the memoirs of an American artillery officer who for several months, served in Villa's ranks: I. Thord-Gray, *Gringo Rebel* (Coral Gables, Fla.: University of Miami Press, 1960), pp. 36–53.

[62] RDS, Letcher to Sec. of State, 812.00/11043, Feb. 21, 1914.

[63] AHDN, C. Eugenio Pasquel, Administrador del Timbre de Chihuahua, to Sec. de Guerra y Marina, Exp. XI/481.5/70, T. I, folios 4–5, Jan. 3, 1914.

[64] AHDN, Arturo M. Elías to Sec. de Guerra y Marina, Exp. XI/481.5/69, T. III, folios 583–589, Dec. 17, 1913.

[65] AHDN, José Reyes Estrada to Estado Mayor, Exp. XI/481.5/70, T. I, folio 12, Dec. 30, 1913.

[66] Amaya, *Venustiano Carranza*, pp. 67, 72. Orozco's opposition to the evacuation

pressure, and the opposition of General Orozco, however, failed to change Mercado's mind. Mercado withdrew the federal garrison as scheduled, on November 29, 1913.[67] A large number of civilians, most of them relatives of the federal soldiers, accompanied Mercado on the withdrawal. Villa took over the city several days later, without a fight, and for all practical purposes the entire state of Chihuahua was in his hands.

After the evacuation of the Chihuahua capital, General Mercado ordered a retreat to Ojinaga, where he established a provisional state government.[68] Orozco and José Inés Salazar, meanwhile, planned a surprise attack on Ciudad Juárez.[69] Because most of Villa's troops had been moved to Chihuahua City,[70] the attack would almost certainly have succeeded, but Mercado refused to authorize the plans. Orozco and Salazar were ordered to Ojinaga to join the main body of federal troops. There were rumors that Orozco had decided to take matters into his own hands, the orders of Mercado notwithstanding,[71] but Orozco, instead, sent a telegram to the Secretary of War, Aureliano Blanquet, requesting that his irregulars be placed directly under the command of the Ministry of War rather than under Mercado.[72] The request was denied.

Pancho Villa began the final phase of his operation to rid Chihuahua of federal troops in late December. Four infantry brigades, supported by artillery and machine-gun batteries, were thrown against Ojinaga.[73] The Constitutionalist generals, Pánfilo Natera and Toribio Ortega,

was not announced in the press until several months after the incident occurred (*El Imparcial*, Feb. 23, 1914).

[67] RDS, Letcher to Sec. of State, 812.00/10054, Nov. 30, 1913.

[68] If Mercado believed the evacuation of Chihuahua City was an unavoidable military necessity, he should have reinforced the small federal garrison at Torreón. The federal foothold at Ojinaga was almost meaningless, with the entire state of Chihuahua under Villa's control and with the entire body of Constitutionalist troops to the south of the federal army. Ojinaga could not be supplied, communication with Mexico City was almost impossible, and it was known that the strategy of the three Constitutionalist armies called for the capture of the capital of the country. There was no military justification for the decision to move the federal troops to the unimportant town of Ojinaga.

[69] RDS, Lindley M. Garrison, Sec. of War, to Sec. of State, 812.00/10085, Dec. 6, 1913.

[70] Barragán Rodríguez, *Historia del Ejército*, I, 268–270.

[71] *El Paso Morning Times*, Dec. 11, 1913.

[72] Amaya, *Venustiano Carranza*, p. 73.

[73] Gutiérrez Santos, *Historia Militar de México*, p. 307.

joined the attack on January 1, 1914, but were unable to dislodge the garrison after seven days of relentless assaults. The stalemate prompted Villa to assume personal command as the siege entered its second week. The federals were able to resist until January 10, when they finally succumbed to the numerically superior Villista force.[74] The new military governor of the state, General Manuel Chao, declared January 10 a state holiday.[75]

The loss of the north-central Mexican state was the most severe setback Huerta had yet sustained, and, in retrospect, must be considered the beginning of the end for the Huerta regime. For the next six months the federal army resisted the steady southward penetration of the three Constitutionalist armies, but it was apparent that the die had been cast in Ojinaga; the resistance of the federals between January and June, 1914, merely postponed the final reckoning. The arms embargo of March 14, 1912 (which earlier had stopped the shipment of arms and ammunition to the Orozquistas), was revoked on February 3, 1914, enabling the Constitutionalists to obtain supplies of war legally from the United States.[76]

With the loss of Ojinaga, the federal army in Chihuahua dispersed. General Salvador Mercado and approximately 5,000 soldiers and their families voluntarily interned themselves in the United States, whereupon they were taken into custody and shipped to Fort Bliss, Texas, outside El Paso.[77] Other federals had been captured by the Villistas at Ojinaga. Of the total fighting force, slightly more than 5,000 men, only 300 or 400 escaped.[78] Orozco, much to the chagrin of the vindictive Pancho Villa, was one of the escapees. Mercado, whom the Huerta government attempted to have released by the United States so that he could be tried for his decision to evacuate Chihuahua,[79] tried to shift the responsibility to Orozco, José Inés Salazar, and Antonio Rojas. Mercado charged the three men with cowardice, insubordination,

---

[74] *El Paso Morning Times*, Jan. 10, 1914, and *El Imparcial*, Jan. 12, 1914.

[75] STC, Informe Que Rinde el Gobernador Militar del Estado de Chihuahua al Primer Jefe del Ejército Constitucionalista, C. Don Venustiano Carranza, Mar., 1914.

[76] *U.S. Foreign Relations, 1914*, pp. 447–448.

[77] Food and housing for the 5,000 refugees who were interned after the battle of Ojinaga cost the United States government approximately $1,600 a day ("The Fort Bliss Camp," *Outlook*, CVI (Jan. 31, 1914), 225.

[78] *El Paso Morning Times*, Jan. 12, 1914.

[79] *El Imparcial*, Jan. 17, 1914.

intrigue, looting, robbery, and the like.[80] The Mexican Ministry of War, however, soon vindicated Orozco by announcing that new military decorations would be conferred upon the general as soon as possible.[81]

Orozco's whereabouts after the loss of Ojinaga was a matter of wide speculation. Pancho Villa at first believed the general had taken refuge in the United States, but since his name did not appear on the list of those who had been taken into custody, Villa cautioned American border officials to be on the watch for the elusive Chihuahuan lest he launch a counterrevolution from north of the Rio Grande.[82] The alleged presence of Orozco on American soil prompted a number of erroneous intelligence reports to the Department of State, pinpointing Orozco at Mineral Wells, Texas; at El Paso, Texas; at Las Cruces, New Mexico; and at New Orleans—at approximately the same time.[83] The story subsequently devised was that Orozco had crossed into the United States shortly after the battle of Ojinaga, hid for several days in Shafter, Texas, and took a train for New Orleans, where he had boarded a ship for Veracruz.[84]

It is possible but not likely that Orozco sought an extended refuge in the United States after the federal defeat at Ojinaga. Fully cognizant that General Villa would turn the Constitutionalist war machine south toward Torreón, Orozco and the followers who escaped with him probably began to work their way south through the Constitutionalist lines almost immediately after the defeat.[85] On January 14 the American press reported that Orozco and the remnants of his once formidable fighting force were marching south and had approached the town of Monclova, Coahuila.[86] Several days later the Mexican press repudiated

[80] *El Paso Morning Times*, Jan. 20, 21, 1914. As late as 1919, Mercado tried to clear himself by blaming Orozco for the debacle at Ojinaga (STC, Salvador Mercado to Silvestre Terrazas, Jan. 13, 1919).

[81] STC, Salvador Mercado to Silvestre Terrazas, Jan. 26, 1914.

[82] *New York Times*, Jan. 18, 22, 1914.

[83] RDS: Special Agent, Pendleton, to Sec. of State, 812.00/10073, Feb. 27, 1914; Special Agent, Fort Worth, to Sec. of State, 812.00/11107, Feb. 21, 1914; Special Agent, El Paso, to Sec. of State, 812.00/11107, Feb. 23, 1914; Special Agent, El Paso, to Sec. of State, 812.00/11179, Mar. 2, 1914.

[84] *El Paso Morning Times*, Aug. 15, 1914.

[85] Several months later, Orozco told representatives of the press in Mexico City that he had spent one night in Presidio, Texas, before beginning his overland march to Torreón (*El Imparcial*, Feb. 23, 1914).

[86] RDS, William Blocker, Consul, Eagle Pass, to Sec. of State, 812.00/10551, Jan. 15, 1914; *El Paso Morning Times*, Jan. 14, 1914.

its earlier reports that had placed the general in the United States and stated that Orozco was marching southward to Torreón.[87] Orozco and his small body of troops did indeed arrive at Torreón on January 25.[88]

By the middle of February, 1914, the Huerta government rested on very shaky foundations. General Álvaro Obregón was the undisputed master of northwest Mexico. Pockets of federal opposition survived in the northeast, but Carranza's Constitutionalists, after an extremely difficult first year, held a number of key outposts in Coahuila and Nuevo León. The greatest immediate danger, however, was in the north-central region, where Pancho Villa, after expelling the federal army from Chihuahua, amassed a huge, well-equipped army that was preparing to march on Torreón.[89] President Woodrow Wilson's revocation of the arms embargo had ensured that the acquisition of supplies of war would no longer be a serious problem for any of the Constitutionalist armies.

President Huerta and Secretary of War Aureliano Blanquet, realized that if the Villistas were to be forestalled, it would be necessary to launch a major counteroffensive in Chihuahua. The first step in the new scheme was to reorganize the Chihuahua military district in such a way that the rivalry between federal regulars and irregulars would be eliminated, or at least minimized. Because contingents sent into Chihuahua would undoubtedly be made up largely of irregular volunteers, the Ministry of War decided to place irregular commanders in charge of the zone. Accordingly, Chihuahua was divided into three military districts, each under the command of an irregular officer. The northern district, with headquarters in Ciudad Juárez, would be commanded by José Inés Salazar; the central district, with headquarters at Chihuahua City, would be commanded by Pascual Orozco; and the southern district, with headquarters at Parral, would be commanded by Benjamín Argumedo.[90] The organizational plan was sound, at least on paper, but the reorganization would never become operative.

[87] *El Imparcial*, Jan. 22, 1914.

[88] *El Imparcial*, Jan. 25, 1914, and *El Paso Morning Times*, Jan. 26, 1914.

[89] Villa's army alone was larger than the entire federal army under Profirio Díaz (Edwin Lieuwen, *Arms and Politics in Latin America* [New York: Frederick A. Praeger, 1960], p. 107). After being forced into exile, Victoriano Huerta stated that the size of his federal army had once reached 180,000 men (Victoriano Huerta, "The Future of Mexico," *Independent*, LXXXII [May 3, 1915], 202). Almost every other figure I have seen would make it appear that a federal army of 180,000 men is a gross exaggeration. Although the federal forces undoubtedly increased after the overthrow of Díaz, they did not reach this figure.

[90] AHDN, Carmona, Official Mayor, to General Jefe de la División del Norte, Exp. XI/481.5/70, T. I, folio 19, Feb. 9, 1914. Argumedo was later replaced by Carlos

Early in February, Orozco was ordered to Mexico City to testify on Mercado's evacuation of Chihuahua and to offer suggestions on how the proposed campaign against Villa might be organized. The general arrived in the capital on February 21 and on the following day consulted with Huerta and Blanquet.[91] In the weeks that followed, Orozco was given a free hand in organizing the new federal offensive, and was awarded his last and highest promotion in the federal army, to division general.[92] Orozco's plans called for the creation of a new, crack battalion that would be trained for guerrilla warfare. While Orozco's special battalion was being recruited and trained, Pancho Villa began his march to the south, and on March 20, 1914, made his long-expected attack on Torreón. The federals, under General José R. Velasco, held the city until April 2, when they were forced to withdraw.

Rather than falling back to Zacatecas, Velasco cleverly moved his troops eastward, toward Saltillo, so that Villa—if he had continued his drive on Mexico City—would have exposed his supply line to a counter-attack.[93] On April 19, with Villa temporarily stalled, General Orozco and his new battalion left Mexico City for the north. The force avoided major engagements during the northward trek because it intended to establish itself in the mountains of Chihuahua and then spread to the neighboring states of Sonora and Coahuila. The plan, however, was doomed to failure almost from the beginning: Constitutionalist victories at Monterrey, on April 24, and at Tampico, on May 12, left only Saltillo in the hands of the federal army by the middle of May.

Because of these unexpected developments, Orozco's orders were changed and he was instructed to join the federal garrison of General Joaquín Maass in Saltillo, the capital of Coahuila. On May 17 and 18 the Orozquistas passed through Ramos Arizpe and Paredón, the towns that guarded the approaches to Saltillo,[94] and entered Saltillo on May 19—just in time to participate in the evacuation of the city. Although Orozco strongly protested General Maass's order,[95] the presence of

García Hidalgo (AHDN, Carmona to General Jefe de la División del Norte, Exp. XI/481.5/70, T. I, folio 40, Mar. 7, 1914).

[91] *El Imparcial*, Feb. 22, 23, 1914.

[92] *El Imparcial*, Mar. 7, 1914, and *El Paso Morning Times*, Mar. 7, 1914.

[93] An excellent description of the battle for Torreón is contained in Quirk, *Mexican Revolution*, pp. 19–24.

[94] *El Imparcial*, May 19, 1914. Orozco had about 2,000 men under his command at this time (Taracena, *La Verdadera Revolución,* II, 190).

[95] *El Paso Morning Times*, May 25, 1914.

Pancho Villa, only a few hours from the city, necessitated the evacuation. Orozco had to choose between two possibilities: he and his troops could return to Chihuahua as originally planned, or he could join General Maass in the retreat to San Luis Potosí. Because the removal of federal troops from Coahuila would greatly reduce his chances for success in the adjacent state of Chihuahua, he chose the second alternative.

The combined forces of Orozco and Maass arrived at San Luis Potosí on the last day of May, 1914,[96] and for three weeks the federal troops held their own. General Orozco's guerrilla battalion defeated small bands of Constitutionalists on a number of occasions, and a major rebel effort to capture San Luis Potosí was repulsed by the Chihuahuan at La Ventura in the middle of June.[97]

During the brief interlude the Constitutionalist command was beset with serious difficulties. Hostility between Venustiano Carranza and Pancho Villa, which had been dormant for almost a year, reasserted itself in early June. Carranza, the "first chief," realizing that the strong Villista force could frustrate his plans, ordered Villa to send 5,000 troops to join General Pánfilo Natera, who was besieging Zacatecas. Villa, suspicious of Carranza's motives, refused to divide his forces, and, against Carranza's order, moved his entire army against Zacatecas. As soon as the news of Villa's insubordination became known in Mexico City, Secretary of War Aureliano Blanquet, ordered General Orozco to Zacatecas.[98] The order came too late, however, for Villa attacked on June 22 and the federal regulars of General Luis Medina Barrón and the irregulars of General Benjamín Argumedo withdrew early the next day. (Many sources place Orozco in Zacatecas at the time of the federal evacuation, but a minutely detailed fifty-page description of the battle of Zacatecas [in Mexico City's Archivo Histórico de la Defensa Nacional] contains the names of all of the participating federal officers, the deployment of their troops, and lists of the weapons they had at their disposal; and General Orozco and his 3,000 troops are not even mentioned.[99])

Orozco received his orders to move to Zacatecas on June 21, and began his march immediately. By June 23, the day of the evacuation, he had passed through Aguascalientes and probably encountered the retreating federals between that city and Zacatecas. Villa entered

[96] *El Imparcial*, June 1, 1914.

[97] *Ibid.*, June 17, 1914.

[98] *El Sol*, June 22, 1914.

[99] AHDN, "Batalla de Zacatecas," Exp. XI/481.5/334, T. II, folios 251–302, June–July, 1914.

Zacatecas on June 24 and immediately dispatched a probing expedition to the south.[100] The main body of his troops, however, was forced to remain in Zacatecas because of a lack of ammunition and insufficient coal for his supply trains. Carranza, to punish Villa for his insubordination, made no effort to replenish the expended supplies.[101]

The military strength of the Huertista forces had so deteriorated by July that their position was completely untenable. General Álvaro Obregón in the west and General Pablo González in the east had made deep penetrations southward, and there was no hope of halting their advances. Villa, who finally persuaded Carranza to replenish his supplies, was ready to resume his march on Mexico City, but before marching on the capital he made several attempts to capture Orozco. The Chihuahua general cleverly avoided the traps, then retreated to the federal stronghold at San Luis Potosí.

By the middle of July, Huerta was powerless; he made no attempt at conciliation, and on July 15, 1914, submitted his resignation to the congress. The combined houses accepted the resignation the same day and named Francisco S. Carbajal, Huerta's Secretary of Foreign Relations, as interim president of Mexico. Huerta left the capital for Puerto México (Coatzacoalcos), Veracruz, where he embarked for Spain.

Pascual Orozco, having committed himself to the Huerta cause, had been tenacious in his support of the federal government. Although his chances for success in northern Mexico, wedged as he was among three hostile armies, were never great, he withstood the rebels' assaults and impeded their advance for more than sixteen months. During the Constitutionalist revolution he demonstrated the same organizational skill, tactical acumen, and field generalship that had made him a hero in the fight against Porfirio Díaz, but Huerta's cause had been unpopular —and unsuccessful. Orozco had picked a loser.

[100] Orozco fought this expedition to a draw, at Estación de Soledad, June 26 (*El Sol*, June 27, 1914, and *El Imparcial*, June 27, 1914).

[101] RDS, Canova to Sec. of State, 812.00/13323, Sept. 22, 1914; Quirk, *Mexican Revolution*, pp. 33–34; Taracena, *La Verdadera Revolución*, II, 212.

# VII

## *Intrigue and Aftermath*

Pascual Orozco's response to Huerta's resignation and exile was completely unexpected: even before the new interim president, Francisco S. Carbajal, had made a policy statement, Orozco declared himself in revolt against the new government and the Constitutionalists who would obviously replace it soon. Soldiering and "revolution" had become a way of life for many Mexicans, and the general's new following numbered approximately 4,000.[1] The new Orozquista army was merely a group of men who believed they had no alternative way of survival.

There was no ideological justification for Orozco's new rebellion; on the other hand, the general's personal motives are easy to understand. Huerta's resignation had made no provision for equitable treatment for his generals and supporters by the victorious Constitutionalists,[2] and it was thought that the federal army in Mexico City might disband because of fear of reprisals.[3] Orozco's position, moreover, was especially perilous because his surrender to Pancho Villa would undoubtedly have meant immediate execution. Villa had vowed on several occasions that he would order Orozco's execution if the general ever fell into his hands —and Villa's military career leaves no room for the speculation that

[1] *El Imparcial*, July 19, 1914; *El Paso Morning Times*, July 18, 1914; *New York Times*, July 19, 1914. A later statement, that Orozco was seconded by only 500 men, should be viewed with caution; the Carbajal caretaker government did everything in its power to minimize the severity of the new movement (*El Imparcial*, July 20, 1914).

[2] In contrast to Huerta's unconcern, Madero had stipulated as one of the conditions of his resignation that his followers should not be harassed because of their political views (Luis Lara Pardo, *Madero: Esbozo Político* [Mexico City: Ediciones Botas, 1937], pp. 342–343, cited in Sherman, *Victoriano Huerta*, p. 78).

[3] Quirk, *Mexican Revolution*, pp. 49–50.

115

this was merely an idle boast.[4] By continuing the military campaigns—his enemies were still the same—Orozco could perhaps avoid an ignominious death before a Villista firing squad.

Orozco was seconded in his movement by one of the most despised men in Mexico, Francisco Cárdenas,[5] who on February 22, 1913, had been in charge of the federal army guard that had escorted Francisco Madero and José María Pino Suárez on the evening they were assassinated. Also fearful for his life at the hands of the Constitutionalists, Cárdenas joined forces with Orozco only a few days after Huerta's decision to tender his resignation. At the end of July the two rebels were joined by a third important figure, the ex-revolutionary general Emilio P. Campa.[6] Additional support came from an unexpected quarter when General Roque Gómez in Chihuahua declared for Orozco and attacked and defeated the Constitutionalist garrison at Palomas in late July.[7] Chihuahua, the once proud bulwark of the status quo, had again taken arms. Other groups withdrew recognition of the new government in August, but it is unlikely that any of them were connected with Orozco.[8]

The strategical blueprint of the new rebellion called for Cárdenas and his men to move into the state of Michoacán; Orozco and Campa would operate in the central states of Guanajuato, Querétaro, and Aguascalientes, and would work their way north to join Roque Gómez in Chihuahua. In late July, Orozco defeated a large force of Carrancistas near the city of León, Guanajuato.[9] León fell to the Orozquistas on August 3, 1914, but they were forced to withdraw from the city on

[4] Villa once set a price on Orozco's head (*New York Times*, Dec. 27, 1913, and Dec. 15, 1914). During the entire Constitutionalist revolution, Villa had singled out the Orozquistas for especially harsh punishment. When the Villistas captured Ciudad Juárez in November, 1913, Orozco's troops who had helped defend the city were shot in the Juárez cemetery. The same fate awaited the Orozquistas who defended Torreón against the Villistas in April, 1914 (Clendenen, *United States and Pancho Villa*, pp. 43, 74).

[5] *El Sol*, July 19, 1914.

[6] *Ibid.*, July 29, 1914.

[7] *El Paso Morning Times*, July 23, 1914.

[8] On August 28, 1914, a group of revolutionary generals, which included Benjamín Argumedo, Higinio Aguilar, and Juan Andreu Almazán, withdrew recognition of the federal government in Tehuacán, Puebla (RDS, Canada to Sec. of State, 812.00/13381, Sept. 26, 1914). There is no evidence, however, that this movement was connected with Orozco's revolt; rather, these officers soon allied themselves with the cause of Emiliano Zapata, who recognized neither Carbajal nor Carranza (*El Sol*, Nov. 26, 1914).

[9] *El Imparcial*, July 25 and Aug. 1, 1914, and *El Sol*, Aug. 1, 1914.

August 6 because a large body of Constitutionalist troops was moving on the city. After evacuating León, Orozco moved his dwindling body of troops northeast, into the state of San Luis Potosí, under hot pursuit by the Constitutionalists.[10]

During the last week of August the futility of the new revolution became more and more apparent; it had no financial backing or hope of assistance from any quarter. The revolt did not have the popular support of Orozco's previous revolutionary endeavors, and the problem of acquiring supplies was insurmountable. In early September Orozco turned directly northward in an attempt to reach the United States border rather than be captured by the enemy. By the time he reached Coahuila, skirmishes and desertions had reduced his army to a mere handful of followers. On September 14, 1914, Orozco was reported to be in Texas, but his exact whereabouts was not known,[11] and the Constitutionalists circulated reports that the Chihuahua rebel was planning to use North American soil as a springboard for a new invasion of Mexico.

Although Mexican officials requested Orozco's extradition on the grounds that he was plotting a rebellion from the vicinity of El Paso, Texas, and Las Cruces, New Mexico,[12] extradition proceedings were not initiated because his exact whereabouts could not be ascertained. Although United States border officials and army contingents stationed along the border were cautioned to be on the lookout for the rebel general, he could not be found.[13] (Even if Orozco had been located and charged with plotting a revolution from United States soil, he would have not been extradited, because he would have had to stand trial in the United States for violation of the neutrality laws.)

The apprehension of the Constitutionalist officials was not without justification. Orozco was not the only political dissident who sought refuge north of the Rio Grande after Huerta's resignation. Félix Díaz, the nephew of the ex-dictator and an active revolutionist since 1911, was residing in Boston. The former interim president, Francisco Carbajal, who had been replaced by the Carrancistas before he had completed his first month in the presidency, was in New Orleans, as was Huerta's Minister of Foreign Relations, Querido Moheno. Two

[10] *El Sol*, Aug. 23, 1914.

[11] *El Paso Morning Times* (Spanish section), Sept. 14, 1914.

[12] *Ibid.*

[13] In early October, Orozco was believed to be in Presidio, Texas, but a positive determination could not be made by the reporting agency (RDS, "Report of Conditions Along the Border," 812.00/13462, Oct. 3, 1914).

generals, José Refugio Velasco and Gustavo Maass, had taken up residence in Galveston, Texas. José M. Luján, who had served in the ministries of Foreign Relations and Gobernación, chose El Paso, Texas, as his new residence, as did a host of other ex-Huertistas and several state governors.[14] Throughout October and November the revolutionary clan continued to grow. After the collapse of the northern segment of Orozco's short-lived campaign against the Constitutionalists, General Roque Gómez moved to El Paso. By the end of November three additional Orozquista generals—Marcelo Caraveo, Francisco del Toro and Emilio Campa—had arrived in El Paso.[15] By early 1915, Orozco and his fellow revolutionaries in exile were planning a revolution of colossal proportions; however, because of important events that were occurring simultaneously within Mexico, this peripheral movement has been almost completely overlooked.

General José Inés Salazar was not a member of the revolutionary circle in the fall of 1914 although he had crossed into the United States after the battle of Ojinaga (January, 1914). Salazar had been arrested near Sanderson, Texas, on smuggling charges, had stood trial at Fort Wingate, New Mexico, for violation of neutrality laws, but had been acquitted. Immediately after his release, however, he was arrested on a perjury charge.[16] The new trial was set for November 30, 1914, at the federal court in Albuquerque, New Mexico, and Salazar was taken to Albuquerque two weeks before the date of his trial and placed in the county jail.[17] On the evening of November 20 (a significant date in the Mexican Revolution) two masked men overpowered the guards at the jail, and released Salazar from his cell on the second floor of the building.[18] The well-planned escape was the work of experts; in all probability the revolutionary circle in El Paso engineered the episode in order to win another well-known revolutionary to its ranks.[19]

By the end of November, Salazar was a member of the El Paso group,

[14] *El Paso Morning Times*, Sept. 18, 1914.

[15] *Ibid.*, Nov. 3, 27, 1914. For a detailed list of prominent Mexicans in the United States at this time, see Antimaco Sax, *Los Mexicanos en el Destierro* (San Antonio: International Printing Company, 1916), pp. 43–73.

[16] Salazar had been responsible for the murder of Thomas Fountain, a United States citizen, approximately two years earlier (see above, pp. 77ff.). Once the general fell into the hands of United States authorities, every effort was made to convict him on one charge or another.

[17] *Albuquerque Morning Journal*, Nov. 16, 1914.

[18] *Ibid.*, Nov. 21, 1914.

[19] Salazar's wife arrived in Albuquerque the day before the escape (*Albuquerque Morning Journal*, Nov. 21, 1914). El Paso newspapermen believed General Roque

and his role in the conspiracy was carefully outlined by the revolutionary headquarters. During the first week of December, in conjunction with Emilio Campa, Salazar was to lead an insurrection in northern Chihuahua. The movement was intended merely to harass the Constitutionalists, who already were hopelessly split.[20] The main revolutionary thrust would come later, after the movement had been coordinated and had achieved sufficient strength to assure some promise of success. The Salazar-Campa statement of revolution, like the Plan Orozquista, mentioned no presidential candidate, decried personalism, and asked for social reform: "The movement is not being made for the purpose of making presidents, but only for the purpose of bringing reforms which will benefit all social classes, and especially the poor. . . ."[21] The campaign of harassment began with an assault on Casas Grandes, and, by December 15, Salazar and Campa had cut the National Railroad line between Ciudad Juárez and Chihuahua City.[22] The strategy was more successful than had been hoped: federal field commanders were convinced that the Salazar-Campa revolt was an all-out attack rather than a preliminary expedition.[23]

Pascual Orozco played several roles in preparing the larger and more important revolution that was to follow. He served first as a coordinator, establishing and maintaining contact with important Mexican exiles in various cities throughout the United States. In addition, he later was given the important and difficult task of securing arms and ammunition in large quantities, and without arousing the suspicions of United

Gómez had participated in the escape (*El Paso Morning Times* [Spanish section], Nov. 26, 1914).

[20] At this early date it was imperative that the revolutionaries in exile be cautious in their expenditure of funds. From the beginning of the movement, United States authorities had been advised that General Luis Terrazas and Enrique Creel were planning to give the rebels financial support (RDS, Edwards to Sec. of State 812.00/14011, Dec. 11, 1914). Creel's participation was confirmed several months later when the revolutionary headquarters in San Antonio sent him to Spain to recruit another famous Mexican exile, Victoriano Huerta (RDS, Gracey, Consul Seville, to Sec. of State, 812.00/14751, Mar. 31, 1915). The contention of Zachary L. Cobb, the collector of customs at El Paso, that British and Spanish capital would finance the movement is untrue (RDS, Cobb to Sec. of State, 812.00/14928, Apr. 15, 1915, and 812.00/14999, May 11, 1915).

[21] *Albuquerque Morning Journal*, Dec. 7, 1914. The Albuquerque press, which had always given good coverage to the Mexican Revolution, followed Salazar's activities with particular interest after his escape from an Albuquerque jail.

[22] *Ibid.*, Dec. 15, 1914.

[23] STC, Col. Tomás Ornelas to Military Governor of Chihuahua, Dec. 17 and 24, 1914.

States authorities. Finally, when the main revolution was launched, he would serve as its supreme military commander and would personally lead its forces. Soon after his arrival in the United States, Orozco visited San Antonio, Texas, a city that for years had been a hotbed of Mexican revolutionary activity.[24] From San Antonio he went to St. Louis, Missouri, another revolutionary center.[25] In early December, 1914, Orozco passed through Washington, D.C., on his way to New York City,[26] the most important stop of his tour.

New York had never before been of major importance to Mexican revolutionists; after the overthrow of Huerta, however, it became a nucleus of anti-Constitutionalist activity in the United States. As early as September, 1914, the United States Department of State had been informed that plots had been hatched in New York City for the overthrow of the government of Venustiano Carranza.[27] Orozco arrived in the city on December 3 and conferred with various Huerta sympathizers; in addition, he placed a large order for arms and ammunition.[28] Several days later the general left for a similar mission in Los Angeles.[29]

As Salazar's movement in northern Chihuahua continued and as Orozco's activities became known through press dispatches, news stories began to connect the two: it was reported that Orozco was purchasing arms for the Salazar revolution[30] and that Orozco was the head of the Chihuahua movement.[31] The reporters, however, failed to recognize that something much bigger and much more important was in the offing. At the end of December, 1914, as the Salazar revolt bogged down, the rebel headquarters in El Paso intensified the recruitment of Mexican exiles along the Arizona, New Mexico, and Texas borders.[32] Orozco crossed into Mexico in January to recruit troops in northern Mexico and to find safe storage facilities for the munitions he had purchased in New York and Los Angeles.[33]

[24] *El Paso Morning Times*, Dec. 4, 1914.

[25] *Ibid.*

[26] *Ibid.*, Dec. 5, 1914.

[27] RDS, A. G. Adams, Special Agent, Dept. of Justice, to Sec. of State, 812.00/13383, Sept. 18, 1914.

[28] *New York Times*, Dec. 15, 1914.

[29] *El Paso Morning Times*, Dec. 10, 1914, and Jan. 8, 1915.

[30] "New Movements in the North," *Independent*, XIII (Dec. 14, 1914), 440.

[31] *El Paso Morning Times*, Dec. 10, 1914.

[32] RDS, "Report of Conditions Along the Border," 812.00/14197, Jan. 2, 1915, and 812.00/14241, Jan. 9, 1915.

[33] *El Paso Morning Times*, Jan. 8, 1915.

Early in 1915 the rebels launched a second diversionary movement, seemingly designed to perplex the United States. This movement consisted primarily of a series of border raids along the lower Rio Grande valley. The revolutionary plan ostensibly was promulgated in the small town of San Diego, Texas, and therefore known as the Plan de San Diego.[34] Some of the stated objectives of the movement were so farfetched that it is exceedingly difficult to take them seriously. The provision most pregnant with international overtones was Article 7, which stipulated that "every North American male over 16 years of age shall be put to death and only the aged men, the women, and children shall be respected."[35] Perhaps the most historically significant aspect of the plan was the incitement of Mexican nationals and American citizens of Mexican extraction to revolt against the government of the United States and to establish an independent republic consisting of "Texas, New Mexico, Arizona, Colorado, and Upper California, of which states the Republic of Mexico was robbed in a most perfidious manner by North American imperialism."[36] When conditions in Mexico were sufficiently stabilized, the independent nation would request annexation.

The Salazar-Campa revolt achieved its purpose in Mexico, but the raids carried out in the United States in the name of the Plan de San Diego did not convince government officials that the intense Mexican activity along the border was being conducted in support of the foolhardy scheme. As border officials and special investigators increased their vigilance, it became obvious that the San Diego plan was a spoke rather than a wheel.

Organization of the larger and more important movement continued throughout February. In the middle of the month the exiles founded a new organization, the Mexican Peace Assembly, with headquarters in San Antonio, Texas. In a statement issued by the directive council and forwarded to President Woodrow Wilson by Toribio Esquivel Obregón, the assembly decried the excesses of the Mexican Revolution and compared them to the atrocities of the Reign of Terror during the French Revolution. The statement also denied the Constitutionalists' charges

[34] The subject of border raids and their connection with the Plan de San Diego is discussed in Charles Cumberland, "Border Raids in the Lower Rio Grande Valley— 1915," *Southwestern Historical Quarterly*, LVII (July, 1953–April, 1954), 290–295; additional information can be gleaned from *Congressional Record*, 64th Congress, 1st sess. (Washington, D.C.: Government Printing Office, 1916), pp. 4846–4848.

[35] *Fall Committee*, I, 1206.

[36] *Ibid.*, p. 1205.

that the revolutionaries in exile were implacable reactionaries: "Be it clearly understood that least of all things do we want a reaction in the sense of bringing back systems which have brought so many [unfortunate] consequences."[37] The statement called for an agrarian reform program that would subdivide large landholdings and establish credit institutions for the small farmer.[38]

The Mexican Peace Assembly, despite its name, was formed to launch a new revolution, and a revolution that would employ a powerful military force. The Constitutionalist victory in July, 1914, had not brought peace or stability to Mexico. The victors, from the outset, began to fight among themselves for the spoils. Carranza did not demonstrate either the ability or the desire to effect a permanent compromise with Pancho Villa or with Emiliano Zapata. Civil war ravaged the states of Sonora and Durango.[39] Civilian and military authorities within the ranks of the Carrancistas themselves seemed unable to agree on any major issue. Villa and Zapata split with the "First Chief," then formed an alliance against a tenuous Obregón-Carranza coalition. The Carrancistas, driven from Mexico City, established a second national capital in the state of Veracruz; and presidents came and went in rapid succession. Mexico City changed hands several times in the spring of 1915. Each time a new army entered or reentered the capital, the citizenry was subjected to looting and other depredations, and the firing squads worked overtime.[40]

By March, 1915, the Revolution had virtually consumed Mexico's meager and badly organized financial resources. Mexicans had been fighting for four and a half years; thousands had lost their lives, presumably for an ideal; and the country and its people were much worse off than they had been in 1910. Under Díaz there had been peace and stability—at the expense of personal liberty—but in 1915 there was neither—only promises whose fulfillment was long overdue. Even within the narrow definition of Mexican patriotism, there was room to believe that drastic measures were justified. Only if all of the divisive factions were subdued by an overwhelming onslaught from the north could peace return to Mexico. Four and a half years of constant fighting seemed to argue that it would not be still another peace without social justice. The possibility that the new revolution might split

[37] RDS, Toribio Esquivel Obregón to Woodrow Wilson, 812.00/14576, Mar. 8, 1915.

[38] *Ibid.*

[39] Quirk, *Mexican Revolution*, pp. 68, 70, 75.

[40] Clendenen, *United States and Pancho Villa*, pp. 137–138.

into opposing factions was not considered. Yet at the same time the movement was unfolding, a separate anti-Carrancista plot, under the leadership of Félix Díaz, was being hatched in New Orleans.[41]

In March and April the pace of revolutionary activity quickened. As a result, Enrique C. Llorente, the representative of Mexico's Conventionist (Villista) government in Washington, D.C., asked the Secretary of State to bring a speedy end to all rebel activities along the Mexican border:

> I am anxious of inviting your attention to the sudden activities in this country of members of the reactionary element, the greater part of whom fled from Mexico during the last days of the Huerta administration. It was, as you so well know, this group of men who were responsible for the *coup d'état* resulting in the overthrow of our first and last really democratic government. . . . The individuals are now arranging to establish headquarters in San Antonio, Texas, and are intent on promoting . . . a counter-revolution; that is a movement to restore themselves in power. My government hopes that . . . you will cause the acts of these persons to be duly observed . . . in order that no armed expedition may be set on foot within this jurisdiction for the purpose of crossing into Mexico with hostile intent.[42]

There was no official response; apparently incensed by President Wilson's lack of interest, Llorente made another appeal several weeks later. Expressing dismay over Wilson's apparent apathy toward rebel activity on United States soil, the Villista representative reported that Generals Marcelo Caraveo and Emilio Campa had rented houses in El Paso, "near the banks of the river," and were secretly assembling implements of war. Llorente said he hoped the "United States government will not fail to adopt all means possible to promptly frustrate this conspiracy."[43]

At approximately the same time, representatives of the Mexican Peace Assembly were trying to move the United States government in the opposite direction. On one occasion when they sought assurance that the United States would not hinder a military expedition against the warring factions in Mexico,[44] Acting Secretary of State Robert

[41] Luis Licéaga, *Félix Díaz* (Mexico City: Editorial Jus, 1958), pp. 350–352.

[42] RDS, Llorente to Sec. of State, 812.00/14571, Mar. 9, 1915.

[43] *Ibid.*, 812.00/14955, Apr. 23, 1915. Llorente also thought the United States should take firm action against the agents of Venustiano Carranza, who also were recruiting supporters in the El Paso area (RDS, Llorente to Sec. of State, 812.00/14641, Mar. 17, 1915).

[44] RDS, Salvador Domínguez to Woodrow Wilson, 812.00/14928, Apr. 21, 1915.

Lansing reminded the would-be rebels of the United States' neutrality laws and cautioned that violations would be punished.[45] However, no attempt was made at this time to bring the rebel activities to a complete halt.

As the projected revolution moved into its seventh month of meticulous planning, it apparently lacked only one requirement for success: a strong political figure who could assume the presidency after victory was assured. The conservative leadership and financial support of the movement dictated that Victoriano Huerta be this man.

Huerta and his family had left Mexico on July 20, 1914, and after brief stops in Jamaica and England had taken up permanent residence in Barcelona.[46] In late March, 1915, the ex-president was visited by Enrique Creel, who had been sent by the revolutionary leaders in San Antonio for the express purpose of informing Huerta of their plans and, if possible, enlisting his support.[47] The ex-president, however, had been considering a return to Mexico, and the potential benefactor of his political comeback was Kaiser Wilhelm II.[48]

Huerta had cultivated a close relationship with Wilhelm during his presidency. After the outbreak of the Constitutionalist revolution and after United States hostility had begun to manifest itself, Germany had been a valuable source of arms for the federal government; indeed, a large shipment of German arms in April, 1914, had been partially responsible for the United States' military occupation of Veracruz. After Huerta had decided upon exile rather than surrender to Venustiano Carranza or Pancho Villa, he chose a German ship, the *Dresden*, to carry him to Europe. The Kaiser did not forget his Mexican friend, and shortly after the outbreak of World War I, in June, 1914, the intelligence department of the German General Staff (Abteilung III B) began contemplating the strategic value of Mexico as an ally. In February, 1915, a German secret-service agent, Franz von Rintelen, visited

[45] RDS, Lansing to Domínguez, 812.00/14928, May 10, 1915.

[46] George J. Rausch, "The Exile and Death of Victoriano Huerta," *Hispanic American Historical Review*, XLII (May, 1962), 133–134.

[47] RDS, Gracey to Sec. of State, 812.00/14751, Mar. 31, 1915.

[48] Strong German interest in Mexico began in the late Díaz period; interest waned during the immediate post-revolutionary period but picked up again during the Huerta regime. For the early activities, see Warren Schiff, "German Military Penetration into Mexico During the Late Díaz Period," *Hispanic American Historical Review*, XXXIX (1959), 568–579, and Alfred Vagts, *Deutschland und die Vereinigten Staaten in der Weltpolitik* (2 vols.; New York: Macmillan, 1955), II, 1766–1781. The most complete coverage of the intrigue in 1915 is contained in Michael Meyer, "The Mexican–German Conspiracy of 1915," *The Americas*, XXIII (1966), 76–89.

Huerta in Barcelona and offered German assistance in restoring Huerta to the Mexican presidency.[49]

The German reasoning was sound. The eventual entry of the United States into World War I, even in early 1915, was a strong possibility. A friendly government in Mexico could give Germany a base of operations in the Western Hemisphere, if and when they needed one, and at the same time would keep the government of Woodrow Wilson occupied with matters closer to home.[50] If United States arms and ammunition could be diverted from the Allies, because of the threat of a hostile government to the south, it would be an added benefit. Although Huerta and Von Rintelen probably did not come to a firm agreement at their February meeting, the possibility of unlimited financial backing was not turned down by the Mexican exile.[51]

When Creel arrived in Spain, the two men debated the pros and cons of the German proposal, and events later proved that they decided to accept German assistance as the final assurance of the success of the revolution they were contemplating. Huerta and Creel left Spain together in late March on the Spanish steamer *López*. Their departure and destination were publicized in the press, and even before their scheduled arrival in New York City (on April 12, 1915), Pancho Villa's confidential agent in Washington, Enrique Llorente, protested that "in view of the present activities of the supporters and adherents of Huerta in the American border states," Huerta and Creel should not be permitted to land.[52] A similar protest was made by Francisco Elías, the Constitutionalist (Carrancista) consul general in the United States.[53] The two men, however, were permitted to land, and Huerta, in interviews with the press, unconvincingly stated that he had no desire to return to Mexico. Asked why he had come to the United States, Huerta said he had come on a pleasure trip and hoped to do some traveling.[54]

Huerta began to hold conferences with German secret-service agents

[49] John Price Jones and Paul Merrick Hollister, *The German Secret Service in America* (Boston: Small, Maynard and Company, 1918), p. 290; Rausch, "The Exile of Huerta," p. 135.

[50] James Brown Scott (ed.), *Diplomatic Correspondence Between the United States and Germany, August 1, 1914–April 6, 1917* (New York: Oxford University Press, 1918) p. 335.

[51] Rausch, "The Exile of Huerta," p. 135.

[52] *U.S. Foreign Relations, 1915,* p. 827.

[53] *Ibid.*, p. 828; *New York Times*, Apr. 13, 1915.

[54] *New York Times*, Apr. 13, 1915.

almost immediately after his arrival. In addition to reestablishing contact with Von Rintelen, who had preceded him to New York, the expresident also held frequent meetings with two members of the German embassy staff: naval attaché Karl Boy-Ed and military attaché Franz von Papen.[55] While in New York, Huerta informed Von Rintelen that "another revolution was being engineered by his friends but that it lacked weapons, or, in other words, money."[56] At approximately the same time the German press began to give some indications of what might be in the offing; the *Frankfurter Zeitung* reported in mid-April:

> Conditions in Mexico defy description . . . . It is difficult to suppress the feeling of bitterness against those [the United States] who fomented where they could have extinguished the smouldering fire. . . . Huerta, although he was no saint, nevertheless represented the least of all evils. . . . There is a vestige of hope in the report that Huerta has left his exile in Spain and has gone to South America [*sic*]. This strong man could save the country if anybody could. . . . We must not lose sight of Mexico, even in the storms of the present war, because Mexico will become the focus of a gigantic movement of world power.[57]

The specific roles of the various German officials involved in the conspiracy are difficult to determine. Count Bernstorff, the German ambassador to Washington, denied that he had been involved,[58] and although such a denial might be expected of a minister, the evidence suggests that the conspiracy was the work of the German military and that the regular embassy staff was not fully apprised of the details. (Secretary of State Lansing later testified that Bernstorff had not been directly involved.[59]) Captain Franz von Papen, the German military

[55] Rausch, "The Exile of Huerta," p. 136; *Papers Relating to the Foreign Relations of the United States. The Lansing Papers* (Washington, D.C.: Government Printing Office, 1939), I, 86. Earlier, Boy-Ed and Von Papen had made trips to the Mexican border. Besides conferring with the leaders of the proposed movement, the two men arranged for the mobilization of German nationals in Mexico and (through their consular agents in Mexico) for the storage of supplies and ammunition (Jones, *German Secret Service*, p. 291).

[56] Franz Rintelen von Kleist, *The Dark Invader: Wartime Reminiscences of a German Naval Intelligence Officer* (New York: Macmillan, 1933), p. 176.

[57] Apr. 15, 1915.

[58] See Bernstorff, *My Three Years in America* (New York: Scribners, 1920), pp. 115–123.

[59] *Official German Documents Relating to the War* (2 vols.; New York: Oxford University Press, 1923), I, 260. Professor Arthur Link has found that there is ample evidence to prove that Bernstorff at least had knowledge of the various intrigues

attaché to both Washington and Mexico City, appears to have been the leading figure in the plot. Von Papen, who spent several months in Mexico City during the Huerta presidency before he assumed his post in the United States, was familiar with the intricacies of the Mexican situation.[60] One of his duties in Mexico was to convince the German minister, Paul von Hintze, a man without respect for the Mexican president, that Huerta's friendship should be cultivated.[61] One year later, in the United States, the interest in Huerta would pay dividends.

The final agreement between the Huerta-Orozco conspirators and the German government was sealed in late April or early May. Huerta's German patrons deposited $895,000 in various bank accounts and promised to supply 10,000 rifles[62] (the total value of the German commitment approached $12,000,000[63]). It was also agreed that "if and when Huerta became president again, they [the Germans] would support him both in peace and war."[64] The exiles on the border had only to set the date for the revolution; June 28, 1915, was chosen.[65]

In early May, Pascual Orozco made a final trip to New York and conferred with Huerta; plans were coordinated and arrangements were made to notify all interested Mexican exiles in the United States of the movement. Orozco returned to El Paso several days later and prepared for Huerta's arrival. By that time *El Presente*, the organ of the San Antonio exiles, was supporting the German cause in its editorials.[66]

The United States government and the representatives of the two Mexican governments in Washington knew of the intrigue; virtually everyone in an important governmental position had been notified well

---

(*Woodrow Wilson and the Progressive Era, 1900–1917* [New York: Harper & Row, 1963], p. 201, n. 11), but this does not suggest that the ambassador participated in them.

[60] *Official German Documents Relating to the War*, I, 260; Franz von Papen, *Memoirs* (London: Andre Deutsch Limited, 1952), p. 17; William James, *The Eyes of the Navy, A Biographical Study of Sir Reginald Hall* (London: Methuen and Co., 1956), p. 133.

[61] Tibor Koeves, *Satan in Top Hat: The Biography of Franz von Papen* (New York: Alliance Book Corporation, 1941), p. 24.

[62] Rausch, "The Exile of Huerta," p. 137.

[63] Arthur S. Link, *Wilson, The Struggle for Neutrality* (Princeton, N.J.: Princeton University Press, 1960), p. 562.

[64] Emanuel Victor Voska and Will Irwin, *Spy and Counterspy* (New York: Doubleday, 1940), p. 195.

[65] *Albuquerque Morning Journal*, June 28, 1915.

[66] *El Presente*, May 26, 1915, quoted in Sax, *Los Mexicanos en el Destierro*, pp. 95–96.

in advance.[67] Huerta's arrival in the United States brought the movement under increased surveillance by the Department of Justice and secret-service agents kept a close watch on the "vacationing" ex-president. Even friends who visited Huerta in his hotel were aware of their presence.[68] The Department of State, of course, had known of the possibility of a revolutionary movement with the arrival of the exiles; when Huerta arrived in New York in April, Secretary of State, William Jennings Bryan commented that the event "indicates some kind of a scheme."[69] Huerta's press-release statement that he had no desire to return to Mexico fooled nobody. As the time for the uprising drew near and as arms began to cross into Mexico at a stepped-up pace,[70] reports of the "new revolution" began to fill United States intelligence channels.[71] In the middle of May, Zachary Cobb, the customs inspector in El Paso, reported:

> Situation now as follows: New revolution is organized, former federal officers in El Paso placed upon salary, men being recruited secretly and ammunition being obtained, Orozoco [sic] in New York conferring with real leaders. . . .[72]

On June 24, Victoriano Huerta left New York on a westbound train, telling reporters he was going to visit San Francisco. At approximately the same time, Mexican exiles from all over the United States began to converge on El Paso.[73] On June 27, the day before the scheduled invasion, Department of Justice agents discovered 14 machine guns, 500 rifles, and 100,000 rounds of ammunition in an El Paso warehouse that had been rented by a Mexican exile.[74] The find, however, was not

[67] The United States Ambassador to Germany, James Gerard, commented upon the conspiracy, as did Secretary of State Lansing (James W. Gerard, *Face to Face with Kaiserism* [New York: George H. Doran Company, 1918], pp. 66, 94–95, and Robert Lansing, *War Memoirs of Robert Lansing* [New York: Bobbs-Merrill, 1935], p. 75).

[68] Luis Lara Pardo, *Matchs de Dictadores* (Mexico City, 1942), quoted in Isidro Fabela (ed.), *Historia Diplomática de la Revolución Mexicana* (2 vols.; Mexico City: Fondo de Cultura Económica, 1959), II, 76.

[69] RDS, Bryan to Cobb, 812.00/14928, Apr. 26, 1915.

[70] "Huerta and Others," *Independent*, LXXXII (May 10, 1915), 236.

[71] RDS, "Report of Conditions Along the Border," 812.00/14899, Apr. 10, 1915, and 812.00/14971, Apr. 25, 1915.

[72] RDS, Cobb to Sec. of State, 812.00/14999, May 11, 1915.

[73] *Albuquerque Morning Journal*, June 27, 1915.

[74] RDS, "Report of Conditions Along the Border," 812.00/161256, Sept. 11, 1915; *Albuquerque Morning Journal*, Sept. 11, 1915.

of great significance, because most of the arms and ammunition had already crossed the border and been deposited at strategic sites in the northern Mexican states.

Because Huerta and Orozco were aware of the large number of federal agents in El Paso, they agreed to meet in Newman, New Mexico, twenty miles north of the border city. Huerta's train arrived at Newman early on the morning of June 27 and Orozco and Huerta's son-in-law, Major Luis Fuentes, who met him at the station, had a car waiting to take him to the border.[75] Before the three men could leave the station, however, Orozco and Huerta were apprehended by Department of Justice agents and federal troops. Zachary Cobb sent the following explanation of the incident to the Secretary of State:

> Last night I learned through railroad of Huerta's plans to leave train at Newman station, twenty miles north of El Paso. With Beckman [a Department of Justice agent], District Clerk, two Deputy Marshals, and Col. G. H. Morgan, accompanied by twenty-five soldiers that he brought to prevent disorder or any attempt to interfere, we went to Newman Station this morning and found Orozco and Huerta's son-in-law awaiting train. We had prepared to use warrants if necessary but found it unnecessary. Beckman invited Orozco and Huerta to accompany us to federal building without arrest which they did. Without display we have treated them with consideration and proper courtesy.[76]

Huerta and Orozco were taken to El Paso and formally charged with conspiracy to violate United States neutrality laws. Nine months of meticulous planning had been undone as the two most important figures in the proposed movement, the political and the military leaders, were arrested within several blocks of the Mexican border.[77] The news circulated rapidly among the Mexican residents of El Paso, and huge crowds gathered outside the federal building. Thomas Lee, the mayor of El Paso, asked that the two Mexicans be detained at the Fort Bliss prison, rather than in the city, and the federal authorities agreed to make the transfer. As the two leaders were taken from the federal

---

[75] *El Paso Morning Times*, June 28, 1915, and *Albuquerque Morning Journal*, June 28, 1915. The two revolutionists were to cross into Mexico at Bosque Bonito, Chihuahua, near Sierra Blanca, Texas (*El Paso Morning Times*, July 5, 1915).

[76] *U.S. Foreign Relations, 1915*, p. 828.

[77] After the arrests, Von Rintelen began to conspire with Villistas in the United States; see Friedrich Katz, "Alemania y Francisco Villa" *Historia Mexicana*, XII (July, 1962–June, 1963), 96–97.

building, "they were cheered vigorously by the crowd of Mexican refugees."[78]

At Fort Bliss, Huerta was released on a $15,000 bond and Orozco on a $7,500 bond, but, because of the proximity to Mexico, the men were placed under house arrest and guarded by Department of Justice agents and army personnel. Despite these precautions, Orozco escaped on the evening of July 3.[79] The Spanish-language edition of the *El Paso Morning Times* described his getaway in detail for an obviously eager Mexican public.

> The most sensational event of yesterday was the flight of Pascual Orozco. It is not known if he has crossed the international line yet. Six guards, three from the Department of Justice and three from the military garrison, were watching Orozco's house with firm orders to employ all means to prevent him from escaping. Neither the exact hour nor the exact means of his escape are known yet. . . . It was at dawn when the guards discovered that they were watching an empty house. . . . When the house was examined . . . it was noted that a window was open. Since about ten yards from the window there is a patch of high grass, it is supposed that Orozco jumped from the window and hid in the grass. It is also supposed that . . . after having walked a short distance . . . an automobile was waiting for him.[80]

As soon as Orozco's escape was discovered, federal authorities canceled Huerta's bond and again arrested him; his trial was set for December, in San Antonio. A painstaking search for Orozco, however, was unsuccessful, for the Chihuahua rebel had many friends in the vicinity of El Paso and was thoroughly familiar with the entire area. Although many reports of Orozco's whereabouts were received by various government agencies, none of them led to his capture.

The second arrest of Victoriano Huerta did not allay the suspicion that the revolution would still take place: it was generally believed that Orozco would launch the movement, the absence of Huerta notwithstanding. Leon Canova, a special representative of the State Department in Mexico, even reported that Pancho Villa and Orozco were contemplating an alliance against Venustiano Carranza[81] (the in-

[78] *Ibid.*, p. 829.

[79] AGO, Frederick Funston to Adjutant General, Doc. File Box 7835, No. 2303485, July 4, 1915; RDS, Special Agent, Dept. of Justice, to Sec. of State, 812.00/15517, July 10, 1915.

[80] *El Paso Morning Times* (Spanish edition), July 4, 1915.

[81] RDS, Canova to Sec. of State, 812.00/15541,1/2, July 7, 1915. An equally fallacious rumor suggested the existence of an Orozco–Carranza alliance against Pancho Villa (*El Paso Morning Times*, Aug. 30, 1915).

tense hatred between Orozco and Villa, however, precludes a valid basis for this interesting report). The representatives of Venustiano Carranza, of course, were especially worried that the revolution might take place even though Huerta was in prison. The Mexican consul in San Diego indicated covert concern in assuring his superior in San Francisco: "Whatever plans this recalcitrant reactionary [Orozco] has they are bound to fail because the Mexican people know who their enemies are."[82] The tone of the message revealed more than the obviously calculated statement of optimism. The dispatches of the consul in Los Angeles during the same period revealed a similar uneasiness.[83]

Despite the uneasiness and uncertainty of the United States and Mexican authorities, the arrest of Huerta temporarily stalled the revolution—Orozco's primary concern was evasion of American and Mexican authorities. Throughout July and August, Orozco was reported in and around El Paso, but he always managed to keep at least one step ahead of the federal agents. On August 30, 1915, the Orozco-Huerta conspiracy was dealt its *coup de grace*. Pascual Orozco and four of his companions—Crisóforo Caballero, General José Delgado, Andrés Sandoval, and Miguel Terrazas—were shot to death in Green River Canyon, Culberson County, Texas, by a posse of federal marshals, deputy sheriffs, Texas Rangers, and troops of the Thirteenth Cavalry.

The story of Orozco's death—the chase on horseback through the rough terrain of the Big Bend country, culminating in a gun battle in which the five "bandits" lost their lives—reads like a western cowboy romance. The circumstances surrounding the episode, however, do not enhance the prestige of early twentieth-century United States law enforcement. Although abundant but conflicting evidence makes it difficult to reconstruct all of the events, there is enough agreement for an accurate summary.

On the morning of August 30, General Orozco and his four companions arrived at the Dick Love ranch, near Sierra Blanca, Texas. The Mexicans, after a hard ride, were in need of food and water. The owner of the ranch and most of the cowhands were absent. Orozco ordered August Franzen, the cook, to prepare some food and had a cowboy shoe his horses. While the Mexicans were eating, Love and several of his men were seen approaching the ranch, and the Mexicans

---

[82] AREM, E. A. González, Consul, San Diego, to Ramón P. de Negri, Consul General, San Francisco, L–E 817, T. 208, No. 128, July 6, 1915.

[83] AREM, Adolfo Carillo, Consul, Los Angeles, to González, L–E 817, T. 208, No. 133, July 2, 1915.

fled. Love and some of his employees gave chase, while another employee called the sheriff to form a posse. During the course of the chase, gunfire was exchanged, until the Mexicans were able to out-distance their pursuers.[84]

By noon, Dick Love and his cowboys had been joined by a federal posse, and the chase continued into the foothills of the High Lonesome Mountains in Culberson County. Early in the afternoon the posse lost sight of Orozco and his men but were able to follow their trail. The Mexicans were spotted several hours later, camped in Green River Canyon, approximately twenty-five miles east of Sierra Blanca. The posse manned the ridges on both sides of the canyon and opened fire. By dusk, all five of the Mexicans had been killed, but none of the members of the posse were injured.[85]

The news of Orozco's death caused a storm of protest among the Mexican inhabitants of El Paso, San Antonio, and the other revolutionary centers in the United States. They believed Orozco had been assassinated.[86] The statement of Zachary Cobb that the identity of the men was not known until afterwards[87] only aggravated the situation because of the implication that a different kind of "justice" would otherwise have been applied. There was fear in the Big Bend area that the deaths would bring reprisals by Mexican residents, and several cattlemen asked the governor of Texas for special protection.[88] Even the anti-Orozco *El Paso Morning Times* expressed indignation at the manner in which Orozco had been brought to justice,[89] and an organ of the revolutionary exiles in San Antonio published an article entitled "Pascual Orozco y la Ley Fuga."[90] The statements released by the United States Department of State and the American press were un-

[84] There is no agreement on who fired the first shots: American sources generally attribute it to the Mexicans and Mexican sources generally attribute it to the Americans (*New York Times*, Sept. 1, 1915; *El Paso Morning Times*, Aug. 31, 1915; *La Época*, Sept. 3, 1915; *La Justicia*, Sept. 4, 1915; Sánchez Escobar, *El Ocaso de los Héroes: Como Murieron Algunos Connotados Revolucionarios* [Tlalpan: Talleres Tipográficos de la Casa Orientación para Varones, 1934], pp. 123–125). Zachary Cobb, the inspector of customs at El Paso, in his initial report stated only that there had been an exchange of fire (RDS, Cobb to Sec. of State, 812.00/15982, Aug. 31, 1915).

[85] *El Paso Morning Times*, Sept. 1, 1915.

[86] RDS, Cobb to Sec. of State, 812.00/16016, Sept. 4, 1915.

[87] *Ibid.*, 812.00/16008, Sept. 2, 1915.

[88] *El Paso Morning Times*, Sept. 1, 1915. It was feared that one of Orozco's men, Eduardo Salinas, might cross into Texas from Bosque Bonito and begin the reprisals (*El Presente*, Sept. 1, 1915).

[89] *El Paso Morning Times* (Spanish edition), Sept. 2, 1915.

[90] *La Época*, Sept. 3, 1915.

convincing: Orozco was said to have raided the Love Ranch, attacked the ranchmen, stolen horses and cattle, and it was reported that he was killed in a "fair fight"—during which the members of the posse had acted in "self-defense."[91] Even a representative of the hostile Carranza government demanded an investigation of the deaths.[92]

If an investigation was made, the findings were never released to the public.[93] It would appear that the Mexicans were taken completely by surprise. They did not know the American posse had manned the ridges overlooking the floor of the canyon until the first volley was fired; they were on foot and their horses were unsaddled when the fight began,[94] and they never reached their horses. Furthermore, although all of the revolutionists were skilled in the use of firearms, none of the Americans were killed or wounded.

The bodies of Orozco and his four companions were loaded into a wagon at Green River Canyon and taken to Van Horn, Texas. After having been embalmed, Orozco's body then was taken by train to El Paso, where burial arrangements were made by his widow. The funeral was held in El Paso, on September 3, 1915, with approximately 3,000 Mexicans in attendance. Orozco was buried in the military uniform of a division general of the Mexican army, the rank he had held under President Victoriano Huerta,[95] and his coffin was draped with the Mexican flag. Orozco's rites were conducted by a Methodist clergyman; those for his companions by a Catholic priest. Prior to the burial, Señora Orozco had received a telegram from Orozco's bitter enemy, Pancho Villa:

> I have always considered Orozco as an enemy of the faction which I sustain and of the democratic cause of the Mexico people, but having

[91] AGO, Funston to Adjutant General, Doc. File Box 7647, No. 2310780, Sept. 1, 1915; RDS, Cobb to Sec. of State, 812.00/15971, Aug. 30, 1915, and 812.00/16008, Sept. 2, 1915; *El Paso Morning Times*, Aug. 31 and Sept. 1, 1915.

[92] RDS, Eliseo Arredondo, Representante de la Agencia Confidencial del Gobierno Constitucionalista de México, to Sec. of State, 812.00/16003, Sept. 1, 1915.

[93] It is likely that the United States was embarrassed about the manner in which Orozco met his death: Senator Fall's detailed investigation of Mexican affairs contains no mention of the death, even though Fall interviewed several persons who resided in the Big Bend country at the time of the incident. This, however, was not the only black mark on United States law enforcement in the border area: many innocent Mexicans were persecuted and killed, especially after the German conspiracy became known. The Texas Rangers were guilty of a number of excesses in 1915 and 1916. See Walter Prescott Webb, *The Texas Rangers, A Century of Frontier Defense* (Boston: Houghton Mifflin, 1935), pp. 473–516.

[94] *El Paso Morning Times*, Sept. 1, 1915.

[95] *Ibid.*, Sept. 2, 1915.

died, all cause for animosity is removed. His family is hereby authorized to bury his body in whatever place they desire in the national
territory.[96]

The widow declined the offer, and Orozco was interred in El Paso on
September 3.[97] The huge crowd which assembled for the ceremony did
not make a public display either during or after the burial.

Orozco's death and Huerta's imprisonment[98] brought an end to a
significant, well-planned movement that could easily have altered the
course of the Mexican Revolution. One can merely speculate on the
success or failure of the movement had it not been frustrated at the
eleventh hour. It is not unlikely, however, that the arrival of Orozco
and Huerta in Mexican territory would have been greeted with sympathy and considerable support. Despite numerous mistakes, Orozco
was still very popular in northern Mexico, and Huerta was not universally regarded as the villain holding the gun at Madero's head. With the
almost unlimited financial backing which the movement enjoyed, and
with the revolutionary factions within Mexico so badly divided among
themselves, the Orozco-Huerta intrigue did have possibilities.

Although in late 1915 and early 1916 a few faint rumblings were
heard from various Mexican exiles in the United States, their energy
and hope was spent. Protests were made against the excesses of the
factions in Mexico, but a plan of action was not developed.

The death of Pascual Orozco ended a significant and eventful career,
but not an epoch of Mexican history; the civil war continued. The
bloodshed, violence, and passion that had engulfed Orozco's career—
since November of 1910—would continue unabated for two years more,
and sporadically afterwards. Orozco, a member and a molder of the
revolution, bequeathed a tradition of violence, which—although a poor
tribute to a man's career—was necessary for the positive accomplish-
ments of a later period.

Orozco has been damned on so many counts, and so vociferously,
the most valid charges that could be leveled against him have been lost
in the heat of passion. The fact that the *guerrillero* possibly believed he
was acting in the best interests of his country (a fact that his detractors
are wont to omit), certainly does not excuse his indiscretions or mis-

[96] Quoted in *El Paso Morning Times*, Sept. 3, 1915.

[97] In December, 1925, Orozco's remains were transferred to the municipal
cemetery in Chihuahua City (Sánchez Escobar, *Ocasos*, p. 125).

[98] Huerta died on January 16, 1916, probably from complications from an
improperly performed operation, in El Paso.

takes. The most serious of them is that he placed himself in the un-enviable position of judging the actions of Madero and Huerta on two completely different scales. It is likely that Orozco revolted against Madero, with the gentle but steady prompting of the Terrazas clique, to be sure, because he was convinced that the president had turned his back even on the modest program of political reform that he had promised. Huerta did virtually nothing to implement any program of reform, but the *guerrillero* from Chihuahua supported him to the end. Orozco's naiveté degenerated into intellectual incompetence, and his dedication to a cause into obstinacy.

The contributions of individuals to the total scheme of history are too often portrayed as manifestations of idealism on the one hand or opportunism on the other, but Pascual Orozco was not an idealist when he fought against Díaz or an opportunist when he rebelled against Madero and supported Huerta. From the time of his rise to national prominence until his death in August, 1915, he was the people's revolutionist. Whether supporting a cause that history has subsequently vindicated or one that it has censured, Orozco had an almost charis-matic appeal. From his position of leadership he was often able to determine the course that the Revolution was to follow.

It has not been my intention to create a new hero or a new villain, or to disparage the positive achievements of the accepted demigods. Rather it is hoped that some light has been shed upon a highly im-portant but little-known aspect of the Mexican Revolution. It is seldom that human actions can be judged totally in terms of good or evil. It is readily admitted that certain simplifications may be necessary if the intricacies of history are to be at all fathomed. Yet, if historical truth is a desirable goal the grey tones must be extended, when applicable, at the expense of the blacks and whites.

# Orozco's Letter of Resignation to Madero

Today I am again addressing myself to you through proper channels to kindly ask that you relieve me of the position which you have conferred upon me so that I can dedicate myself to my private affairs.

The kindness which you have shown me makes it incumbent upon me to apprise you personally of the decision I have made for the reason expressed and because I am convinced that at the present my services are of little use to the country. Since the country is at relative peace it is necessary that citizens, instead of living off the state treasury, try, by whatever honest means within their reach, to dedicate themselves to some job which while covering their expenses also helps to fill the public treasury so that it can meet the unavoidable expenses of administration.

On separating from my position I would like to carry with me the assurance that the government emanating from the Revolution will continue to move forward, unflinchingly, and against all obstacles, always doing honor to its high ideals, using Justice and Law as the norm for its actions, and obtaining with true patriotism the well-being of the people. Only in this way will the country become great and the citizens consecrate a Revolution that has cost so many lives and so many tears.

As a private citizen I appeal to your patriotism, to you as First Citizen of the Republic, to bear in mind the immense responsibility that rests upon you. Try to surround yourself with truly impartial, learned, and patriotic men who will work with you in the great chore of saving the people in this period of transition. It is necessary that each and every one of your associates be eminently qualified, through their patriotism as well as through their ability and prudence, to bring to a happy conclusion the difficult and transcendental problems which exist today. The ruin or prosperity of our beloved fatherland will depend in large measure on the resolution of these problems.

I ask you to pardon the frankness of this letter because of the good intentions which caused me to write it. I am among those who would give his life with pleasure for the happiness and well being of your fellow citizens.

I remain your fond friend.

*January 26, 1912*

PASCUAL OROZCO, JR.

# Plan Orozquista

MEXICANS: The definitive triumph of the Revolution, which began with the seizure of Ciudad Juárez, has progressed rapidly and it is necessary, therefore, to make known to the nation, in a complete and detailed manner, its true tendencies, expanding upon the proclamation made on the eighth of this month and bringing to light the detailed program which synthesizes the desires of the people and the sincere principles which the present revolution is pursuing. The revolution, localized in its beginning, has converted itself into a general uprising of discontent with President Madero and his cabinet. It has the support of . . . public opinion and of an organized and disciplined army of more than ten thousand men in the northern part of the Republic and thirty or forty thousand in the remainder of the country. It has at its disposal an entire state unanimously allied to the revolution; a constitutional legislature which has withdrawn recognition of the federal government; and a government, also constitutional, which supports the revolution. It has issued decrees which guarantee the dominion of law; it has been able to contract, easily and spontaneously, a loan of one million two hundred thousand pesos. In every region occupied by revolutionary forces, all public services, administered by constituted authorities, function regularly; municipal officials and police ensure order and morality. Taxes are collected regularly. Security for the lives and interests of nationals and foreigners is guaranteed and severe punishment awaits any misbehavior or abuse of those who, hiding beneath the liberating banner, have tried to pillage and rob. We wish to demonstrate that this is not a barbaric or an anarchic movement but a sacred revolt against despotism. The revolution has been victorious in all the actions where it has been necessary to fight. It has treated the heroic and daring federal prisoners with the dignity and respect that they deserve. It will exercise reprisals and punishments only against traitors, *ambiciosos*, and the executioners of the people.

With all these elements which glorify and exalt it, the revolution is moving forward with assurance of victory and the certainty that it will fulfill its duty and its promises. It calls to the people without fear or distrust to support the movement with applause, with sanction, and with force.

When the unhealthy impulse of man's passion leads a people to error, to shame, and to slavery, it is a sacred duty to remove them from error, to cast them aside from shame, and to free them from slavery.

The Mexican people's sacrosanct desires for Liberty and Justice, vilely exploited by the most ambitious, inept, and miserable of men, resulted in sacrifice. Believing incorrectly that the false apostle was leading them to the Tabor of restitution, the people were crucified, like a pleiad of martyrs and heroes, on the calvary of the blackest of treasons.

Francisco I. Madero, the Pharisee of Democracy, the Iscariot of the fatherland, because of ambition and because of heredity—since he is the offspring of a wicked breed of brothers fighting brothers—has pulled the dignity and honor of the country through the mud. He has stained the history of our race, procreative of heroes, and has sold the dignity and independence of our nation.

Francisco I. Madero has purchased the fratricidal bullets with gold from the coffers of our only enemies.

Francisco I. Madero has taken twenty thousand lives with the dynamite of his filibusters.

Francisco I. Madero has profaned our flag with the sacrilegious hand of the Yankee.

Francisco I. Madero has ripped from our coat of arms the glorious eagle devouring the serpent, substituting the vulture which devours all of Spanish America.

Francisco I. Madero has usurped power with the help of our exploiters, reaching it not by the smooth road of democracy but by the tortuous paths of deceit and treason, by a pyramid of bodies and debris, all the while laughing at the good faith of the people who by error converted their hangman into an idol.

When the rope of the tyrant or the whip of the ruler causes men or nations to bend their backs and fall to their knees in the face of the tyranny or abomination, it is because they have ceased to be men; they have ceased to be nations.

When the mark of the rope or the welt of the whip ignites the ire of men or nations, and they rise up with pride, challenging destiny serenely, defying the future, it is because those men are moving toward dignity and those nations toward glory and greatness. And our nation . . . will move toward that glory and greatness.

Virile and rejected sons of Juárez and Morelos! Through our veins the blood of the stoic and firm Aztec runs mixed with that of the noble and brave Spaniard. Let us demonstrate to the world once again that we still know how to accept martyrdom as Cuauhtémoc; we can still thrust the dagger into the enemy, as Guzmán el Bueno, even though revenge might befall our children. People who live on their knees are infamous; those who die on their feet are examples.

It is for this reason that we call you: so that on our feet we will die for the race and for the fatherland, with law for a shield, dignity for a guide, with our valor as a norm, and our faith in victory as the only reward for our effort.

We call you together, fellow countrymen, for a great revolution of principle and emancipation. You are not going to fight under the banner of a personalist faction but rather under the noble teachings which protect the rights of men.

The Maderist revolution was harmful to the country because from its beginning it was seething with germs of treason; because it used Yankee money and the phalanx of mercenary filibusters as its main element of combat. Mercenaries, without law, without honor, and without conscience were sent to assassinate our brothers. The leaders of the movement were greedy, unscrupulous status-seekers; they deceived the people, engaged in nepotism and robbery, and sold out the fatherland.

It is already well demonstrated that this disreputable and unprincipled man has sold out the country, and that he, and the infamous body of ministers that surround him, constitute a government that is no more than a dependency of the government of Washington.

Because of these facts, as heralds of national dignity, with arms in hand and representing the revolutionary junta, we declare before the nation that:

(1) The initiator of the Revolution, Francisco I. Madero, falsified and violated the Plan de San Luis Potosí.

(2) Francisco I. Madero made the Revolution with the money of American millionaires and with the indirect or covert assistance of the government of the United States. This is shown even in Madero's own declarations.

(3) Francisco I. Madero used Americans and other foreign nationals in his lines as filibusters to assassinate Mexicans.

(4) Francisco I. Madero, together with other members of his family, robbed the nation on the pretext of raising an armed force during the elections which carried him and José María Pino Suárez to the presidency and vice-presidency of the Republic.

(6)[1] Francisco I. Madero imposed interim governors by armed force

[1] None of the copies of the Plan Orozquista that I have seen contain Article 5. It is probable that the original was incorrectly numbered. (*Author's note.*)

and sanctioned fraudulent elections in violation of the sovereignty of the states.

(7) Francisco I. Madero contracted for and received FOURTEEN MILLION dollars from Wall Street within two days after assuming power on the pretext of expanding the services of the National Railroad Lines (something that was not of great urgency). The true object of this loan was to pay debts contracted [by Madero] through two attorneys of the Water, Pierce Oil Company of the United States during the Revolution. Earlier Madero had named these two attorneys advisers of the National Railroad Lines.

(8) Francisco I. Madero, in a manner prejudicial and humiliating to the nation, placed the destiny of the fatherland in the hands of the American government by means of contemptible complacency and promises that encumbered our nationality and integrity.

(9) Because of the above-mentioned indiscretions and crimes, Francisco I. Madero and his accomplices are declared traitors to the fatherland and outside of the law.

(10) Because both fraud and armed force intervened in the elections of October, 1911, the election for the presidency and vice-presidency are considered null and void. As a consequence Francisco I. Madero is not recognized as president nor José María Pino Suárez as vice-president.

(11) In honor of the principles of equity—and so as not to injure various interests—loans contracted with foreigners up to the date of this pronouncement will be recognized; however, it is solemnly declared that after the date of this proclamation no loan, concession, or contract made with foreigners residing in or out of the country will be recognized, even though it may be the cause of great conflict.

(12) The revolution does not recognize, and declares null and void, all concessions and contracts made by the usurping government with members of the Madero family or with blood relatives or relatives through marriage and with the so-called ministers of this cabinet. And in order to recover the capital gains made by these concessions they will be confiscated and adjudicated, one-half going to the denouncer and the other half to the orphans and widows of the victims of the revolution.

(13) In order to avoid disturbances in the civil administration of towns and cities, the revolution recognizes all present authorities as long as they adhere to the revolution and recognize its principles. If they refuse, they will be considered rebels against the fatherland and accomplices of the usurping and disloyal government; as such they will be punished with the full rigor of the law.

(14) The congress of the union and the local legislatures are recognized as legitimate, as are the judicial powers of the entire Republic. They must, however, recognize the revolution, withdraw recognition of

Madero, and pledge their concurrence with the principles proclaimed in this manifesto.

(15) This being a revolution of principles, in the interest of democracy and national sovereignty, personalism is absent. As a consequence there is no provisional president nor candidate for the presidency. The revolution recognizes as operative only the legislative and judicial branches of government. As stipulated in the previous article, the executive branch is considered acephalous.

(16) The revolution declares the constitutional reform which established a vice-presidency of the Republic abolished and places in force the constitutional precept which invests the president of the senate as a substitute for the executive; but since at the present time there is no legislative president of the senate, since the so-called vice-president Pino Suárez was acting in that capacity, this constitutional arrangement will be temporarily suspended until a legal regime begins to function regularly at the triumph of the revolution.

(17) By virtue of the previous [article], and in agreement with the principles of the most pure form of democracy, when the revolution triumphs it will declare as interim president of the United Mexican States, the citizen designated in an election of the following type: all of the generals, chiefs, and officers of the National Revolutionary Army and civilian members of the army which occupy the capital of the Republic, will elect a junta, composed of fifteen individuals; this junta— by secret ballot—will designate the person who will occupy the first magistracy as interim president, or, it will determine if it should establish a government junta of three members following the Swiss system, which would function temporarily as the executive; neither the interim president in the first instance, nor any member of the government junta in the second, will be eligible for election as constitutional president in the following elections.

(18) The interim period will last one year, beginning on the date that [the revolution] takes possession of [Mexico City]. This will be sufficient time for complete pacification of the nation so that the people may freely exercise the right of suffrage.

(19) The revolution considers the elections for deputies and senators held during the administration of the usurping government illegal because it considers those elections as the spurious fruit of a government of traitors. It therefore declares that at the moment of triumph it will recognize the present members of both chambers as legitimate representatives of the people only until the end of the interim government. At that time their terms will be prorogued and new elections will be held simultaneously with those for the executive. In this way the performance of the new government will be uniform and will emanate totally from the will of the people as expressed freely in the voting. This will be the

case if the legislators have adhered to the revolution in accordance with Article 14. [If they do not adhere to Article 14] the revolution will dissolve the chambers and the executive will assume legislative powers during the interim period.

(20) The armed elements of the revolution, upon its triumph, will remain intact under the command of their own chiefs. These armies will remain in the areas in which they have been operating in order to serve as a guarantee for the aspirations of the revolution and for the sovereignty and rights of each of the states to which they belong. Their mission is not to support the ambitions of a single man, who arbitrarily alters the destiny of the fatherland, but rather to defend and contribute to the effectiveness of the suffrage and the sovereignty of each one of the entities of the federation in agreement with the general interests of national unity (not subordinating one to another but harmoniously consolidating them). It is necessary that these forces support the legitimate desires of the people. With this support the interim government will be able to carry out the promises of the revolution.

(21) The militarization of the country is unconstitutional and contrary to democratic principles; therefore Madero's despotic law of obligatory military service (which takes sons away from widows and fathers from infants to support the ambitions of a despot) is abolished. Citizens are obliged to serve their country in a foreign war, but under the [principles] laid down in the constitution. In such a manner the glorious federal army will continue standing up as the guarantor of sovereignty and national dignity as well as a defender of institutions, but it will be filled with volunteers who are well paid and well fed. Its standing size in time of peace will not exceed 28,000 men in the three arms.

(22) All of the states of the federation will comply with the obligation imposed upon them by the constitution of organizing and maintaining a national guard. This guard will be formed by the revolutionary forces of each state. So that the guard will not be burdensome on the treasury, the states will maintain in active service only that number indispensable to an [efficient] veteran corps.

(23) The instruction of the national guard will be conducted by the federation so that it will be uniform and efficient. Recruiting and organization will be determined by the respective organic laws [the state constitutions].

(24) The remaining revolutionary forces, after the formation of the veteran corps of the national guard, will be gradually discharged after the president, having been freely elected by the people, takes office.

(25) The presidential term of Señor General Don Porfirio Díaz will be declared terminated at the end of the interim presidency. As a consequence, the president elected by the people will begin a new term which will last six years in accordance with the law.

(26) In a like manner the remaining federal functionaries, after the popular election, will be restored to the terms provided by law.

(27) The executive will not be given extraordinary powers to legislate in any branch of public administration for any cause or motive, imperative as they may seem, except in the field of war so that he can mobilize and direct the army and the national guard in the case of a foreign invasion.

(28) The revolution will make effective the independence and autonomy of the town councils so that they can legislate and administer their taxes and other funds.

(29) The duties of the *jefes políticos* throughout the entire Republic are eliminated. These duties will be performed by the municipal presidents.

(30) In order to improve the federal system of the Republic, the territories of Tepic and Baja California will be incorporated as states of the federation. The opinion of the inhabitants will first be consulted. Their economic resources will be studied so that their estimated debits will not be encumbered in any harmful manner.

(31) The territory of Quintana Roo will be reincorporated with the state of Yucatán from which it was separated for reasons which no longer exist.

(32) In order to prevent the reduction of government control over the National Railways, the government will not, for any motive, alienate the stock which it already possesses. On the contrary, in order to accelerate complete nationalization of the lines in an effective manner, it will create an annual fund in the budget for the purpose of purchasing a greater number of shares in that corporation.

(33) In a like manner, in order to make the nationalization of personnel effective, the government will encourage the practical and technical advancement of Mexican personnel and will demand that the company make substitution of Mexican for foreign employees. Taking ability into consideration, Mexicans will be paid the same wages as foreigners.

(34) In order to improve and raise the conditions of the working class the following measures will be adopted:

(I) The company stores, with their systems of notebooks and charge accounts, are abolished.

(II) The wages of workers will be paid totally in effective money.

(III) Working hours will be reduced to a maximum of ten hours for those who work by the day and twelve hours for those who do piecework.

(IV) Children under ten will not be permitted to work in factories and those between ten and sixteen will only work a maximum of six hours a day.

(V) [The government] will try to raise the daily wage of workers, harmonizing the interests of capital and labor, so that it does not cause an economic conflict which would obstruct the industrial progress of the country.

(VI) [The government] will demand that the owners of factories provide hygienic working conditions which guarantee the health of the workers.

(35) Because the agrarian problem in the Republic demands the most careful and violent solution, the revolution guarantees that it will gradually proceed to resolve that problem according to the following principles:

(I) The property of persons who have lived peacefully on the land for over twenty years will be recognized.

(II) Revalidation and improvement of all legal titles will be made.

(III) Lands seized by despoilment will be returned.

(IV) Uncultivated and nationalized land throughout the Republic will be redistributed.

(V) All of the land which the large land owners do not regularly keep under cultivation will be expropriated in the public interest after being appraised. The land thus expropriated will be partitioned to improve intensive agriculture.

(VI) In order not to burden the state treasuries, nor use up the reserves of the national treasury, and in order not to increase the national debt by contracting foreign loans, the government will float a special agricultural bond in order to pay for the expropriated land. The holders of the bonds will be paid four percent interest annually until their amortization. This will occur every ten years. The proceeds from the redistributed lands will form a special fund earmarked for the amortization.

(VII) A regulatory organic law will be dictated on this subject.

(36) The Official Register in the Federal District, the territories, and the states of the federation will be reorganized in an efficient manner so that an equitable leveling of taxes can be made. These will be graduated with the intervention of consulting boards for each branch or source of tax. The system of annual fees of contributors will be completely eliminated because this system is harmful, improper, and constitutes a monopoly or privilege prohibited by the constitution.

(37) Freedom of the press and of thought in all its forms will be made operative without restrictions other than those imposed by Article 7 of the Constitution [of 1857] before it was reformed.[2]

[2] Article 7 of the Constitution of 1857 provided that freedom of the press was inviolable except in cases of lack of respect for life, public morality, or public peace. See Francisco Zarco, *Historia del Congreso Constituyente* (Mexico City: El Colegio de México, 1956), pp. 526–548, 1346. (*Author's note.*)

The present revolutionary plan duly satisfies national needs and aspirations. We are confident that the public will respond to our call.

The parties which go to the peaceful electoral fight with a previously designated candidate exercise a democratic right.

The revolutionary parties which, with anticipation of triumph, hoist a personalist banner do no more than ruin the country and enslave the people. In advance they place enormous power into the hands of a single individual. They factionalize the revolution and reinforce the strength of a single individual who can later convert himself into their executioner.

It is for this reason that this program does not proclaim any provisional president, but merely expresses the manner in which a citizen or governing junta will be chosen to exercise the executive power of the Republic during an interim period. In this way [the revolution] guarantees compliance with and realization of national desires.

FELLOW CITIZENS: We call all patriots to our ranks; we call all those who have holy faith and who dare to offer their lives for the happiness of the country; and we call all those who have abstained from participating in the fight. For the salvation of the country and national dignity there should be no distinctions between parties in this moment of common danger. In democratic countries [parties] should only fight before the election urns and not on the fields of battle.

SOLDIERS OF THE REPUBLIC: Your sacred mission is to guard the institutions of the nation and not to serve and sustain a man who criminally deceives it, robs it, floods it with anarchy, and turns it over to the foreigner, impoverished and manacled.

We don't call you to insult your duties or loyalty because we do not exhort you to violate laws or overthrow constitutions but to withdraw recognition of the government of an ominous man who is carrying the country to ruin and slavery.

Your heroism and discipline in the last contest won you the admiration of the world!

If the chivalrous spirit in your souls evokes scruples about having to shoot fellow Mexicans, we ask that you bear in mind that this is a true fight of emancipation. Remember Colonel Morelos and the other victims who sacrificed their lives in a fratricidal war. You will be judged by the sublime Niños Mártires, who sacrificed themselves for our honor and our liberty.

*Chihuahua Headquarters, March 25, 1912*

GENERAL PASCUAL OROZCO, JR.; GENERAL INÉS SALAZAR; GENERAL EMILIO P. CAMPA; GENERAL J. J. CAMPOS;

General Benjamín Argumedo; Colonel Demetrio Ponce; Colonel Gonzalo C. Enrile; Colonel Félix Díaz; José Córdova, Secretario.

# Historiographical Note

There is a vast amount of historical literature on the Mexican Revolution of 1910. Multifarious secondary accounts, all purporting to be deeply grounded in historical fact, hit every gradation from childish fantasy to genuine scholarship. Unfortunately, the literature, all too often, has been colored by passion, prejudice, questionable methodology, faulty logic, and—worst of all—deliberate distortion. Even the questionable works cannot be discarded, however. Critically used, they often provide important guides to the chronology of events and are at times valuable for their insights into motivation, historical settings, and personal responses to historical stimuli.

In addition to abounding secondary information, there is a wealth of primary evidence—some of it scarcely tapped—that treats the revolutionary period: government documents (in a number of archives), diaries, travel accounts, newspaper files, and letter collections, all available to researchers. The abundance and availability of primary source material would, in part, seem to explain the large number of secondary accounts. The investigator with only the most cursory familiarity with the literature, however, is immediately aware that until quite recently historians of the Revolution have not generally availed themselves of documentary evidence.

Between 1910 and 1950 most Mexican and United States historians were members, as it were, of a pro-Revolutionary school. The apotheosis of the revolutionary phenomenon—long after it ceased to be a revolution—critically affected the scholarship of the period. Biographers of men who had in some way opposed the "apostles of the Revolution" depicted their subjects as traitors, Judases, heretics, renegades, turncoats, and the like. The word "counterrevolution" was used to characterize mild schismatic tendencies. Mexican reportage of the relations between the revolutionary governments and the United States was typified by an extreme nationalism that often degenerated into chauvinism. As late as 1951, the noted Mexican lawyer and author Ramón Beteta was still calling for *menos explotación y mas nacionalismo.*

United States coverage of the Mexican Revolution for forty years followed a similar pattern, but with several noteworthy modifications. As Mexican nationalism began to manifest itself in the economic sphere and United States interests began to be threatened, there was a new look into the early years of the Revolution. Although no major attempts were made to modify the general pattern that had been constructed by the pro-Revolutionary school, new features were added. Atrocity stories began to find their way into historical tracts. Newspaper accounts with vivid descriptions of the occasional murder of a United States citizen in Mexico were used to intensify a latent race sensitivity. In the late 1920's and early 1930's the specter of "Communism in Mexico" colored much of the United States reportage of the Revolution. Once again, it was often the threats to foreign economic interests that caused reporters to blame "Bolshevik agents."

The literature on the Orozquista insurrection is typical of the distortions, half-truths, and oversimplifications the Mexicanist must guard against. Much of it was compiled by persons with a blind faith that the overthrow of a long-despised dictatorship must result in political and social amelioration. (Perhaps it is only since the Castro revolution that Latin Americanists have been made acutely aware that such a generalization is not necessarily valid.) Deviation from Maderismo was therefore simple political heresy. In addition, the contemporaneous accounts often were colored by the fact that the historians had a personal interest in the outcome; an anti-Madero press further aggravated the problem.

It was not for personal reasons that Pascual Orozco was systematically vilified: the reasons were much more profound. History became a tool, a pragmatic device for keeping the Revolution alive and for exalting its "success." It was therefore imperative that the accepted "heroes" of the Revolution be defended and that those who opposed the movement, their reasons for doing so notwithstanding, be condemned. The crimes of the Revolution had to be overlooked, or excused, on the grounds of political necessity; and those of the opposition had to be portrayed as barbarities. All "enemies of the Revolution" were depicted as pawns in the hands of satanic "counterrevolutionists." If the Revolution embodied all virtue, its "enemies" had to be considered depraved.

The clearly propagandistic motives of the pro-Revolutionary school precluded genuine scholarship. Facts were carefully selected to fit a preconceived outline. Attempts were made to defend the indefensible and to evaluate all human actions by a rigid yardstick of good and evil. The few voices that decried the distortions were faint—and soon they too became involved in the endless polemics, and were equally guilty of distortions. Objectivity could scarcely have served their purpose in the face of such overwhelming opposition.

The last decade and a half of revolutionary historiography, in both Mexico and the United States, has been characterized by refinement and improvement of the investigative process. Newly available guides and improved methodology have yielded more mature analyses in which the blacks and whites give way to the more subtle gray tones. The paladins are more fallible and the heretics less malevolent. All United States–Mexican relations are no longer portrayed as determined by the evil machinations of Wall Street.

The Revolution is losing its sacrosanctity as its shortcomings are revealed. Its justification, for example, on the grounds that it was a Mexican solution to a series of Mexican problems—and therefore should be exalted—is not upheld by historians of the late 1950's and the 1960's. Tentative balance sheets now show the credits as well as the debits and, in addition, indicate that both existed from the beginning of the movement.

The bibliography that follows does not purport to be comprehensive. I consulted many other studies in writing the book, but because they had only marginal value for the specific historical problem at hand, they have not been included. In addition to the standard bibliographies, guides, and aids for the revolutionary period, only the documentary collections, books, and articles that are cited in the footnotes have been included. English rules for the capitalization of titles have been followed throughout for purposes of regularization.

# Selected Bibliography

## I. BIBLIOGRAPHIES, GUIDES, AND AIDS

ALMADA, FRANCISCO. *Diccionario de Historia, Geografía, y Biografías Chihuahuenses*. Chihuahua: Talleres Gráficos del Gobierno del Estado, 1927.

ARNADE, CHARLES W. "The Porfirio Díaz Papers of the William Clements Library," *Hispanic American Historical Review*, XXXIII (May, 1953), 324–325.

CARRERA STAMPA, MANUEL. *Archivalia Mexicana*. Mexico City: Universidad Nacional Autónoma de México, 1952.

CASTILLO, IGNACIO B. DEL. *Bibliografía de la Imprenta de la Cámara de Diputados para Servir a los Historiadores de la Epoca de Madero, Huerta, y la Convención, 1912–1915*. Mexico City: Oficina Impresora de Hacienda, 1918.

———. *Bibliografía de la Revolución Mexicana de 1910 a 1916*. Mexico City: Talleres Gráficos de la Secretaría de Comunicaciones y Obras Públicas, 1918.

CLAGETT, HELEN L. *A Guide to the Law and Legal Literature of the Mexican States*. Washington, D.C.: Library of Congress, 1947.

CUMBERLAND, CHARLES CURTIS. "The United States–Mexican Border: A Selective Guide to the Literature of the Region," Supplement to *Rural Sociology*, XXV (June, 1960).

DIRECCIÓN GENERAL DE ESTADÍSTICA. *Bibliografía Mexicana de Estadística*. 2 vols. Mexico City: Talleres Gráficos de la Nación, 1942.

ESTRADA, GENARO. *200 Notas de Bibliografía Mexicana*. Mexico City: Imp. y Ed. Secretaría de Relaciones Exteriores, 1935.

FERNÁNDEZ DE CÓRDOBA, JOAQUÍN. *Tesoros Bibliográficos de México en los Estados Unidos.* Mexico City: Editorial Cultura, 1959.

GONZÁLEZ, LUIS (ED.). *Fuentes de la Historia Contemporánea de México.* 3 vols. Mexico City: Colegio de México, 1961–62.

GONZÁLEZ, SILVINO M. *Algunas Fichas para una Bibliografía General de la Secretaría de la Defensa Nacional.* Mexico City: Talleres Nigromante de González, Martínez y Cía., 1943.

HARRISON, JOHN P. (ED.). *Guide to Materials on Latin America in the National Archives.* Washington, D.C.: General Services Administration, National Archives Record Service, 1961. (2d vol. in preparation.)

HERRERA GÓMEZ, NESTOR, and SILVINO M. J. GONZÁLEZ. *Apuntes para una Bibliografía Militar de México, 1536–1936.* Mexico City: Talleres Gráficos de la Nación, 1939.

KER, ANNITA M. *Mexican Government Publications.* Washington, D.C.: Government Printing Office, 1940.

*List of National Archives Microfilm Publications, 1961.* Washington, D.C.: General Services Administration, National Archives Record Service, 1961.

MEYER, MICHAEL C. "Albert Bacon Fall's Mexican Papers: A Preliminary Investigation," *New Mexico Historical Review,* XL (April, 1965), 165–174.

MILLÁN, JESÚS S. (ED.). Secretaría de Guerra y Marina. *Manual para la Clasificación Decimal de los Archivos de Ramo.* Mexico City: Imprenta Escallada, 1930.

MILLARES CARLO, AGUSTÍN, and JOSÉ IGNACIO MANTECÓN. *Ensayo de una Bibliografía de Bibliografías Mexicanas.* Mexico City: Biblioteca de la II Feria del Libro y Exposición Nacional del Periodismo, 1943.

*New York Times Index.* 1910–15 (cumulative).

OSWALD, J. GREGORY. "La Revolución Mexicana en la Historiografía Soviética," *Historia Mexicana,* XII (July, 1962–June, 1963), 340–357.

PARSONS, MARY D., and ROBERT A. GORDILLO. *Directorio de Bibliotecas de la Ciudad de México.* Mexico City: Mexico City College Press, 1958.

PERAL, MIGUEL ÁNGEL. *Diccionario Biográfico Mexicano.* 2 vols. Mexico City: Editorial P.A.C., 1944.

POTASH, ROBERT A. "Historiografía del México Independiente," *Historia Mexicana,* X (July, 1960–June, 1961), 362–412.

———. "Historiography of Mexico Since 1821," *Hispanic American Historical Review*, XL (1960), 383–424.

PRIESTLEY, HERBERT INGRAM. "Mexican Literature on the Recent Revolution," *Hispanic American Historical Review*, II (May, 1919), 286–314.

RAMOS, ROBERTO. *Bibliografía de la Revolución Mexicana*. 3 vols. Mexico City: Talleres Gráficos de la Nación, 1959–1960.

ROSS, STANLEY ROBERT. "Aportación Norteamericana de la Revolución Mexicana," *Historia Mexicana*, X (July, 1960–June, 1961), 282–308.

———. "Bibliography of Sources for Contemporary Mexican History," *Hispanic American Historical Review*, XXXIX (1959), 234–238.

———. "El Historiador y el Periodismo Mexicano," *Historia Mexicana*, XIV (July, 1964–June, 1965), 347–383.

SECRETARÍA DE GUERRA Y MARINA, Comisión de Estudios Militares. *Apuntes Para una Bibliografía Militar de México*. Mexico City: Talleres Gráficos de la Nación, 1937.

SECRETARÍA DE RELACIONES EXTERIORES. *Fórmulas Clasificadoras de Asuntos Consulares*. Mexico City: Imprenta de la Secretaría de Relaciones Exteriores, 1931.

URIBE DE FERNÁNDEZ CÓRDOBA, SUSANA. "Bibliografía Histórica Mexicana," *Historia Mexicana* (1956–60).

## II. PRIMARY SOURCES

### A. MANUSCRIPTS

Albert Bacon Fall Collection. University of New Mexico. Papers from the Senate Office Files of Senator Albert Bacon Fall Relating to Mexican Affairs.

Archivo General de la Nación. Ramo de la Secretaría de Gobernación. Various *legajos* and *expedientes*, 1910–1914.

Archivo Histórico de la Defensa Nacional. File Series XI/481.5. Various sections and volumes, 1910–1915.

Archivo Particular de Enrique Meyer Orozco. Monterrey, Mexico.

Archivo de Relaciones Exteriores de México. Revolución Mexicana durante los Años de 1910 a 1920. Informaciones Diversas de la República y de las Oficinas de México en el Exterior. File Series H/513-1910-20/1. Various sections and volumes, 1910–1915.

Biblioteca Nacional, Archivo Madero. Correspondencia del Presidente Francisco I. Madero, Mayo a Junio, 1911. Four Boxes.

Records of the Adjutant General's Office. Department of War. Record Group 94, 1911–1915.

Records of the Department of State Relating to the Internal Affairs of Mexico, 1910–1929. National Archives Microfilm Publications (Microcopy No. 274), 1910–1915.

Silvestre Terrazas Collection, Correspondence and Papers. Bancroft Library, University of California, Berkeley.

### B. PUBLISHED DOCUMENTS

*Archivo del General Porfirio Díaz: Memorias y Documentos.* 29 vols. Mexico City: Editorial "Elede" S. A., 1947–60.

Casasola, Agustín Victor. *Historia Gráfica de la Revolución, 1900–1940.* 6 vols. Mexico City: Archivo Casasola, n.d.

*Congressional Record.* 64th Congress, 1st sess. Washington, D.C.: Government Printing Office, 1916.

Fall, Albert Bacon. *Claims Against Mexico.* Washington, D.C.: Government Printing Office, 1912.

González Ramírez, Manuel (ed.). *Manifiestos Políticos, 1892–1912.* Mexico City: Fondo de Cultura Económica, 1957.

———. *Fuentes Para la Historia de la Revolución Mexicana.* Vol. I: *Planes Políticos y Otros Documentos.* Mexico City: Fondo Cultura Económica, 1954.

*Official German Documents Relating to the War.* 2 vols. New York: Oxford University Press, 1918.

Scott, James Brown (ed.). *Diplomatic Correspondence Between the United States and Germany, August 1, 1914–April 6, 1917.* New York: Oxford University Press, 1918.

Secretaría de Guerra y Marina. *Campaña de 1910 a 1911: Estudio en General de las Operaciones que han Tenido Lugar del 18 de Noviembre al 25 de Mayo de 1911 en la Parte que Corresponde a la Segunda Zona Militar.* Mexico City: Talleres del Departamento de Estado Mayor, 1913.

Special Claims Commission. United States and Mexico. *Opinions of the Commissioners Under the Convention Concluded September 10, 1923, Between the United States and Mexico as Extended by the Con-*

*vention Concluded August 17, 1929.* Washington, D.C.: Government Printing Office, 1931.

TENA RAMÍREZ, FELIPE (ED.). *Leyes Fundamentales de México, 1808–1957.* Mexico City: Editorial Porrua, S.A., 1957.

UNITED STATES DEPARTMENT OF STATE. *Papers Relating to the Foreign Relations of the United States, 1910.* Washington, D.C.: Government Printing Office, 1915.

————. *Papers Relating to the Foreign Relations of the United States, 1911.* Washington, D.C.: Government Printing Office, 1918.

————. *Papers Relating to the Foreign Relations of the United States, 1912.* Washington, D.C.: Government Printing Office, 1919.

————. *Papers Relating to the Foreign Relations of the United States, 1913.* Washington, D.C.: Government Printing Office, 1920.

————. *Papers Relating to the Foreign Relations of the United States, 1914.* Washington, D.C.: Government Printing Office, 1922.

————. *Papers Relating to the Foreign Relations of the United States, 1915.* Washington, D.C.: Government Printing Office, 1924.

————. *Papers Relating to the Foreign Relations of the United States. The Lansing Papers.* 2 vols. Washington, D.C.: Government Printing Office, 1939.

UNITED STATES SENATE. *Investigation of Mexican Affairs. Report and Hearing before a Sub-Committee on Foreign Relations, Senator Albert Fall, Presiding, Pursuant to Senate Resolution 106.* 66th Cong., 2d sess., Senate Document No. 285. 2 vols. Washington, D.C.: Government Printing Office, 1919–1920.

C. MEMOIRS, DIARIES, AND CONTEMPORARY ACCOUNTS

BELL, EDWARD I. *The Political Shame of Mexico.* New York: McBride, Nast, and Company, 1914.

BERNSTORFF, COUNT [JOHANN]. *My Three Years in America.* New York: Charles Scribner's Sons, 1920.

BULNES, FRANCISCO. *The Whole Truth About Mexico. President Wilson's Responsibility.* New York: M. Bulnes Book Company, 1916.

CALERO Y SIERRA, MANUEL. *Un Decenio de Política Mexicana.* New York: Middleditch Co., 1920.

CASTILLO, JOSÉ R. *Historia de la Revolución Social de México: Primera Etapa, La Caida del General Díaz; Apuntes y Observaciones Para Formar la Historia de México de 1908 a 1915.* Mexico City, 1915.

[DeBekker, Jan Leander]. *De Como Vino Huerta y Como se Fué. Apuntes Para la Historia de un Régimen Militar.* Mexico City: Librería General, 1914.

Esquivel Obregón, Toribio. *Democracia y Personalismo: Relatos y Comentarios Sobre la Política Actual.* Mexico City: Imprenta de A. Carranza e Hijos, 1911.

Fernández Rojas, José. *De Porfirio Díaz a Victoriano Huerta, 1910–1913.* 2d. ed. Guadalajara: Tip. de la Escuela de Artes y Oficios del Estado, 1913.

Figueroa Domenech, J. *Veinte Meses de Anarquía* (July, 1911–February, 1913). Mexico City, 1918.

Gerard, James. *Face to Face with Kaiserism.* New York: George H. Doran Company, 1918.

Gimeno, Conrado. *La Canalla Roja: Notas Acerca del Movimiento Sedicioso.* El Paso, 1912.

González, Antonio P., and J. Figueroa Domenech. *La Revolución y Sus Héroes.* Mexico City: Librería de Ortega y Compañía, 1911.

González Blanco, Pedro. *De Porfirio Díaz a Carranza.* Mexico City: Imprenta Helénica, 1916.

Guzmán, Martín Luis. *Memorias de Pancho Villa.* Mexico City: Compañía General de Ediciones, S.A., 1960.

[Huerta, Victoriano]. *Memorias del General Victoriano Huerta.* Mexico City: Librería de Quiroga, 1915.

Lansing, Robert. *War Memoirs of Robert Lansing.* New York: The Bobbs-Merrill Company, 1935.

Márquez Sterling, M. *Los Ultimos Días del Presidente Madero.* Mexico City: Editorial Porrua, 1958.

Maytorena, José María. *Algunas Verdades Sobre el General Álvaro Obregón.* Los Angeles, 1919.

Molina Enríquez, Andrés. *Revolución Agraria de México.* Vol. 5: *El Principio de la Verdadera Revolución.* Mexico City: Talleres Gráficos de la Nación, 1936.

Obregón, Álvaro. *Ocho Mil Kilómetros en Campaña.* Mexico City: Fondo de Cultura Económica, 1960.

O'Shaughnessy, Edith. *Intimate Pages of Mexican History.* New York: George H. Doran Company, 1920.

ORTIZ RUBIO, PASCUAL. *La Revolución de 1910*. Mexico City, 1919.

PAPEN, FRANZ VON. *Memoirs*. London: Andre Deutsch, Ltd., 1952.

PRIDA, RAMÓN. *De la Dictadura a la Anarquía*. Mexico City: Ediciones Botas, 1958.

PUENTE, RAMÓN. *Pascual Orozco y la Revuelta de Chihuahua*. Mexico City: E. Gómez de la Puente, 1912.

RESENDI, SALVADOR F. *La Revolución Actual: Sus Causas y Tendencias, Sus Triunfos y Fracasos*. Mexico City: Librería Vda. de Ch. Bouret, 1912.

STARR, FREDERICK. *Mexico and the United States*. Chicago: The Bible House, 1914.

THORD–GRAY, I. *Gringo Rebel*. Coral Gables, Fla.: University of Florida Press, 1960.

UGALDE, R. A. *Vida de Pascual Orozco: Orozco, General y Caudillo*. El Paso, 1915 (?).

VÁSQUEZ GÓMEZ, FRANCISCO. *Memorias Políticas, 1905–1913*. Mexico City: Imprenta Mundial, 1933.

## III. SECONDARY ACCOUNTS

### A. MONOGRAPHS, GENERAL STUDIES, AND SPECIAL ACCOUNTS

AGUIRRE BENAVIDES, ADRIÁN. *Madero el Inmaculado*. Mexico City: Editorial Diana, S. A., 1962.

ALMADA, FRANCISCO R. *Gobernantes de Chihuahua*. Chihuahua: Talleres Gráficos del Gobierno del Estado, 1929.

———. *La Revolución en el Estado de Chihuahua*. Mexico City: Talleres Gráficos de la Nación, 1964.

———. *Resumen de Historia del Estado de Chihuahua*. Mexico City: Libros Mexicanos, 1955.

AMAYA, JUAN GUALBERTO. *Madero y los Auténticos Revolucionarios de 1910 Hasta la Decena Trágica y Fin del General Pascual Orozco*. Mexico City, 1946.

———. *Venustiano Carranza, Caudillo Constitucionalista*. Mexico City, 1947.

ARENAS GUZMÁN, DIEGO. *Del Maderismo a los Tratados de Teoloyucan*. Mexico City: Talleres Gráficos de la Nación, 1955.

BAERLEIN, HENRY. *Mexico, Land of Unrest.* Philadelphia: J. B. Lippincott Company, n.d.

BANCROFT, HUBERT HOWE. *History of the North Mexican States.* Vol. XVI of *The Works of Hubert Howe Bancroft.* 39 vols. San Francisco: The History Company Publishers, 1884–89.

BARRAGÁN RODRÍGUEZ, JUAN. *Historia del Ejército y de la Revolución Constitucionalista.* 2 vols. Mexico City: Talleres de la Editorial Stylo, 1946.

BLAISDELL, LOWELL. *The Desert Revolution, Baja California, 1911.* Madison: University of Wisconsin Press, 1962.

BONILLA, MANUEL. *El Régimen Maderista.* Mexico City: Talleres Linotipográficas de El Universal, 1922.

BRADDY, HALDEEN. *Cock of the Walk: The Legend of Pancho Villa.* Albuquerque: University of New Mexico Press, 1955.

BRANDENBURG, FRANK. *The Making of Modern Mexico.* Englewood Cliffs, N.J.: Prentice-Hall, Inc., 1964.

CALZADÍAZ BARRERA, ALBERTO. *Hechos Reales de la Revolución.* Chihuahua: Editorial Occidental, 1959.

CLENDENEN, CLARENCE C. *The United States and Pancho Villa: A Study in Unconventional Diplomacy.* Ithaca, N.Y.: Cornell University Press, 1961.

CLINE, HOWARD. *The United States and Mexico.* Cambridge, Mass.: Harvard University Press, 1953.

CORONA DEL ROSAL, ALFONSO. "Las Fuerzas Armadas de la Revoulción," in *México: Cincuenta Años de Revolución.* Vol. 3: *La Política.* Mexico City: Fondo de Cultura Económica, 1961.

CUMBERLAND, CHARLES CURTIS. *Mexican Revolution: Genesis Under Madero.* Austin: University of Texas Press, 1952.

DROMUNDO, BALTASSAR. *Emiliano Zapata.* Mexico City: Imprenta Mundial, 1934.

FABELA, ISIDRO. *Historia Diplomática de la Revolución Mexicana.* 2 vols. Mexico City: Fondo de Cultura Económica, 1959.

FUENTES MARES, JOSÉ. *... Y México se Refugió en el Desierto, Luis Terrazas: Historia Y Destino.* Mexico City: Editorial Jus, S. A., 1954.

GARCÍA GRANADOS, RICARDO. *Historia de México Desde la Restauración de la República en 1867 Hasta la Caida de Huerta.* 2 vols. Mexico City: Editorial Jus, 1956.

GONZÁLEZ NAVARRO, MOISÉS. *El Porfiriato: Vida Social.* Vol. IV of *Historia Moderna de México*, ed. Daniel Cosío Villegas. 7 vols. Mexico City: Editorial Hermes, 1955–65.

GUTIÉRREZ SANTOS, DANIEL. *Historia Militar de México, 1876–1914.* Mexico City: Ediciones Ateneo, S.A., 1955.

JAMES, WILLIAM. *The Eyes of the Navy, A Biographical Study of Sir Reginald Hall.* London: Methuen and Co., Ltd., 1956.

JONES, JOHN PRICE, and PAUL HOLLISTER. *The German Secret Service in America.* Boston: Small, Maynard and Company, 1918.

KOEVES, TIBOR. *Satan in Top Hat: The Biography of Franz von Papen.* New York: Alliance Book Corporation, 1941.

LARA PARDO, LUIS. *Madero: Esbozo Político.* Mexico City: Ediciones Botas, 1937.

———. *Matchs de Dictadores.* Mexico City, 1942.

LICÉAGA, LUIS. *Félix Díaz.* Mexico City: Editorial Jus, 1958.

LIEUWEN, EDWIN. *Arms and Politics in Latin America.* New York: Frederick A. Praeger, Inc., 1960.

LINK, ARTHUR S. *Wilson: The Struggle for Neutrality.* Princeton, N.J.: Princeton University Press, 1960.

———. *Woodrow Wilson and the Progressive Era, 1900–1917.* New York: Harper & Row, 1963.

LIST ARZUBIDE, ARMANDO. *Apuntes Sobre la Prehistoria de la Revolución.* Mexico City, 1958.

MAGAÑA, GILDARDO. *Emiliano Zapata y el Agrarismo Mexicano.* 3 vols. Mexico City: Edición de la Secretaría de Prensa y Propaganda del Partido Nacional Revolucionario, 1934–46. (Vol. 3 published posthumously with the collaboration of Carlos Pérez Guerrero).

MANCISIDOR, JOSÉ. *Historia de la Revolución Mexicana.* 2d. ed. Mexico City: Libro Mex Editores, 1959.

MÁRQUEZ MONTIEL, JOAQUÍN, S.J. *Hombres Célebres de Chihuahua.* Mexico City: Editorial Jus, 1953.

MENDOZA, VICENTE T. *El Corrido de la Revolución Mexicana.* Mexico City: Talleres Gráficos de la Nación, 1956.

MORENO, DANIEL. *Los Hombres de la Revolución: 40 Estudios Biográficos.* Mexico City: Libro Mex Editores, 1960.

OCHOA REYNA, ARNULFO. *Historia del Estado de Durango*. Mexico City: Editorial del Magisterio, 1958.

PALACIOS, PORFIRIO. *Emiliano Zapata*. Mexico City: Libro Mex Editores, 1960.

PONCE DE LEÓN, JOSÉ M. *Chihuahua y sus Distritos: Datos Geográficos y Estadísticos*. Chihuahua: Imprenta de Simón Alarcón, 1909.

———. *Resumen de la Historia Política de Chihuahua*. Chihuahua: Imprenta Gutenberg, 1922.

PUENTE, RAMÓN. *La Dictadura, La Revolución y Sus Hombres*. Mexico City: Ediciones Bocetas, 1938.

QUIRK, ROBERT E. *The Mexican Revolution, 1914–1915*. Bloomington: Indiana University Press, 1960.

RAMÍREZ, FÉLIX C. *La Verdad Sobre La Revolución Mexicana: Segunda Etapa*. Mexico City: Casa Ramírez Editores, 1958.

RAMÍREZ PLANCARTE, FRANCISCO. *La Revolución Mexicana*. Mexico City: Editorial B. Costa-Amic, 1948.

RINTELEN VON KLEIST, FRANZ. *The Dark Invader: Wartime Reminiscenses of a German Naval Intelligence Officer*. New York: The Macmillan Company, 1933.

ROMERO FLORES, JESÚS. *Anales Históricos de la Revolución Mexicana*. Vol. I: *Del Porfirismo a la Revolución Constitucionalista*. Mexico City: Ediciones Encuadernables, 1939.

ROSS, STANLEY R. *Francisco I. Madero: Apostle of Mexican Democracy*. New York: Columbia University Press, 1955.

SALAZAR, ROSENDO. *Del Militarismo al Civilismo en Nuestra Revolución*. Mexico City: Libro Mex Editores, 1958.

SÁNCHEZ ESCOBAR, RAFAEL. *Narraciones Revolucionarias Mexicanas Histórico—Anecdóticas*. Tlalpan: Talleres Tipográficos de la Casa Orientación Para Varones, 1934.

———. *El Ocaso de los Héroes: Como Murieron Algunos Connotados Revolucionarios*. Tlalpan: Talleres Tipográficos de la Casa Orientación Para Varones, 1934.

SAX, ANTIMACO. *Los Mexicanos en el Destierro*. San Antonio, Texas: International Printing Company, 1916.

SCHUSTER, ERNEST OTTO. *Pancho Villa's Shadow*. New York: The Exposition Press, 1947.

SHERMAN, WILLIAM L., and RICHARD E. GREENLEAF. *Victoriano Huerta: A Reappraisal.* Mexico City: Mexico City College Press, 1960.

SILVA HERZOG, JESÚS. *Breve Historia de la Revolución Mexicana.* 2 vols. Mexico City: Fondo de Cultura Económica, 1962.

SMITH, LAUNA M. *American Relations with Mexico.* Oklahoma City: Harlow Publishing Co., 1924.

TANNENBAUM, FRANK. *Mexico: The Struggle for Peace and Bread.* New York: Alfred A. Knopf, Inc., 1956.

TARACENA, ALFONSO. *La Verdadera Revolución Mexicana.* 6 vols. Mexico City: Editorial Jus, S. A., 1960.

————. *Madero: El Héroe Cívico.* Mexico City: Ediciones Xochitl, 1946.

VAGTS, ALFRED. *Deutschland und die Vereinigten Staaten in der Weltpolitik.* 2 vols. New York: The Macmillan Co., 1955.

VALADÉS, JOSÉ C. *Imaginación y Realidad de Francisco I. Madero.* 2 vols. Mexico City: Antigua Librería Robredo, 1960.

VOSKA, EMANUEL VICTOR, and WILL IRWIN. *Spy and Counterspy.* New York: Doubleday, Doran, and Co., Inc., 1940.

WEBB, WALTER PRESCOTT. *The Texas Rangers: A Century of Frontier Defense.* Boston: Houghton Mifflin Co., 1935.

ZARCO, FRANCISCO. *Historia del Congreso Extraordinario Constituyente, 1856–1857.* Mexico City: El Colegio de Mexico, 1956.

## B. PERIODICALS

ALESSIO ROBLES, VITO. "La Primera Página Militar de la Revolución," *Todo,* No. 1072 (March 25, 1954), p. 12.

ALMADA, FRANCISCO. "Ciudad Juárez al Través de la Revolución Mexicana," *Boletín de la Sociedad Chihuahuense de Estudios Históricos,* VI (September, 1949), pp. 1–17.

BROWN, LYLE C. "The Mexican Liberals and Their Struggle Against the Díaz Dictatorship: 1900–1906," *Antología MCC* (1956), pp. 318–362.

BUTTERFIELD, DOLORES. "The Conspiracy Against Madero," *Forum* (July–December, 1913), pp. 464–482.

CHRISTIANSEN, PAIGE W. "Pascual Orozco: Chihuahua Rebel," *New Mexico Historical Review,* XXVI (April, 1961), 97–120.

CUMBERLAND, CHARLES. "Border Raids in the Lower Rio Grande Valley—1915." *Southwestern Historical Quarterly*, LVII (July, 1953–April, 1954), 285–311.

―――. "Mexican Revolutionary Movements from Texas," *Southwestern Historical Quarterly*, LII (July, 1948–April, 1949), 301–324.

"The Fort Bliss Camp," *Outlook*, CVI (January 31, 1914), 225.

GARCÍA, RUBÉN. "La Máquina Loca," *El Nacional* (October 7, 1934), Magazine Section, p. 1.

HUERTA, VICTORIANO. "The Future of Mexico," *Independent*, LXXXII (May 3, 1915), 202–203.

"Huerta and Others," *Independent*, LXXXII (May 10, 1915), 236.

KATZ, FRIEDRICH. "Alemania y Francisco Villa," *Historia Mexicana*, XII (July, 1962–June, 1963), 88–102.

KENNER, ALVIN R. "Mexican Revolution," *Mining and Scientific Press*, CII (May 6, 1911), 621–624.

LARA PARDO, LUIS. "Orozco contra Madero," *Excélsior* (August 22, 1953), p. 6.

―――. "Pascual Orozco," *Excélsior* (August 18, 1953), p. 6.

MEYER, MICHAEL C. "The Mexican-German Conspiracy of 1915," *The Americas*, XXIII (July, 1966), 76–89.

MUÑOZ, RAFAEL F. "Pascual Orozco: Caudillo Olvidado," *Así*, XXIII, XXIV, and XXV (April 19, 26, and May 3, 1941), 22–23, 19–20, and 35–36.

―――. "Pascual Orozco y Emiliano Zapata," *El Universal* (December 9, 1929), p. 5.

"New Movements in the North," *Independent*, LXXX (December 14, 1914), 400.

NIEMEYER, VIC. "Frustrated Invasion: The Revolutionary Attempt of General Bernardo Reyes from San Antonio in 1911," *Southwestern Historical Quarterly*, LXVII (July, 1963–June, 1964), 213–225.

ORESTES, OTILIO. "Una Farsa la Campaña de V. Huerta," *Novedades* (July 8, 1962), p. 12.

"Orozco: Maker and Unmaker of Mexican Presidents," *Current Literature* (June, 1912), pp. 645–646.

PAZ, OCTAVIO. "Vásquez Gómez, Pascual Orozco, y Emiliano Zapata," *El Universal* (December 1, 1929), Magazine Section, pp. 1 and 8.

PÉREZ GUERRERO, CARLOS. "Cuando Transiguió Zapata," *El Universal* (September 6, 1933), pp. 3 and 8.

"A Procession of Presidents," *Outlook*, CIX (February 10, 1915), 304.

RAUSCH, GEORGE J. "The Exile and Death of Victoriano Huerta," *Hispanic American Historical Review*, XLII (May, 1962), 133–151.

ROMERO, MANUEL. "La Epopeya de Pascual Orozco," *Boletín de la Sociedad Chihuahuense de Estudios Históricos*, VI (June–July, 1949), 250–256.

SCHIFF, WARREN. "German Military Penetration into Mexico during the Late Díaz Period," *Hispanic American Historical Review*, XXXIX (1959), 568–579.

TISCARENO, JESÚS J. "Porque Venció Huerta a Pascual Orozco," *El Legionario*, III (October, 1953), 11–13.

TORRES, ELÍAS L. "Un Espía de la Revolución," *Jueves de Excélsior* (January 9, 1936), pp. 24–25.

VARGAS PIÑERA, LUIS. "El Gobierno Maquinó la Sublevación de Pascual Orozco Contra Madero," *Excélsior* (September 5, 1938), Magazine Section, pp. 1–2.

————. "Pascual Orozco Forzado a Sublevarse," *Excélsior* (September 11, 1938), Magazine Section, p. 1.

## IV. NEWSPAPERS

*Albuquerque Morning Journal*, 1915.

*El Correo* (Chihuahua), 1912–1913.

*El Paso Herald*, 1912.

*El Paso Morning Times*, 1910–1915.

*La Época* (San Antonio), 1915.

*Frankfurter Zeitung*, 1915.

*El Imparcial* (Mexico City), 1912–1914.

*La Justicia* (El Paso), 1915.

*Mexican Herald* (Mexico City), 1910–1914.

*New York Times*, 1910–1915.

*El Noticioso* (Guaymas), 1913.

*El País* (Mexico City), 1910–1914.

*El Presente* (San Antonio), 1915.

*San Antonio Light*, 1912.
*San Francisco Examiner*, 1911.
*El Sol* (Mexico City), 1914–1915.
*El Tiempo* (Mexico City), 1911–1912.
*La Verdad* (Mexico City), 1912.

# Index

DISCARD

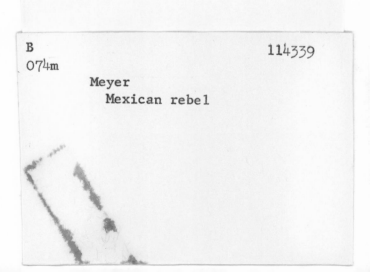